Dancing in the Street

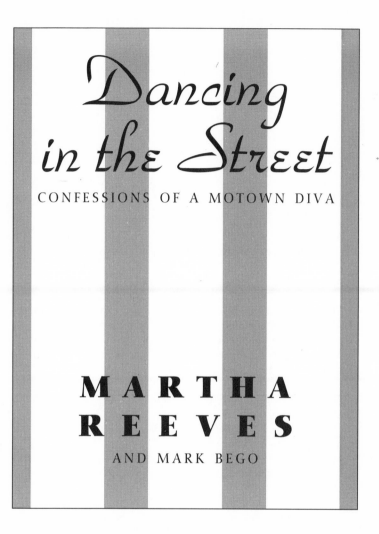

Dancing in the Street

CONFESSIONS OF A MOTOWN DIVA

MARTHA REEVES

AND MARK BEGO

HYPERION

NEW YORK

Library of Congress Cataloging–In–Publication Data
Reeves, Martha.
    Dancing in the street : confessions of a Motown diva / by Martha Reeves and Mark Bego.
        p. cm.
    Includes index.
    Discography: p.
    ISBN 0–7868–6024–3
    1. Reeves, Martha.   2. Singers–United States–Biography.
  3. Rhythm and blues music–History and criticism.   I. Bego, Mark.
  ML420.R333A3   1994
  782.42′1644′092–dc20
  [B]   94–10765
                                                             CIP
                                                             MN

Designed by Claudyne Bianco

FIRST EDITION

10 9 8 7 6 5 4 3 2 1

To my parents,
Ruby Lee Reeves and
Elijah Joshua Reeves;
and to my son, Eric

Contents

Acknowledgments   ix

Prologue   3

1   My Childhood   11

2   Come and Get These Memories   37

3   The Motown Revue   63

4   Heat Wave   85

5   Dancing in the Street   101

6   Nowhere to Run   121

7   Love Makes Me Do Foolish Things   133

8   I Can't Dance to That Music You're Playin'   151

9   In and Out of My Life   169

10 Wild Night   187

11 Free Again   209

12 *I'm Ready for Love* 225

13 *This Time I'll Be Sweeter* 241

Epilogue 256

Martha Reeves Discography 259

Index 275

Acknowledgments

When I realized the time had finally arrived for me to write *my* book, I started collecting bits of excerpts from notes and diaries kept for twenty or thirty years. I found a special nudge from Gary Spicer, my adviser and corporate attorney, to be a big inspiration. I was upset after inaccurate information in various manuscripts was brought to my attention. He advised me that lawsuits were fruitless and that I'd best get busy and accept the challenge of writing my own facts.

Ace Lichtenstein, my manager for the past seven years, assured me that it was a necessity, and he helped me regulate my schedule to make time to reflect. So I took on the task.

Mark Bego, however, showed me the light and encouraged me, letting me know that my opinions and memories would be delivered in print exactly as I desired, to lift my burden of being understood. Whenever I stretch, yawn, and look his way, Mark comes up with this tremendous surge of ideas, and we know that this book will be a good workout, maybe just one of a million autobiographies, but our very best effort!

Legendary thoughts have poured from the lips of my generation, and opinions now flow from my imaginings as I attempt to go back as far as I can. It's between me and the Lord just as it has always been. As I call on God for everything, He strengthens me to go onward and upward.

Simply being a product of good teachers, I have enjoyed my lessons—some of them learned the easy way and some the hard way. It is my hope and desire that this effort encourages everyone I have met on the road to eternity—as I have worked, prayed, loved, and watched as God turns dreams into reality.

*The authors would like to thank these people
for their contributions to this book:*

Margaret Baker, Bill Baran, Stanley Bernstein, Joe Billingslea, Laura Chittenden, Leslie Clark, Otis Clover, Connie Conley, Paul Eaves, Oliver Givens, Ron Goldfarb, Nina Graybill, Wilma Harkness, Gladys Horton, Gloria Jones, Jai Jackson, Liz Lands, Rochelle Lewis, Ace Lichtenstein, John Malveaux, Cary Mansfield, Bob Miller, Eldora Montgomery, George Stevson Montgomery, James Moore, Mary Ann Naples, Michael Ochs Archives, Marc Raboy, Eleanor Rigby, James Roberts, Claudette Robinson, Anthony Rossi, Randy Rossi, Richard Rossi, Joe Schilliar, Ron Strasner, Hugh Staveil, Ron Taylor, Tony Vaughn, Linda Warn, Louis Wendrick, Mary Wilson; and all the Vandellas: Rosalind Ashford, Annette Sterling, Betty Kelly, Lois Reeves, Sandy Tilley, Delphine Reeves.

And Martha would like to give additional thanks to:

Otis Caver, Helen Duncan, Betty Bullock, Bryant Gumbel, Stanley Bernstein, Louis Wendruck, Katherine Anderson, Jackie Kern, Andrea Jovin, Robert Carter, James Roberson, Rod Spencer, Dorothy Mackey, George Clinton, Hugh Stancil, Little Richard, Shirley Alston, Eudora Reeves, Jessie Reeves, Janice Singleton, Jaison Johnson, Regina Carghill, Jacque Shelby, Voncielle Faggett, Patty Howard, Alphanette Silas, Sandra Bomar, Kristie Gaither, Shirley Walker, Noby Weaver, Patricia Smith, Marion Matthews, Mildred Vancy, Tracey King, and all whoever . . . Barry Lee, Otis Williams, Amin Hasson, Reverend H. V. Hill, Reverend Fred K. Price, Reverend Anthony Campbell, Reverend Eugene Guy, Cholly Atkins, Lon Fontaine, Lester Wilson, Charlie Aikens, Brigid Bianco, Emanuel Esparza, Debbie and Dave Weitz, Linda Solomon, Isaiah Thomas, Kim Weston, Theadore Harris, Billie Jean Brown, Faye Hale,

Francis Heard, Francis Thomas, Joe Schaffner, Evelyn Johnson, Ardena Johnson, Burnice Morrison, Jim and Jack Holland, Ivy Joe Hunter, Calvin Brooks, Darrell Smith, Alonza Mckenzie, Larry Crockett, Abe Able, Leno Jaxon, Bert Dearing, Geraldine Matthews, Charlotte, Karen, and Shirley Thompson, Billy Dale, Eugene Brown, Eugene Robinson, Rick Inatone, Kevin Kendal, S. Gary Spicer, Barbara Ann Colding, Tehran Boldon, Clyde Rivers, Eric Kronfeld, Ewert Abner, Edna Anderson, Rebecca Nichols, Jack Ashford, Stanley Bernstein, Ahmed Mohmoud, Darlene Love, Billy Bannister, Jerry Butler, Beatrice Buck, Lela Bomar, Renaldo Benson, John Birge, Thomas H. Bowles, H. B. Barnum, Rudy Calvo, Mikiah Dargin, Roderick Chandler, Jim, Cathy, Lisa, and Mark Dondero, Loren Ashley Graham, Cheryl Daniels, Carmine Delligatti, Cardella DeMilo, Marc Warren, Arthur Bricker, John Tunis, Roz and Sherm Becker, Esther Edwards, Roweena Stewart, Margo Engle, Bernadine Vida, James Colver, Gene Keyes, Lawrence Johnson, George Solomon, Sparkle Maharris, Herb Fame, Eli Fountaine, Jack Gibson, Doris and Lincoln Holland, Ray Henderson, Lonnie Hicks, Cornelius Haliburton, Michael Godden, Susan Jenkins, Maye James, Eddie O'Jay, Arnie Kaye, Sunil Kuruvilla, Dee Dee Kennibrew, John Knowles, Thomas A. Lane, Ramsey Lewis, Dusty Springfield, Sue Marks, Mort Misner, Ed Marcus, Arthur Mitchell, Wendell Rayford, Ronald McDowell, Ed Nelson, Karen and Doug Niethammer, Mose and Marie Primus, Maxine Powell, Tony Patterson, Howard Porter, Curtis Posuniak, David Prible, Mariantee Randolph, Bettina McKinney, Bertha Roberson, Marie Reeves, Rudy Robinson, Charles Rice, Dr. Velton Robinson, Lloyd Storey, Jeribu Shahed, Scipio Solomon, Emanuel Steward, Dick Scott, Don Shipps, Lottie Smith, Fred Schneider, Bonnie Raitt, Vonny Sweeney, Ron Scott, Ronnie Spector, Ike Turner, Faye Treadwell, Scott Taylor, Jeff Allen, Margo Lewis, Eric J. Graham, Sunnie W. Wilson, Lyman Woodard, Skip Williams, John Whyman, Stanley Washington, David Winans, Tony Wilson, Dancing Boy, Billy Wilson, Tom Turner, Benjamin Wright, Anthony and Delores Young, Louvain Demps, Marlene Barron, Jackie Hicks, and all of my instructors.

The Essex House Hotel, New York City
December 18, 1975

MARK BEGO: *Do you find that you strongly believe in the lyrics that you've sung?*

MARTHA REEVES: *A song has to become as much a part of you as a tailored suit becomes a part of you. It's something in you that you'll have for the rest of your life.*

Dancing in the Street

I WANT TO HOLD ON TO YOUR LOVE

I'm not greedy, that's not my style
I'm not selfish, if you give me an inch, I'll give you a mile.
Whatever I try to keep, I always lose
But I want to hold on to your love

I'm not guessing, it's a natural fact
When it comes to me, you've got the knack
You can rock my soul, if I must I will get bold
I want to hold on to your love

I'm not picky, just hard to please
And I can't seem to get enough of you as I try to hold on
I seem to lose you in between
Loneliness and the heartbreaks
I can't deny the truth
You shake my self-control aloose

It's no guess, it's a natural fact
You push my will on, and I react
You know how to rock my very soul

$\mathcal{P}$rologue

$\mathcal{I}t$ is Monday, October 5, 1992, and it seems that no one wants to just let me sleep in late. For some crazy reason I get more rest when I am on the road, because when I am in my own bed in my condominium in Detroit–like I am now–the world seems to take it as a signal to call me up first thing in the morning. Don't they all realize that we Motown divas need our *glamour* sleep!?!

Again I find myself at home, tolerating the ringing of the telephone. I find it unnecessary to be awakened anytime before the banks open for business–especially after I have planned a late rising to follow a night out on the town.

Still half asleep, I grab the ringing phone next to my bed. It's not that I want to find out who is on the line, so much as the fact that I want the ringing to stop this morning.

The first call of the day is thankfully a fast one about a business meeting that evening. "Yes, yes, I can meet with Rick at his home at seven o'clock," I reply. "Yes, you have a good day, too," I say in closing, still hoping that I will be allowed to drift back to sleep.

No sooner do I hang up the receiver than the high-pitched squealing of my fax machine begins. "I've got to move that thing out of my bedroom," I think to myself for the umpteenth time. As I bat my eyes to clearly see the digital clock that sits near the fax machine, I can see that it is 8:30 A.M. Just as this thought registers, the telephone rings again.

"Hello," I answer, still intending to continue my sleep right after this call. It is Susan Jenkins, the executive director of the Rhythm-

and–Blues Foundation. Susan is a lovely young lady, so intent on paying respect to the living legends of R&B music. Unfortunately, dear Susan becomes the target of my disgruntled attitude.

"I *love* the fact that the Foundation wants to honor Martha & the Vandellas next February," I tell her, so that she is aware of my heart-felt gratitude. "However, be aware of the facts: I am a lead singer, with background singers, and, including myself, there have been seven official Vandellas all total. You can't just give the award to myself and two girls," I explain. Unlike the lead singers of some musical groups, I genuinely care about each of my background singers. Although my relationships with them haven't always been rosy 100 percent of the time, I still stick up for them.

"We must remember Rosalind for her ten years as a Vandella, as much as we need to acknowledge Annette for her two," I explain. By now I'm wide awake, and sitting up in bed. "Besides, this will give me the chance to reunite with Betty and thank her for her six years, and for singing on one of our biggest hits, 'Dancing in the Street.' And, my younger sister, Lois, for being with me all the way since 1967. For over twenty years she has made herself available to replace any Vandella who couldn't go out on the road. She even recorded on my last three albums at Motown."

I should not have to explain all of this to Susan personally. I think to myself, "She should have just called my manager in the beginning." Instead of graciously accepting the invitation and honor, I find myself taking all of my frustrations out on poor Susan. My anx-iety, however, has nothing to do with the upcoming award, nor the hour at which I have been awakened. Ever since last Friday, I have been feeling light–headed, on edge, and in pain. There had been at least fifteen calls informing me that Eddie Kendricks has taken a turn for the worse in his bout with cancer. After undergoing major surgery and the removal of one lung, the other lung is now riddled with infection, and he has been given but a few days to live. I have been upset ever since then, dreading the inevitable.

Turning my attention back to the phone call on hold, I continue, "Then of course there is Sandra Tilley and my younger sister, Del-phine Reeves . . ." After I finish stating my case, Susan informs me that she will have to call me back with a revised plan to honor each of my famed Vandellas.

No sooner do I hang up from that call when the phone rings again. Obviously my scheduled morning of slumber is not to be.

Well, I can't spend the entire day dwelling on events that might happen, so I begin planning my day. One thing that I am certain of is that tonight I don't want to be alone, so I ask my friend John if he will come over in the evening after my meeting. He can't, he says, and just as he is apologizing, we are interrupted by the beep that signals a caller on the other line. It continues like this all day long.

It was nearly 11:00 P.M. that evening when I receive the call I have been dreading. It is Billy. "I have some bad news," he begins. I already sense what the bad news is. Eddie is gone. Although it is "bad news," we both realize in our hearts that Eddie's death also means freedom from his pain. Eddie is now free from the trials and tribulations of the profession we all surrendered to way back in the fifties. When I pull myself together, I tell Billy, "I can be strong," and ask him to do the same. "Let us pray for strength," I advise him as we say good–bye.

As I hang up from Billy's call, my friend John, who has patiently held the line, assures me: "Eddie is in a better place, and your love for him will forever keep him alive in your memory. Eddie has brought pleasure and joy to the whole world with his special gift, and we are all the better for knowing him."

When we get off the phone, I find myself caught up in a whirlpool of emotions. We all had just said a sad farewell to Motown's musical director, Earl Van Dyke, earlier that year. Not long afterward Mary Wells, to paraphrase one of her biggest hits, "beat me to the punch" by getting into the gates of Heaven before me. David Ruffin had tragically just left us last year. My heart was already heavy remembering all of the good friends from the glory days at Motown who are gone forever. I haven't really gotten over the deaths of Marvin Gaye, Tammi Terrell, Florence Ballard of the Supremes, Sandra Tilley, Paul Williams of the Temptations, Georgeanna Tillman of the Marvelettes, Loucye Gordy Wakefield, Hubert Johnson, musicians Benny Benjamin and James Jamerson, just to name some of God's favorite and most blessed children who are no longer with us. Now my precious Eddie Kendricks has gone on to be with the Lord, and all I can do is sit here on my own, feeling numb, with this heavy pain in my heart, as if I have been stabbed in the chest with a tree trunk.

As I think about Eddie, I feel some of the true love that we have for each other come forth and shine through some of the dust and film that old things collect in time.

Adrift in a sea of thoughts I find it hard to believe that it has only been three short years since I toured the country with Eddie, David Ruffin, and Mary Wells. Just recently I had looked at a poster from 1989's highly touted Dancing in the Street tour that reunited the four of us "legends" from Motown.

Reminiscent of our first Motown Revue tour of 1962, the 1989 reunion tour was unfortunately besieged with problems. I kept referring to it in my diary as "the bus tour from hell."

We never knew for sure, from one night to the next, whether or not David was going to appear at show time. Although we never spoke openly about it, it appeared to me that he had a severe drug problem. When he would finally arrive he would stand there, swaying, slightly wheezing, and breathing hard. You could visibly see the toll it was taking on his body, destroying any common sense that he had ever possessed.

Most nights I would share a dressing room with Mary Wells. When I had first come to Motown, she was an exotic, vital, and exciting young woman. However, I had recently witnessed her self-confidence erode along with her vocal cords. Each night when she sang, her voice became fainter and fainter. On song after song she would ask the audience to "sing it along with me" so that she didn't have to use up her voice. Offstage I would watch helplessly as she smoked one cigarette after another, destroying what precious little voice she had left.

Eddie and David had always been tall and handsome. The Temptations in their heyday resembled basketball players. Although he and David performed their showstopping set together every night and appeared to be two devoted comrades in the spotlights, when the curtain came down it was a different story. Most evenings, Eddie was furious with David for his irresponsible behavior, and wouldn't speak to him at all. When I asked Eddie why he ignored him, he replied, "David knows."

Then there was the physical side of things. Struck with different maladies, they both slowly grew thinner and thinner. Although they were each over six feet tall, I don't think they weighed 250 pounds between the two of them.

What should have been a glorious reunion in '89 became a downward spiral of loss. Mary lost her voice, Eddie and David were losing their health, and Eddie was losing his patience with David. It took all of the concentration I could gather to keep myself from getting tangled up in this tragic circle.

As news of Eddie's passing had spread, the phone continued to ring. Friends and well-wishers called giving me their condolences. Writers and reporters phoned for my comments for their obituaries. The next morning, Susan Jenkins called back to tell me that the Foundation had agreed to honor all five of my surviving Vandellas. I, in turn, told her the news of Eddie's passing. She told me that she would see if she could get the Foundation to assist Eddie's mother with the funeral arrangements–any way she could be of help to the family during this troubled time.

Each time I hung up the phone, my thoughts returned to that last tour with Mary, Eddie, and David. "Was it only three years ago?" I kept asking myself. "Three short years, and I am the only survivor!" As the day passed I became more and more mired in my own disbelief. In June of 1991 the drugs had caught up with David in Philadelphia. In June of '92 my dear sweet Mary Wells succumbed to throat cancer, after living a full year with her voice silenced by the disease. And now, Eddie's lung cancer had ended his once-brilliant career.

I thought back to the first time I had met each of them at Motown in the early sixties. How we had proudly toured America in one single bus, each with our own dreams of stardom. I flashed back to the glory that we all achieved. Mary had become the Queen of Motown in 1962 when she placed three singles in the Top Ten, including "You Beat Me to the Punch." She was a star on both sides of the Atlantic when "My Guy" hit Number 1 in 1964. That was the year the Beatles named her their favorite singer. My turn came next when Martha & the Vandellas sold millions of recordings of our songs: "(Love Is Like a) Heat Wave," "Jimmy Mack," "Quicksand," and "Dancing in the Street." In 1963 and 1964 we were the top female singing group in the world. Eddie and David, along with the other three Temptations–Otis, Melvin, and Paul–hit it big with "The Way You Do the Things You Do" in 1964, and went on to become the top American male group of the decade. Along with Marvin Gaye, the Marvelettes, the Four Tops, Smokey Robinson & the Miracles, Stevie Wonder, and the Supremes, we created "the Motown sound." We broke down racial barriers with our universal songs of love, risked our lives touring the South at the same time as Martin Luther King Jr.'s Freedom Riders, sold millions and millions of records, and provided the soundtrack for an entire generation.

Mary Wells left Motown in 1964, and her artistry soon lacked the Motown producers' touch. Smokey Robinson had had the right formula for her voice and singing style. Her career was never the same after that.

David was literally thrown out of the Temptations in 1968 because he wouldn't conform to the group's rules and regulations. Eddie, tired of the fighting within the group, quit in 1971 and later teamed up with David. Things were never quite the same for them once they began to question Motown's policies.

Likewise, what I experienced was also a two-edged sword. On one hand, Motown had signed us all to ironclad contracts, and they turned us into international stars. Yet after several years of million-selling records and sold-out concerts, in 1969 I realized that my personal income was but a fraction of what it should have been. I became known as the first Motown star to ask the question, Where is all of this money that Motown was collecting from all the hits? I suddenly experienced a lack of personal and professional attention, and it grieved me. I was left to fend for myself in this shark pool they call show business.

But I was deep in thought this day. My memories continually drifted from the incredible good times we all had when our fame was new, to the sad outcomes so many of my friends had met. Mary Wilson of the Supremes, Smokey Robinson of the Miracles, and Otis Williams of the Temptations had each in turn written autobiographies, telling their own version of what it was like to become a star at Motown. We had all intended to do this one day. That afternoon I realized that Mary Wells, David Ruffin, and Eddie Kendricks had each missed their chance. I knew right then and there that I couldn't let the parade pass me by. I started collecting my memoirs and started to write my book.

I've had experience in going on with life, and it only gets more and more intense as time goes by—and the challenges only multiply. I know that I have truly been blessed thus far: to have had the adventures that I have had, to live the exciting and unpredictable life that I do, and to have been touched by so many wonderful people–some of them famous and some of them unknown. There have been times that I have played the role of a victim, and there have been times when I have emerged victorious. I still marvel at how God turns dreams into reality. Time and time again I have been referred to in print as "a soul survivor." There have been times when I have been extremely successful in my endeavors, and other times I have been humiliated, wronged, and hurt.

Good and bad–this is the story of my life. There are parts of it that are painful to recount, and there are episodes too wonderful not to share. For better or for worse, on the following pages here is my life the way I lived it: the true confessions of this Motown diva.

CHAPTER 1

My Childhood

THROW THE OLD AWAY

You remember because your mind
    won't let you forget.
That was then, and here is now
    and tomorrow seems to promise
    its own brand of whatever it is.
Nothing is new under the sun,
    so let's sing Auld Lang Syne.
And try not to be unforgotten
    when new grooves turn you on.
Take what you've saved for a rainy day
    and throw that old away

Yesterday's just doesn't feel right—
    dust and cobwebs everywhere
The same place you were yesterday,
    don't let tomorrow catch you there.
In this race called "keep up,"
    have some mercy on yourself
Pain will go and never be felt
    if you let your heart go out and play
Throw all of that old away.

It won't come back in style—
    if it does, you won't see it
Could be younger than its future
    but you'll never be it
Grow old graciously, relax
    and when gray from wisdom is at play
Get a good grip on yourselves
    and throw the old away.

$\mathcal{The}$ world I was born into was one filled with music. My mother, Ruby, and my father, Elijah, were two youngsters who fell in love and used music to court with. Together they would sit under the moonlight on that big front porch in Abbeville, Alabama. When Elijah came courting, he would bring his guitar. He'd play and sing, and Ruby would join in. Her parents would leave them alone as long as they could still hear music coming from the porch.

If the music stopped, that instantly signaled the arrival of my grandparents, "Big Daddy" Grover Gilmore and "Big Mama" Jessie, who would appear at the doorway to chaperon. Ruby's brother, Junior, or her sisters, Juanita and Jewel, would make some joke about the music having ceased. Then Elijah—or E.J., as everyone called him—would commence to pick at his guitar, and Ruby would begin singing along. I wasn't born yet, but I can vividly picture this scene, since one of my favorite childhood memories is of my mother's sweet voice singing us to sleep nearly every bedtime.

Ruby was just fifteen years old and E.J. was nineteen when they got married on June 5, 1937. They were just a couple of children themselves. Ambitious newlyweds, they tended a farm just as their parents had. The white boss and his family lived at one end of his property, and on the other side of his field, somewhere back near the woods, there was a shack where the boarders' family could live as long as they met their quota. If they didn't harvest a set amount of crops, they lost their space and had to move on. The house and a few bushels of the produce they managed to draw from the fertile ground they tilled were their pay.

That's where E.J. and Ruby started their family. They hadn't been married long when Benny, my oldest brother, was born on April 2, 1938, at Richard's Crossroad, Alabama. That tiny town at the center of Barbour and Henry counties was named after one of a pair of men killed there in a legendary dispute. The fight happened before my mother's time. She told the story this way: "My great uncle on my father's side of the family, Uncle Ben Gilmore, was fighting with a white man named Richard. After Richard cut his throat, Ben asked to be raised up to speak his last words, saying: 'Lift me up just one more time.' He cut the white man's throat in that instant. They both died, one on top of the other."

My brother Thomas was born next, on December 10, 1939, in Parker's Alley, out in the country. The family had moved to Batesville, where Elijah was hired to work in a sawmill. Moving from place to place, wherever they were hiring, E.J. would work temporary jobs slaughtering hogs, cutting wood, and sometimes going on ahead of the family and sending for mother and children later.

I was the third child and the family's first girl. I was born on July 18, 1941, in Eufaula, Alabama, at 505 Washington Street, in a two-family building. Back then we couldn't afford a doctor, so my midwife was Granny Russau. Her sons Buck and Ball were local farmers, and she served as doctor to all of my cousins. Although she usually arrived late, she was known as the best midwife in the county.

I wasn't even a year old and "the great exodus" from the South had already begun. Since cotton gins were cutting into sharecroppers' jobs, work was becoming scarce in the South. My grandfather's cousins, the Davises, went up north and sent word back that there were many job opportunities awaiting them in Michigan. My father and his three brothers all decided to move their families there. Uncle Adron and my dad's oldest sister, Ella Mae, were the first to move from the South to set up housekeeping in the Big "D"–Detroit. They were later joined by their brothers Ben Thomas, Sylvester, and my dad Elijah Joshua Reeves Jr. Dad sent for my mother and their three children–now four years old, two years old, and eleven months old–in 1942.

After the whole family made it safely to Detroit, we all lived in a three-bedroom house on Illinois Street, even using a closet as a room to make it accommodate three families. Uncle Sylvester and his wife Ola were the acknowledged heads of the house. Along with their children Eloise, Bertha, Arvester, Eunice, and Irene, they occupied the first two rooms.

The room shared by Aunt Ella Mae and her four-year-old daughter, Juanita, was no larger than a walk-in closet itself. The living room had a big bay window, and as you reached the kitchen, our room was just off to the left.

In Detroit my family continued to grow, one new sibling after another, until there were twelve of us in all. Shirley Ann, born August 14, 1942, died from pneumonia at two months old, our first real tragedy. Samuel Elijah was born January 12, 1945, during a very cold winter. Melvin Douglas arrived on February 25, 1947, and then Sandra Delores ("Lois"), the sister I had prayed so hard for, came next—on April 12, 1948.

We had two chests of drawers, lots of trunks, and boxes in that one room where we slept in two double beds. Mom and Dad's bed was near the back window and the rear door. With so many people living in that tiny house, it took a lot of patience and scheduling to get everybody's kids fed, and with one bathroom, there was always a dispute going on. If you were lucky enough to get a turn in the bathroom, you could count on someone banging on the door to hurry you along.

Momma was, and still is, our main source of entertainment. On special nights, she sat with us until we went to sleep, telling us all about the world she so proudly brought all of us into. She idolized Billie Holiday, who was the most popular blues singer when sweet Ruby was courting and growing into a beauty herself. My first remembrances of Momma were of a vanilla wafer–colored angel with long, shoulder-length wavy hair, an hourglass figure, bowed legs, and slightly pigeon-toed. She walked as if she were listening to music, always seeming to step on her own toes.

Ruby worked from sunup to sunset. After bathing us all, refereeing us as we took turns, and attempting to keep the young ones up long enough to get them suited up in pajamas and gowns, she would tell us these wonderful recollections about our ancestors, and her and Dad's romance. Dear heart that she is, she would then sing to us until we had all fallen asleep. She was so exhausted that she would take occasional naps just to get through the day.

My father was handsome and quite popular with the ladies in the neighborhood because he was handy. He not only played his guitar, but he was able to repair cars, washing machines, radios, refrigerators—anything electric—without any training whatsoever. He just had the knack and was good with his hands. I inherited some of that talent. I can definitely say that I have my father's hands.

Dad was rarely home. It seemed as if he were always coming from or going back to work. He was a man of few words, but at special rare times, when he felt like it, he would take his guitar down from the wall where it would hang and play us some down-home blues. My favorite was "Good Evening, Little School Girl," which he would sing just for me. I remember "Oh Lawdy Lord," "One Day, Baby," "I Ain't Gonna Worry My Life Anymore," and "John Henry," to name a few of his classic songs that took us into his world. He tuned his guitar in a style he called "Vassapoo." In our crowded household only he and Mom could play any musical instruments, or "pick the guitar," as they lovingly called it.

When they tired of playing, we would "look at" the radio and listen to Walter Winchell, Gabriel Heatter, "Lights Out," "Inner Sanctum Mysteries," or "The Shadow." On special nights we heard "The Amos and Andy Show," thinking that we were listening to blacks—not knowing that the voices we heard were those of white actors. In actuality, the only black actor we had to identify with on the radio then was Rochester on "The Jack Benny Show."

Every summer, the minute school was out, we packed up all of our summer clothes, and with our box lunches in hand, we rode the "choochoo train" down south to visit our relatives. I really do miss the big steam engines. There was nothing like them. You could hear those long passenger trains coming for about an hour. When they would finally make their approach, the engine would chug down slowly, giving off this last big-sounding "Choooooooo!"

The summer after my brother Samuel was born, we left Dad behind and headed back to Alabama to see our grandparents. Dad continued to work at his new job at Packard, the car factory. Momma cried a little when we left, but we soon turned our concentration to the other passengers. It was the end of June 1945, and the train was crowded mostly with passengers in uniform. These men were all bandaged up, on crutches, some of them with limbs missing, going home from World War II. This was the first time I had ever seen a sling on someone's arm, and it fascinated me. Momma was quick to tell us not to bump into them or annoy them, just to "sit down and be still."

Well, that command lasted about ten minutes, and Thomas, who was always friendly and curious, asked the closest soldier how he was feeling, because one could see that they were in pain and depressed. He responded by saying, "I'm all right, just anxious to get home. I have a son who should be about your age now." With a warm smile, he invited my brother to join him on the empty seat next to him.

Once the train crossed the Mason–Dixon line, we "colored folks," as we were referred to then, had to move to the back of the train. This unfair law applied to these war-torn heroes as well. Tom's newfound friend managed to make the move quite easily with his crutch supporting his one good leg. He even offered to help Mom—a pretty lady with her four small kids.

The rear cars were not as spacious or as comfortable as the front ones, and we sat even closer to the wounded men. Momma with all her persistence tried to make sure that we did not bug the other passengers. Thomas had his adopted friend, and they sat across from us, talking and making each other laugh. The soldier pulled out a harmonica from his pocket and started to play "Sentimental Journey." We all knew the words, for it was one of Mom's favorites, and we started to sing along. To everyone's surprise and delight, Thomas then stood up and went from person to person getting them to join in the singing. That trip turned into a pleasant experience, as we sang "Saturday Night Fish Fry," "Mona Lisa," and "Route Sixty-six," to name a few of the songs we had learned from listening to Randy's radio broadcast from Nashville, or from Ruby and E.J.

It was just like a regular gathering on that train, and then Thomas brought the evening to a close with his rendition of "Choo Choo Cha-Boogie." The men enjoyed his singing so much that they soon began to wipe tears from their eyes. They beckoned to him and dropped coins into the pocket of his miniature navy blue suit. He was so happy with the change he received, because he could now buy a whole bag of penny candy. Thomas was always bighearted, and he shared the candy he bought with the rest of us kids.

Life was so different in the South. I remember being down on my grandparents' farm, watching as sweet potatoes were rolled out of the hot coals with a poker, rinsed off, and put on the table. Our mouths would water as "Big Mama" Jessie flipped her whole cake of cornbread. Her kitchen had a flat wood-burning stove, the kind you used a tool to pry open and fill with wood. On it she would fry chicken, brown bacon, and boil vegetables, and you'd know there was good eating to come when the big stew pot was placed among the readied coals to simmer all day long.

On visits to the farm every year, we hardly ever wore shoes except to town to shop, or in church. I loved those summers we spent in Alabama.

Back in Detroit, before television was invented, we would visit close relatives on Sunday after church services, and in our best clothes, we'd sit on sofas and mind our manners. Whenever someone would make a request, we'd sing, recite, or dance just as our mother and father had instructed us to do.

I certainly had my moments of glory as a child, too. I always rejoiced to see the smiles of approval and hear my parents shout, "That's my girl!" I felt confident that I had a talent to sing. At the age of three, Benny, Thomas, and I had won some chocolate-covered cherries in a church talent contest, singing "Jesus Met the Woman at the Well." At that young age I was already hooked on pleasing a crowd with my singing.

Beatrice Lockett was my first godmother, and she was the one responsible for introducing me to the wonderful world of show business. I can remember her coming and taking me by the hand as we walked to the Paradise Theater on Woodward to see my first live stage show.

Inside the theater I was just too short to see over the seat in front of me, so Beatrice would pick me up and say, "See, that's Louis Jordan. . . . Watch Pegleg Bates dance, he only has one leg! . . . Eddie 'Lockjaw' Davis picks up everything with his teeth–look baby! . . . Isn't that Cab Calloway something?"

Then the curtains changed colors, and parted to reveal a screen. There, live on stage, was a scene just like one out of a movie. Several people entered the stage with umbrellas. Then I saw the most beautiful woman I had ever seen in my whole three little years. Beatrice said, "Now here's my girl Lena Horne. Isn't she pretty?" As she sang "Stormy Weather," I heard a great voice sing the blues. In the lyrics of the song, she was crying over a man, and I couldn't associate that sad song with such a lovely angel-like grown woman. She could have had anything she wanted, she was so beautiful. I never forgot my first taste of entertainment and movie stars—that fantasy world! It was a world I never dreamed that I would one day be a part of.

We had walked from the corner of Riopelle and Leland to Woodward—maybe a half of a mile—and the cold walk home was like dreaming. I called Beatrice regularly and pestered her to take me back to the Paradise. We only went one or two more times, then she moved out of the state. I was sorry to see her go, and I was without a godmother for a lot of years.

From a very early age I have been aware that "guardian angels" watch over us. My brother Thomas was my first guardian angel, and throughout my life he has walked and talked with me. As we grew up, he would teach me the facts of life as he learned them. My first awareness of my being watched over came when my brother Thomas and I were in the city one cold day before winter. I wasn't even school age yet. Thomas wanted to go to Woolworth's to get a jigsaw puzzle. You see, my Aunt Bernice, Uncle Sylvester's second wife, had taught us to work puzzles, but warned us against touching even one piece of the 500- and 1,000-piece puzzles she'd leave undone on tables for weeks. So we wanted our own, and Thomas worked real hard hauling the neighbors' coal into their house to earn enough money. He came and got me, and away we started walking toward where we thought the Woolworth's five-and-ten-cent store was.

Thomas was only nineteen months older than I, but as we walked down the street, he dutifully held my hand. When we reached the Eastern Market, where farmers brought their goods to sell them directly to the public, we were confused, because we were used to people being there. Every morning would find the place filled with local farmers selling their wares. Now, however, the market was closed, and since the stalls were deserted, we were confused and didn't recognize where we were.

Thomas was brave all during our adventure, but I began to cry, and very loudly in fact. He tried to wipe my tears with his hands and kept telling me not to cry, but it was getting to be around 5:00 P.M., and it starts to get dark early at the beginning of winter. We walked around for another hour, and I cried all my tears. My face was so streaked with dry salt streams that I gave up on trying to wipe them away.

All of the sudden we walked up to this huge building. Thomas still had my hand, and these real big white men (blacks were not firemen in our neighborhood yet) met us and asked us, "Where are you kids headed?" Then it was Thomas's turn to break down and cry. He was crying so hard that he couldn't speak, and only nodded his head when the firemen asked, "Are you lost?" They took us inside, warmed us by the biggest potbellied stove I'd ever seen, except for the huge one at the entrance to Belle Isle.

We ate the candy canes they gave to each of us, and as Thomas warmed up he began to talk, and told them where we lived. They laughed among themselves, for it seems that we had been only going in circles around the same four to six blocks–and not far from home–because we were told never to cross any big streets. We were taught to obey orders, or get whippings. We didn't get a whipping that night, though. We were too excited and tired when we rode up to our house on Illinois and Leland in that big fire truck, with all the lights on and the sirens going full blast, at our request!

When I was old enough to begin school, I was very excited. Momma couldn't leave the younger children, so my two older brothers were given the task of delivering me to kindergarten. My first day at school was an event I always remember when I take on a new challenge. No one explained to me what to expect. Mom had already seen Dad off at the crack of dawn. That September morning of 1946 was a chilly one, and I was told to button my coat. My brothers Benny and Thomas were told to take care of their baby sister, and my two oldest brothers took it to heart–one on each side, holding my hands and taking me to kindergarten.

I was introduced to my teacher, Mrs. Walker. She had also been their teacher, and they felt confident that she would do me swell, so they left me there with all those new little kids. I knew that they would come to retrieve me when school was out, so I didn't cry or make a fuss. I did whatever Mrs. Walker instructed us to do, and rather enjoyed it. We sat in rows on the floor, painted, had milk and cookies, and then we were asked to put on our coats, line up, and go outside. I didn't know what "recess" was, so as soon as we were led to the playground, I just kept walking and went home.

I was really hurt because my "heroes" were not there to retrieve me like they promised. My brothers were safety patrol boys, and I had been told how to walk to the corner, look both ways, and when the traffic cleared, walk across the street. So that's what I did. I was so glad when I got home to Momma that I ran to her crying, my heart beating like a drum. However, when I got there, I was startled to find that she was *not* happy to see me. In fact, she scolded me for crossing the street alone. She called the lady next door to come over and watch the little ones so she could walk me back to Mrs. Walker's class. I couldn't figure out why she was so upset: I wasn't told about recess. What a lesson to learn the hard way! I was teased about this over and over again until I tired of it.

I enjoyed school, and the teachers always made me feel special. As early as the third grade, I was chosen from among the thirty or thirty-five students in my class to sing solos by our music teacher, Mrs. Wagstaff, a lady not very much taller than we students. I cherish the smile that she would have on her face as I remembered the lyrics to songs like "This Is My Country," "America the Beautiful," and "Only a Rose," and I can still call them to mind. Mrs. Wagstaff recognized that I could not only remember song lyrics, but I could also hold melodies in my memory. The other kids didn't like the extra attention she gave me, but I enjoyed pleasing our teacher, and their opinion didn't sway me.

I considered myself blessed having older brothers. I adored them, and they would come to my rescue whenever the school bullies would get out of control. Ernest, a little boy who sat behind me in the fourth grade, tried to get my attention in class a number of times by tugging at the back of my hair, taking my braids loose, and kicking me any opportunity that the teacher didn't observe. He really was getting on my nerves and disturbing me, causing me to lose my concentration. One afternoon he chose to dip his pen into the inkwell and squirt me with indelible ink.

When I got home I got a whipping for ruining my white ruffled blouse, and wasn't given a chance to explain myself until afterwards, as Thomas consoled me. He told me, "Don't cry, Sis. I'll meet you after class tomorrow, don't you worry." As we got out of school the next day, there they were: my big brothers asking me, "Point him out. Which one is he?" When Ernest appeared, I showed them this fright-ened-looking guy, and when he saw what was happening, he started to run. He was Tom's size, so it was Tom who pursued him, catching him just as Ernest reached the six-foot-high fence that surrounded the public school.

Whenever any one of us had to fight in our neighborhood, we would do so bravely—unless we were outnumbered or mismatched. The unwritten law was to run to the front of our house, and the one who best matched the size of the adversary would accept the respon-sibility to "kick butt." This time there was no fight. My brother just grabbed Ernest by the collar, and I never knew what was said, for I stayed with Benny and observed from a distance. All I know is that from that day on, Ernest was as sweet as he could be to me, and tried to be my boyfriend. He had a complete change of attitude, thanks to my heroes coming to my rescue again.

Education was always emphasized in our house. Momma, during a quiet time, explained to us children how lucky we were to be able to attend school. After all, it hadn't been so long ago that black chil-dren in the South were not even allowed to receive an education. Momma said that as a girl she used to cry to go to school.

No mere cough or cold ever bought any of the Reeves children a free day off from school. I can remember being sick one morning with a fever and chills. When I announced that I was too sick to go to class, my daddy poured a glass of cold water on my face, just wetting me enough to make lying there impossible. Believe me, I got up and went to school. I felt better than I thought I would.

After some time, the communal living in our house on Illinois Street was becoming impossible because of the subsequent births of Victor Tyrone (June 14, 1949) and Jessie Pecola (July 11, 1950), so we gathered our meager belongings to make our big move. It was just around the corner to a single family flat on Riopelle Street—still a small dwelling, but this time it was ours alone. We rented it from a man named Joe Bermas, who, after deciding to paint the whole house blood red—trimming and all—made us the spectacle of the neighbor-hood. We were referred to as "the bunch of kids who lived in the red house."

E.J. had landed a job with the city water department, which was a step up, and we thought we had it made. When Delphine (November 22, 1951), Eudora (February 22, 1954), and William (June 1, 1955) were born, there were further adjustments to be made. Benny and Thomas now slept on a pullout couch, while the four little boys–Samuel, Melvin, Victor, and William–slept in a double bed in the first bedroom. All of the girls including me slept in a double bed in the second bedroom. Mom and Dad's bed was in the dining room that had no door, and the only rooms in the house that weren't occupied were the kitchen and the bathroom. That was a tight household, baby!

Laundry day would consist of me on my knees in front of the bathtub with a rubbing board. Mom would operate the faucets. She would fill the tub, and on one rubbing board, scrub each piece diligently and pass it to me. I would in turn rub it on my rubbing board, squeeze it and toss it into a number 5 washtub. Then, after washing, we used the same procedure to rinse the clothes, then carry them to the backyard to hang them on clotheslines with clothespins. We worked our way up from tub washing to our first washing machine with an agitator. Our first machine was a bucket on four wheels, rolling with a clothes wringer that could catch your fingers and sometimes your arms.

Because of the horse stable directly in back of the house, we would constantly have to fight the flies. All my friends–Elaine, Shirley, Kaline, Della, Geraldine, Pluckey, Ray, Sweet, Little Junior, Marcus, and Bert, Jr.–teased us about living in front of a horse stable. We had the last laugh, though, for when the junkers would empty their wagons, we'd get the best of the treasures that they had found.

With so many of us in the house, we kids sure did have a great time–especially when Momma and Daddy left us on our own. We had this little game we called "Ten-X" where the guys and the girls were on opposing sides. We would collect throwable things, stack them up in a pile, and whichever team got really fed up with the other's jazz, would initiate "the attack." With all those children, imagine how many shoes were available for warfare. It was usually the girls, unable to retort to some of the boys' teasing, who would pass the first lick and yell: "Ten-X!!!" This was our battle cry! We would completely wreck the house, but we had common sense enough to have everything straight and in its proper place by the time Mom and Dad were scheduled to arrive home. Sometimes we'd even turn the lights off at night during one of our "Ten-X" brawls. We'd scream at the top of our voices with delight and throw things into the darkness, and get hit repeatedly.

One day one of the stronger boys hit me squarely on target with a cushion from the chair. He knocked me into the molding of a door frame, and the center of my forehead made direct contact. No blood, just a great big welt that looked like a "hickey." I was Daddy's first born girl, and being the authority figure among us kids, this also meant getting the blame when pandemonium hit. Panic struck. Suddenly we all bound together, fearing the whipping that hurting me would surely bring. Quickly we went into action: Upon my swollen forehead they put shoe polish, alcohol, witch hazel, ice, flour, and everything else in the house that they thought would make the swelling go down. They were so concerned that as a last resort, they went into one of the bedrooms and prayed to God that He would let that hickey go away. The moment I heard Mom's and Dad's footsteps on the porch, I got prepared for what was to come. I began to cry all over again, and was the first to the door. As they entered, Mom asked, "What's wrong with you, girl? What are you crying for?"

I mumbled something through my tears and pointed to my head, only to hear her say, "What hickey?" Boy, was that a close call!

When I went outside to play, I always carried along four brothers and four sisters: one on the hip, one on my hand, and the rest walking ahead of me. At that time "skate boxes" were the latest craze. A precursor to skateboards, skate boxes were old vegetable crates with broken roller skates attached—homemade in construction and design. It was an honor to have the best of the skate boxes. Also, we were lucky enough to have a perfectly smooth street just around the corner—the rest were cobblestone. When the weather permitted, we got to see a colorful parade. The self-taught inventors would use bottle tops, the rubber from inner tubes, and a bunch of ten-for-a-penny nails to create their masterpieces. Some skate boxes even had windshields, fenders, and ornaments.

I loved to watch the big boys and their customized skate boxes, so we'd make a trip around the block once a day, stopping on Leland to watch all the action. There were about ten racing on this particular hot summer day. I was there with seven of my usual eight siblings. Mom and I had just tidied them up, a regular operation on hot days.

We were walking around the corner when suddenly there was a loud screech of tires and someone yelled, "There's been an accident!"

I immediately began grabbing up everybody to return home. I could account for everybody but Jessie. "Where's Jessie?!" I screamed. I soon found out that she had wandered into the street and had been hit by a car! The second the discovery was made, there was Mom yelling from the porch to me: "You let my baby get killed! I told you to watch these children! It's all your fault!! You were supposed to be watching them!!!" Dad was there, so they got Jessie into the car and drove off to the hospital. "You'd better watch all of them this time!" they warned me as they drove away. My first thought to myself was, "None of these are my children!"

Luckily, it wasn't serious. Jessie had only been knocked against the curb. The black mark on her yellow dress was just dirt and not a tire mark.

Back then, in the Detroit of the 1950s, there was a strong sense of neighborhood, where everybody knew everybody else and looked out for each other. As it was, my family—including aunts, uncles, and cousins—and the other families were full of self-appointed "mothers." If you were sassy, disobedient, or just demonically inspired, somebody would whip you. Then they would take you home, knock on your front door, and inform your parents of your wrongdoing. They'd leave you at your doorstep, only to have your own parents get just as angry and wallop the living daylights out of you, too! This was your worst nightmare.

One day while at play and watching my younger sisters and brothers, I heard a voice call out, "Hey, little girl!" At first I thought I was hearing things. So I twirled round and round, and then I looked up into the direction the voice came from. Through a screened window that was slightly ajar, I could see the eyes and cheekbones of a person peering down at me. At eleven years old I was imaginative. Although my first instinct was to run, I walked closer to the house and heard the voice say, "Come up the stairs for a moment. I want to ask you a favor." I knew to ask my Mom first, and I informed the woman of this. After Momma said that she didn't mind as long as she knew where I was, I came back as fast as I could and climbed that tall flight of stairs.

The door to this house was open, and I stepped inside. There sitting on the edge of a bed was an oversized woman with two long braids hanging to her waist like an Indian. She pleasantly greeted me, saying, "My name is Mrs. Williams, and I was wondering, could you do something for me?"

I said, "I guess so."

She asked, "What's your name?" and started up a friendly conversation. As we got acquainted, I saw that she really needed someone there to help her from time to time. She was a very nice woman, and I was glad I was there to lend a hand. I soon discovered that Mrs. Williams was a paraplegic and that she was divorced from the man who lived in an apartment that was upstairs in the back of the same house. Although they were no longer married to each other, they owned the house together and rented out most of the rooms.

Mrs. Evelyn Williams had a daughter and three grandchildren, and when they were not available to assist her, she would call me from the upstairs window and ask me to do chores for her. She weighed at least 300 pounds, was either half white or half Indian, and had a temper to match the length of her hair, which was long and thick and needed combing every day. I soon began stopping by every day after school. She told me fascinating stories of her life, and I would earn money from her to buy much-needed school supplies and unmentionables. I washed her hair at least once a week, changed her bed, and washed her bedsheets. I guess I was a nurse of sorts.

She earned money as an illegal numbers runner. She would write down the neighbors' bets or "numbers," and take a cut of the winnings. Some people phoned in their bets and others dropped by. While it was illegal, it was still considered an "honest" way for some of the poor to make enough money to survive on.

Years before I met her, Mrs. Williams had been in a car accident in which she was thrown from the vehicle. In the process she had injured her spleen, legs, and spine. Because of her size and her lack of exercise, she was plagued by rheumatism and arthritis. Yet she still had the spunk to get up every morning and run her numbers operation.

If I think about it, and inhale, I can still smell the liniment that she rubbed on her swollen joints. Since she wasn't able to do it properly, I often rubbed the liniment on her. I could always be of help, which made me feel good about doing something for someone less fortunate than I. I would cook for her, and from time to time she sent me to buy things for her at either Mr. Edward's or Mr. Mack's stores. After I was finished doing chores for her, I would leave as fast as she would count out forty or fifty cents as my pay. She never gave me more than a whole dollar for hours of sweating, turning her, changing her bed, and doing her laundry. She was demanding and always wanted things done for her exactly her way. But my real pay was in learning to do a lot of things for myself in addition to what I learned at home from Momma.

Mrs. Williams would sit on the side of a double bed, day in and day out, looking out her window at the neighborhood below. She made note of everyone's comings and goings, and she would always have reports and gossip for anyone who gave her an audience. I learned about nearly everybody's business in the neighborhood. She was quite a character, and I grew very fond of her.

Unfortunately, she was one of the first people I ever knew who died. One day she had heart failure and died alone in her room. I was thirteen, and I never knew how much I really cared about her until I saw her lying very still, waxen and pale. I had gone to the funeral parlor to pay my last respects and promptly fainted when I saw Mrs. Williams laid out and looking decidedly dead. That was the last funeral I attended for a long time. When I arrived at Mrs. Williams's house just after she had died, I saw three men skillfully carry this 300-pound woman down the stairs as if she were a delicate glass figurine. That helped ease the pain of losing someone whom I still consider to be one of my "godmothers." Being with her those two years kept me out of a lot of teenage trouble that I could have gotten into, and I am thankful for her having been in my life. I know that my education was a little greater than the average child's because of Mrs. Williams and her attention.

In my last four years at Russell Elementary School, I was taken from the regular classes and put with several other students who had been selected by the teachers to become part of what they called an "Open Air" program. The children were there because certain handicaps or afflictions made it difficult for them to attend regular classes. Some of the students in the program were hard-of-hearing, blind, malnourished, or neglected. A few had Down's syndrome. Although it was never made clear just why I was placed there, I have always sus-

pected that it was because I wasn't properly nourished. Back then I
had very poor eating habits. I was always skinny and never seemed
to have much of an appetite. Mom made me sit at the table sometimes when everyone else had finished, instructing me to clean my
plate. After I was treated for a case of bronchitis, I overheard a doctor
tell my mother that I was "anemic." Regardless of the reason, I was
happy to have been chosen for this program, as it provided us with a
light breakfast, a hearty lunch, recess on the open-air roof, and an
afternoon rest period. It was almost like attending a private school
within the public school system.

Our teacher was Mrs. Keys, a beautiful silver-haired lady who
had a face that looked as if it belonged on the front of a cameo. In
one room she taught the fifth, sixth, seventh, and eighth grades in
separate rows. She would go from one grade to the next, controlling
every situation with a stern rule and zealous determination. I found
myself among some very intelligent people and I was encouraged to
learn even more. I even won the district spelling contest. The prize
was a collegiate dictionary, which I dearly cherished.

Mrs. Keys was a gem of a teacher who never stepped out of the
guise of educator. She had no sense of humor or any patience for
fooling around or not paying attention. I can still remember her smiling when we gave the correct responses to her questions. She usually
wore a navy blue two-piece suit and a white blouse. The blouse style
would vary—sometimes nylon or ruffled—but it was always white.

In my four years with Mrs. Keys, we only had a handful of sub-
stitute teachers. One of the substitutes was the sister of Detroit's
world-famous boxer, Joe Lewis. I remember how impressed we all
were to have Miss Lewis instruct us for a couple of days. Detroit was
filled with celebrities, and it was always inspiring to encounter them—
or anyone closely related to them. This reinforced my realization that
people of working-class beginnings could rise up and attain stardom—right in my hometown of Detroit.

When the weather permitted we would go onto the roof to play
during our recess. There was a tall chain-link fence that kept us from
any dangers, but it was merely a screen and didn't stop the voices of
the regular students from below. They taunted us and called us rude
names, as if we had a choice about being in this special classroom.
Sometimes it felt like prison, and at other times I was glad to be there

because we had fewer students and the attention of our fine Mrs. Keys.

For school one warm spring day, I had worn a sundress selected from a bundle of discarded clothes that my mother's cousin, Veola Culver, had brought over. They had been given to Veola by her rich employers. At least we thought they were rich. God rest her soul, Veola considered us poor, and she would give us a lecture every time she came to our house with her secondhand gifts. She would throw it up in Mom's face in conversation whenever she and Mom didn't agree. I remember hearing her tell my mom, "You should not have laid down and had all of those children."

Mom has always had a lot of pride, and she passed it on to me. She never asked Veola for anything, and she was probably taking these discarded rags off of Veola's hands. We could wash some of them and wear them once or twice. In a large family, we often wore "seconds," and it was all right as long as we knew they were clean. I had washed, starched, and ironed this lovely-looking little dress, placing the pleats in the skirt just so and making it look as new as possible. However, I didn't notice how thin the cotton fabric was. The day I wore it, I had on my first garter belt and my first silk stockings, but no slip. I didn't know anything about slips yet.

It was a hot day and I thought I looked cute in that dress until I stood in that slow-moving line. When the boys caught the sight of my body through it, they started teasing me. Little did I know that the sun shone through the thin material, turning it transparent and undressing me from the waist down. When the boys started laughing, making snide remarks, and pointing at me, I became miserably sick to my stomach. Too embarrassed to tell Mrs. Keys what happened, I asked her if I could be excused, and she let me go into the restroom where we took our daily naps on cots. After thanking her for her kindness, I was lying there feeling much better when I spotted a roll of paper towels. There was no one around, so I tore four long sheets off the rolls and placed them just right under my dress and returned to class. The roll of paper saved the day. Sure, the paper towels rustled when I walked, and that prompted more amusement from my peers, but they couldn't see through my dress anymore. Although the whole thing fell apart as I neared home, that day I had learned a valuable lesson about the necessity of linings and slips!

The one thing I missed while being in the Open Air program was the music teacher who taught the regular classes. However, I loved to hear Mrs. Keys read us poetry. Sometimes I would sing melodies as I read the works of James Weldon Johnson, Ralph Waldo Emerson, Edgar Allan Poe, or any classic compositions that she enlightened us with.

The only opportunity to hear music was in church and around the house. My whole family would sing when the radio was on. We would all sing whenever Mom or Dad would play the guitar. I had stopped going to church four times a week as I once did, mainly because I was now needed more and more to help Momma at home in the kitchen. Sunday always meant a big meal day, with five- or six-course meals and all kinds of fancy desserts. The preacher would always come to eat, and he usually claimed the drumsticks for himself.

I was now in my teens, the rebellious age when you get to have your way sometimes–with a little extra whining. Mom would wear me out trying to work with her. She spent all of her time cooking, cleaning, and making sure we were neat and cared for.

Dad had recently been struck by an out-of-control automobile while working a jackhammer with his back toward oncoming traffic. Using the money that the insurance paid for his accident suit, we moved into a house on Townsend Street in 1956.

Meanwhile, Dad worked every day for the city and brought the money home. He left for work around 6:00 A.M. as we were awakened to rise and get ready for school. Every morning the older boys were expected to start the fire and warm the house for all of the younger kids. I would get dressed and then I'd have to help the other four girls, who were all in need of a "do." We were glad to be in our new house, although Daddy still had terrible pain from the accident and had to wear a back brace for most of the rest of his life. We even had a coal-burning furnace in the basement, something our other house didn't have, and we could sit in the living room and not have to face that big potbellied stove that everyone got burned on trying to get warm. We eventually converted the furnace to gas. Hallelujah, no more piles of the sooty coal to shovel into the bin. We had really moved up in the world!

There were three bedrooms on the top floor of our new house, and a half-finished storage room that was just the supplement we needed. (We referred to it as "the outer room.") All five of us girls shared the long front bedroom. With two double beds, we did swell. Jessie and Lois slept in one bed, and I and the two youngest ones, Delphine and Eudora, slept in the other. Sometimes morning would find us all in one bed because my sisters liked for me to tell them stories that I would make up. I would use different voices, sometimes scaring them, mostly making them laugh, until we all fell asleep.

The high school that I attended, Miller, was a predominately black school and is noted for all the great people who attended there, like former Detroit mayor Coleman Young, Little Willie John, Clifford Fears, and Motown singer Kim Weston.

Thomas and I had some classes together in high school. We both eventually transferred from Miller to Northeastern High when Miller became a middle school, and he graduated just before I did. He was just a year older than I and fell behind trying to work and go to school too at the same time. Benny had gone to join the navy upon graduation, so Tom occupied the smallest of the three bedrooms, and the one designated to the next child to leave. Victor, Melvin, Samuel, and William (in the baby's bed) held down the other room. We could finally spread out and no one had to sleep on the couch anymore.

I was very active in extracurricular activities, even making the varsity cheerleading team. Not only were we the best sports team in the city competitions, our cheering team was great. I remember slip-jointed Elsie Williams and her double flips and handstands. She taught me how to do the splits, but I couldn't quite get down like she could. She always got applause from both sides of the field. I joined the Y-Teens and Junior Achievement, and becoming a member of the choir was a must.

I spent many wonderful moments dreaming of being famous one day. I learned all I could about music, hoping one day to be as great as local singing star Little Willie John ("Fever," 1956). I would sometimes see him after school, singing in front of the candy store just across the street.

My cousin Marie Reeves attended Northeastern also, graduating the year I arrived, and she was a lifesaver. Marie was special because she had been ill most of her life with attacks of asthma. While other children were outside playing, she was in the house reading or sewing. She always had labored breathing, so she excelled at indoor activities.

She was a good student for most of her teachers. Some of them asked me if we were related. When I said yes, they spoke very highly of her, and expected great things from me. Marie could really sew, and made a lot of her own clothes, which she would graciously hand down. I wore her creations gladly. When I was in high school, she really saved the day by loaning me one of her winter coats.

My mom and Marie's mother often talked on the telephone. Speaking about my upcoming graduation ceremony, Mom said, "I was barely able to get her a dress, but she sure needs a coat, and there just isn't enough money for one." My Aunt Eunice replied, "Marie has lots of coats. We'll drop one of them by for Martha." I don't think Marie liked the idea too much, but she complied anyway and loaned it to me.

My high school graduation ceremony was very important for me. Not only was I going to get my diploma, but my choir would be singing, and today marked one of my first public solo singing performances. Momma and I were late arriving because the full-length black wool coat came late. Nevertheless, I hurried and made it to the choir stand just as the introduction to my song was beginning. The choir instructor, Mr. Abraham Silver, gave me big eyes as though he were thinking, "Thank God, you finally made it!" I adored him and his choir class, and music was my favorite subject. We were also the first choir ever to be featured in a live broadcast at Northeastern, and we performed at the Ford Auditorium before 4,000 people. We had just given a great spring concert in the school auditorium.

That day I was the featured soloist after being chosen from a group of eleven sopranos to sing "Allelujah." All of the school's choirs were combined, and I was so proud to see my name in the program. I put all my heart into my singing. This was only my fourth performance in front of people, so my knees knocked together as I nervously shook those beautiful notes and Bach's "allelujahs" out.

Mom was the only immediate family member there, and Aunt Eunice obliged me with her presence. Momma stayed up with me real late that night, curling my hair and helping me lay out my clothes for the big day. From where I stood on the stage, I looked for her approval. She had stayed awake pretty well through all the speeches, but the moment I began my aria, I could see her head was tilted back and she had fallen asleep. The applause for our efforts woke her, but she had missed my song. I couldn't be concerned about that, for she had tolerated me rehearsing all of these weeks, and I was just glad that she was there. She saw me get my diploma, and that was all that really mattered.

I didn't go to my prom because I didn't have a date, so Mom and Dad gave me permission to give a graduation party in the basement if I agreed to clean it up. Some of my fellow students showed up on short notice, but didn't stay very long because I ran out of Kool-Aid and bologna salad sandwiches too quickly. This was the best that we could afford. As my elite guests were leaving, I heard comments about the condition of our well-lived-in house, and references about other parties that they had on their lists. I stood in the doorway saying good-bye to some of them forever. Charlesetta Solomon, Marstella Hicks, Francis Thomas, Modestine Simmons, and Marzene Kendricks must have given parties themselves, because none of my cheerleading partners showed up.

The morning after my high school graduation found me up early job hunting. I ran to the County Building to apply for a Social Security card, and with my new credential, filled out as many applications as I could for open positions there. I even took a test at Wayne State University for a job where I could work and attend school at the same time. This is what my counselor at Democracy House, Mr. Graves, had suggested. I didn't pass the exam, and at that time there were no tuition grants available to me, so I put the dream of college on the back burner.

Next I tried the want ads and found a housecleaning job on the East Side. It was for a family with two small children. Both parents worked, and I was to clean their house and take care of two little boys for $8 a day. That was not enough for carfare, lunch, and other expenses like a winter coat that I direly needed. This job didn't last long, however. I had a high school diploma, and I wanted to do something more challenging than housework.

I went back to the ads and read one that made selling Stanley Home Products seem like the opportunity of a lifetime. I tried selling door to door, and since it was a good line of products, I sold them easily after a good demonstration. Although many housewives felt that they deserved the very best household aids, they just didn't seem to have the money ready when it was time for delivery. We sales reps worked on a commission basis, and I never got to the "getting paid" stage because I was to be paid out of my nonexistent sales profits.

For a while I worked in my Uncle Adron's restaurant on Canfield Street. I tried to do my best at being a waitress. The restaurant was near the railroad tracks, and Uncle Adron regularly gave credit to senior citizens on welfare and would keep their accounts in a spiral notebook. For these people, it was always a long time before the first of the month when they would get their Social Security checks. For me, it meant no tips. As anyone who has ever waited tables can tell you, tips are at least half of one's salary. I knew from the start that I was wasting my time, especially since I never received a salary from my uncle. Oh well, I owed his daughter Marie so much for loaning me all those clothes, and for being such a good friend as well as my cousin. I added waitressing to my growing résumé, and moved on.

My next job came from the want ads. There was an opening for a "telephone solicitor." After a brief inquiry on the phone, I was given an address and showed up bright and early for a desk job. I was shown to a cubicle and given the same white-paged telephone directory that I had at home. I was assigned to specific pages and given a pitch to read. Reluctantly I started dialing, after being informed that this too was on commission. My instinctive first thought was: Oh no, not again.

"Good morning, I'm calling you from the All Right Construction Company–" . . . *click.* "Good morning, I'm calling from the All Right Construction Company and we are offering a free home inspection to see if you need any of our improvement services." A man answered sharply, "Listen, babe, I'm in the business!" . . . *click.* Or, "Don't you call my house no more, my child is crying, I don't want to talk to you" . . . *click.* After a week of this–and not one single sale–I didn't receive a cent for my labor. With that, it was back to the want ads again.

In the meantime, I had met a girl named Shirley Walker, who was forming a "girl group" called the Fascinations, and we became best friends, "running buddies," almost sisters-in-law. Singing was my first love, and when she asked if I was interested, I jumped at the opportunity. I never thought that Shirley could sing, but she was the organizer and kept everybody rehearsing, even booking us gigs at small local clubs. We met some real gentlemen in the band at the Sports-man Lounge, and they helped us tremendously with their sugges-tions and advice. T.J. and his friends helped us a great deal, and Shirley continued to work hard to get new engagements and keep us going. Two girls in the group, Bernadine and JoAnne Bradley, were sisters, and we sounded pretty good together. After I left the Fascina-tions, they went on to record with Curtis Mayfield of the Impressions.

This is what I did to survive the years 1959 to 1960, being led by some powerful force. Somehow good would always emerge from every situation. Although I still hadn't successfully landed a steady paying job, I learned something new from everything I tried. I had already had so many revelations over the years as my dreams had come true, and I knew that I was meant for bigger and better things. I just had to find out what they were.

CHAPTER 2

Come and Get These Memories

I'M GONNA TAKE ADVANTAGE OF YOU

I'm not greedy, it's not my groove
Everything I've ever tried to keep
Was the very thing I'd lose
That's one sin I'm not guilty of
But when I'm resting in your arms
Wrapped up in your unchanging love
I want all I can get and more
So I'm gonna do something
I have never chosen before to do
I'm gonna take advantage of you.

I don't take it for granted
How you thrill my soul
Make me tingle inside
From my head down to my feet
I was ready to say "I love you"
As you sincerely said it to me
Your eyes give me confidence
I'm filled with happiness through and through
Don't be surprised if I follow
In your footsteps all the way
I'm gonna take advantage of you.

I have always thought of music as a way out of the ordinary mundane obligations of life. While in high school glee clubs and choirs, our singing time always seemed to end too soon. Those were two classes that were just not long enough! Long before I was ever satisfied, the loud bell would ring and we'd rush off to our next class. Many days after school, in the park just across the street, I would stand around singing harmony parts with my friends Pat, Barbara, and Charlene. We would meet just to blend our voices, while everyone else in the park courted, gambled, or did homework.

The park was the place where all of the neighborhood would sit on benches under big maple trees or stand in groups and sing. We even had an old man who would flash you if you strayed away from the crowd. Throughout the years several groups were created there in that park, including the Peppermints, who later became Little Joe and the Peps. Mary Wilson and Florence Ballard, then of the Primettes, spent some leisure hours doo–wopping in that park. Bobby Rogers and Claudette Robinson spent time there also. We all had the expert training of the same music teacher, Abraham Silver, I'm happy to say.

Mary and Florence eventually invited this girl named Diane Ross to join their group as a Primette. She later changed her name to Diana, but to any of us who knew her back then, she'll always be just Diane. Bobby and Claudette later became two of the Miracles, along with Claudette's husband, William ("Smokey"). Little Joe Harris would later work at Motown as lead singer for the Undisputed Truth, known for their 1971 hit "Smiling Faces Sometimes."

It was a magical era for Detroit. I didn't know it then, but many of the people I was encountering at this time were destined to write their own pages of musical history. Detroit had never seen it happen before, and would never see it happen again. I was already on my way to becoming part of the scene. For me, though, the road to Motown–or "Hitsville U.S.A.," as it was called back then–would be a bumpy one.

After graduation in 1959, while changing jobs every two or three weeks, I kept finding ways to sing on the side. I followed the music whenever I got the chance. Once I went to a schoolmate's house just to stand around and watch a group called the Four Tops. She bragged about how good they were, and she knew how much I loved hearing group harmonies. And this group was on its way to Las Vegas. I had never seen four more handsome men in one place, and they had a harmony reminiscent of the Four Freshmen. I thought to myself that they were the best singers I had ever heard.

I was only nineteen years old then, so I would borrow someone's identification card and pretend that I was twenty-one. Using the fake ID, I would sneak into the local nightclubs to watch the singers, in hopes that I might get a lucky break or meet someone who could help me launch a career in music. Occasionally there were showcase nights where anyone could get up on the stage and sing, play an instrument, dance, or do comedy. There was a four-piece band who could play anyone's music–or do their best to fake it. The announcer would bring the acts on, and he would tell jokes in between.

After one of my performances one night, I met a man who called himself Wine Head Willie. He was a comedian who would pull his hat over his ears and do an act that was so convincing you did not ever want to get drunk. He told me that he liked my singing, and promised to get me a spot on one of the shows he worked on. So I gave him my phone number.

When he called me from Boston saying that he had a job for me there, I asked my parents if I could go. They warned me of my previous disappointments. Several times I had already let my hopes fly too high, anticipating big things. I told him of their concerns. While I held the phone, they questioned me: "What would the pay be?" "How long will you be in Boston?" Boston was somewhere I had never dreamed of going, but I figured that this could be my lucky break. I wanted to be in show business so badly.

Wine Head Willie sent me a telegram filled with lies and misconceptions, and I fell for it hook, line, and sinker. With that invitation I packed a bag and headed for Massachusetts. I arrived at the Greyhound bus station in Boston with $5 and a suitcase–scared, cold, and adventurous. He had told me to get a cab from the station, but a man I had befriended while riding on the bus told me that the club was within walking distance. So I set off on foot, and in five minutes made it there safe and sound. When I arrived, I found a showroom at a big old dilapidated hotel, but I wasn't booked in it. I called Willie from the lobby and he gave me his room number. He had been the house comedian at this club for a month, and Milt Buckner was the headlining act.

I knocked on his door, and he asked me into his tiny double room. There was an ironing board standing upright, slightly blocking the doorway. A clothesline ran from wall to wall, and the room smelled like a gymnasium locker room.

"Where is my room?" I immediately asked. He replied, "You'll stay right here with me."

I may have been only nineteen, but I instantly sensed something to my disliking.

"The telegram you sent said that you had a gig for me," I said, "and now you are trying to tell me that this is it?" I started waving my arms around, pointing to his tacky room at this dive.

He suddenly became loud and violent. "You'll work all right–work the bar! If you pick up fifteen or twenty dollars a night, it should get you a room at the beginning of next week. For now you will stay here with me. So shut up and do as I tell you." I was in shock. I had come all this way only to find out that he expected me to become a prostitute, picking up tricks in a dive bar! I panicked.

That very second, he started to attack me, choking me with one hand and drawing his fist back to hit me. I had seen the iron on the ironing board when I came in, and it proved to be a good weapon at the right time. I managed to get a hold on it and swing it, hitting him upside the head. The lick didn't kill him–as I had hoped. It only angered him more, and holding the side of his head he yelled, "You crazy bitch, get your s—— and get your ass out of here. I tried to help you, but you ain't ready. Get out of here."

Glad to be free of him, I ran into the hallway and slammed the door behind me. *Oh my God, what am I to do now?* I thought to myself. I couldn't stay in the hallway, so I went back downstairs to the show-room. Just then, famed organist Milt Buckner was finishing up his first set, and I knew that the newly christened "Iron Head" Willie was up next. So I sat off to the side in an unlit area to avoid him, because I feared he might try to hurt me. Just then Maurice Sinclair, Milt's drummer, walked by and asked me, "What are you doing here, young lady? Aren't you a little young to be in a place like this?" I broke down and started crying. I could hardly contain my shaking, skinny body, but I managed to tell him that I had been tricked to come to Boston and I didn't know what to do. He took pity on me and tried to get me to call my parents. I told him that all I had was $5 to my name, and he shook his head and said, "Come on, child. This was definitely a dumb move, but I'll help you."

After his last set, Maurice was heading home for his three off days–Tuesday, Wednesday, and Thursday. He took me to a phone to call my parents. They were very distressed with my collect call and offered to bail me out. The soonest Dad could send for me was after payday Friday.

Maurice took me upstairs to see his friend Mary, who lived on the top floor of the hotel. She worked as a sewing machine operator in a garment factory in the daytime and would serve meals for a fee to a lot of the people who lived there. Most of her customers were on pensions, and she kept them eating between checks. Maurice asked her to feed me, and promised that he would pay her when he came back.

Acting like a ship's stowaway, I stayed in Maurice's rented room. He told me I had to be out of the room before the maids came every day, and that I must avoid the owner of the building because I wasn't a registered guest. The first day went all right. After he left I slept well, rose early, and went to apply for temporary employment where Mary worked. It was a real drag waiting around eight hours until Mary got off work. I guess I had expected a miracle, thinking that I could breeze in from Detroit and go right to work. I was so naive! The garment factory placed me at the bottom of a waiting list of about a hundred names. I hadn't planned to be in Boston that long! In this factory I saw the women sewing different pieces of cloth together, then tossing them to the next operator. After watching that assembly line action, I was glad there was no job waiting for me. The pace was maddeningly fast and demanding. That evening I offered to wash dishes and help Mary clean up after meals. She agreed, although she insisted I stay out of the kitchen when she was cooking. No one was allowed in there. I will always remember Mary as if she were an angel. Because of her kindness to a stranger like myself, she saved my life. I've always prayed for her, but I never saw her again.

Maurice had warned me to watch out for the hotel owner because he ran his place like a boardinghouse. However, the second morning, Wednesday, as I prepared to leave for the day, the room door was suddenly opened with a passkey. In walked the most obnoxious creep that I had ever met. His clothes were seedy and he was shifty-looking. Of dark complexion and undetermined national- ity, he had a big stomach that seemed to lead him around. "Who are you and what do you think you're doing?" he demanded.

I was too scared to say anything.

"You are not supposed to be in here," he said sternly. "How did you get in here, anyway?"

While I was explaining that Mr. Sinclair had given me permission to wait for him here, he stared at me, looking me up one side and down the other. He started moving in on me. As he spoke, he came closer and closer, looking sleazier with each step. He was mumbling something about "if you act right . . ." as I moved closer to the dresser where my knife was lying. It was not large, and I mainly used it to cut apples or things like that, but I genuinely feared this evil spirit now in my face.

"What will you do with this?" he asked, snatching up my blade, opening it, and laughing slightly. He closed it and tossed it back down on the top of the dresser. I stood there frozen with fear. He left me there scared to death, retorting as he left, "You be out of here by tomorrow, or I'll have you thrown out by the police."

This was one of those times that I wanted to abandon my dream of a career in show business. I was alone, in danger, and feeling like an absolute fool for trusting Willie, for believing that I had a job but not having sense enough to ask for a contract or a deposit. In time I learned that these are both very necessary things in show business. This was one lesson I learned the hard way.

Mary had a friend not far away who let me bring my suitcase and dilemma to him. I was able to use his address to get my letter of deliverance from Mom and Dad. The days seemed to crawl by. This man worked evenings in a club along with his costar, Little Miss Cornshucks. I was used to tricks by now, and when he too tried to get sleazy with me, it was time for me to leave Boston.

After my money arrived I walked back to the bus depot alone, just as I had come nearly running that brisk Monday morning. I was sure happy after the twelve-hour ride back home. Detroit never looked so good. Next morning, it was back to the *Detroit Free Press* want ads for me.

One evening late in the summer of 1960, one of the guys managed by my friend Fred Brown gave me a telephone number and suggested I call a girl named Rosalind Ashford. She was looking for someone to replace a member of her singing group, the Del-Phis. A group member's family had to move out of state, so I agreed to audition for them. I went to Rosalind's house, and after being introduced I found that I knew most of the popular songs on their list. Also, our voices blended really well together. Right off the bat it was an automatic fit.

Gloria Jean Williamson, the group's leader, was around my age. She could play gospel keys on the piano well enough to conduct her church choir, and she'd give out harmony parts with ease. We all had good ears, and she had a real good voice. She sang with all of her heart, and definitely held your attention.

After that meeting, I officially became one of the Del-Phis. Alternating from house to house, our parents would listen to us and serve us bologna sandwiches and sometimes potato chips. All the neighbors would come in to compliment and encourage us.

We would rehearse three times a week, and we tried to keep busy singing at any celebration: birthday parties, weddings, anniversaries. Any occasion and we'd be there. We later worked the Masonic lodge, the Elks' hall, and several banquet halls around the city. We even played at YMCAs and YWCAs—virtually anywhere we could get an audience.

When Gloria was singing songs of heartbreak on stage, she would get so emotionally carried away that big tears would run down her cheeks, and we all would wind up boohooing. We were all young and in love with love, so we could identify with her sorrow.

Annette Beard, the quiet one in the group, was the alto. She was neither as friendly as Rosalind nor as solemn as Gloria. I was the outgoing member of the quartet. We lived a long distance from each other, but we were dedicated and rehearsed at least three or four times a week and got together every weekend. I miss those times. With our different personalities, we were never easy around each other, but we sang like angels, and our voices blended together as one. I had more pleasure singing backup to Gloria's lead than anything. She had great crowd appeal, and our three-part harmonies behind her were outstanding. I always believed that before you could effectively sing lead, you had to perfect background singing.

We all competed in local talent contests back then. All of us future Motown stars were local contest winners first. We went through that amateur stage together, and we had all competed at one time or another at the Warfield Theater, where the shows were judged by an applause meter. We often competed with Mary Wilson and Florence Ballard's group. Sometimes we would win as the Del-Phis, sometimes they'd win as the Primettes. Sometimes the Primes would take the show, and nobody could get on. Other winners included the Voice Masters, who later became the Originals. They *really* kicked butt! Everybody had a turn to win.

When we finally made it to Motown, the Primettes became the Supremes, the Primes became the Temptations, and the Del-Phis were destined to become stars as Martha & the Vandellas.

One night Gloria, Annette, Rosalind, and I had fun riding all the way to Flint, Michigan, to sing. Flint was about 100 miles from Detroit, and upon arrival there we were taken to a dark and shabbily furnished house that was to be our dressing facility and rest stop. The ladies' dressing room was small but adequate to change in. The men had the larger room, which was the living room. There were several couches pushed up against the walls, and the room was cluttered with a lot of other broken, scattered, well-used furniture.

Tony, the redheaded featured male vocalist, was the first to begin protesting, but we only laughed as he described this place, putting it down with some choice words. We changed into our homemade costumes and went to put on a good show at a large auditorium. It had a ceiling that was so high the sound just bounced from wall to wall, but we managed. Judging by the sound system that night, the young black business group who gave this affair knew very little about the technical side of things, and were just as green as we were.

When the gig was over and we gathered once again at the "haunted house," Fred Brown, one of our managers, took us aside. He poked at his glasses, perspired, chewed gum, and spoke fast—his usual manner. Fred proceeded to tell us that there was a problem with the pay, and we had to call our parents and tell them that we had to stay overnight. This was obviously another painful show business lesson to learn: It's called "get paid first—before showtime." We would be able to return to Detroit as soon as the banks opened, but some of us had to go to work or school, and there was a lot of grumbling at this point. This was a strange place, and it was supposed to house fifteen or more performers, plus our managers, Katie and Fred. Just where were we all supposed to sleep?

Gloria and her boyfriend, James, found themselves a space in the corner of one of the other rooms, and Annette, Rosalind, and I tried bedding down in the small room we first changed in. Pulling the covers back to the bed that was sitting in the middle of the room, we found dingy, ragged sheets with traces of past loungers. The springs were so worn that the bed sank in the middle, so we passed on it. We found it easier to pull the mattress from the bed to the floor. Sleeping under our coats, we tried to relax. I didn't like show business very well that night. The noises from a party in the other room kept us awake all night long. The laughter and talking was as loud as the guitars and radios that were constantly playing. We killed several roaches and prayed there were no rats about. The four of us made a pact never to tell our parents how horribly we had been accommodated, or they'd never let us leave town again. In the morning after a bank transaction was completed, our pay came, and we safely made it back to Detroit.

Gloria and James were having a torrid affair at the time, and they had equally passionate lovers' quarrels. They soon moved in together, and whenever they didn't get along, neither did we. We didn't rehearse or sing anywhere if Gloria and James were amid one of their arguments. That became annoying real fast, and put a strain on our relationship.

Realizing that the Del-Phis might not have the unity to last, I began seeking out other musical opportunities on the side. I started singing the blues and light jazz with local quartets, both in and out of Detroit. I attended sessions held at Mrs. Rogers's Rappa House. She taught music, dance, and drama, having once been a professional dancer in the thirties and forties. She once had an act with her husband, who had since passed away. He would lift her up in the air in gorgeous costumes. She was really beautiful, God rest her soul.

Mrs. Rogers also acted as a booking agent for her pupils, and she booked me in Canada as Martha LaVaille. Also on a show with me was Yvonne Thomas, a snake dancer who worked with a boa constrictor and who kept the snake in her hotel room. Yvonne was well versed and taught me a lot in the week that we played at that roadside "Holiday Out," as I called it (as opposed to Holiday Inn). I will always be grateful to her for being so protective, and watching out for me. The club owner was the kind who wanted sex with the women who worked his club. I didn't and never have operated that way, so after a week, I formally *booked*. By now I had learned to get paid before I worked, after one too many times going home empty-handed.

As the Del–Phis, we did have a fleeting moment of glory, recording one song on Checkmate records, "I'll Let You Know." We had sung background vocals on a record by J. J. Barnes called "Won't You Let Me Know," and our recording was the "answer song" to it. Now we knew what it felt like to hear ourselves on the radio, but in the end it received very little airplay and no one could seem to find it in the record stores. This did not discourage me, but the disappointment was painful. We had no contract, no compensation, just experience. Things looked doomed for our group as we all went our separate ways to seek income. I started working for City Wide Cleaners in 1960 and moved to six different locations during the week, filling in during each of the regular clerks' days off.

In October 1961 I entered another talent contest, and won a perfect opportunity: a short gig for three nights at the fabulous Twenty Grand during happy hour: 5:00 till 8:00 P.M. On my last and final evening, a knight in shining armor came into my world, and I have never looked back since.

People talk about unsung heroes in their careers. Well, one stepped into my life that night. It was just like the fairy tales I have learned to believe in–and the glass slipper was about to fit *my* foot! Here I was, in the fabulous Twenty Grand. All of the stars of the sixties in our category were formed, shaped, and/or discovered in this popular establishment, so I was overwhelmed when I finally got a chance to sing there. I was especially excited because this was my first "legitimate" gig.

I was only twenty at the time, and a minor, so my friend Melvelyn Mance let me borrow her identification. Although I had won the contest and would probably be admitted to the club, I carried her ID just in case a policewoman made a surprise visit and stopped me from working.

That night I felt a little sad. It was the last of my three nights, and I dreaded the thought of going to City Wide Cleaners the next morning. I had never found the adage "Money breeds money" so true as it was in this nightspot. This place was a combination of a bowling alley, dance hall, lounge, and showroom.

My big break at the Twenty Grand consisted of a two–song set. My first number, "Fly Me to the Moon" in B–flat, had gotten a nice response. Just as I finished the tag of "Gin House Blues," I started to exit to retreat to the nice dressing room backstage. My very own dressing room at the club was attractive and private. It gave me a taste of what being a "star" was all about.

From out of the darkness this real good–looking man approached me, and he extended his hand to help me down the three steps from the stage.

"Your name is Martha. Martha what?" this handsome guy asked me kindly.

I was so stunned that I could barely utter "LaVaille" and accept the business card he handed me. MOTOWN RECORDS, the card read. Below that, it said: *William Stevenson, A&R Director, Hitsville U.S.A., 2648 West Grand Boulevard.* I had never heard of Motown or Hitsville U.S.A., but I did love the Miracles, Marvelettes, and Mary Wells. I knew of Marv Johnson, Barrett Strong, and how Eddie Holland's "Jamie" had just gone to Number 1. These artists' songs were burning up the airwaves. You heard Mary Wells's "Bye Bye Baby" at least six or seven times a day on radio stations WCHB, CKLW, and WXYZ every day. It wasn't until later that I realized that these stars were all with Motown.

William Stevenson had walked into the door of the Twenty

Grand as if he owned the place, looking as if he had just starred in a movie or had just posed for a photo session. He was well tailored in the neatest silk suit I had ever seen, and his hair was perfection: combed-out finger waves that were as natural-looking as they could be. He looked as if he had just left Benny Mullins's barbershop, since Benny had all of the stars for clients.

He questioned the origin in my stage name. With a smile and a chuckle he asked me, "What kind of name is that?" I assured him that it was a name I was given by my Auntie Bernice, Uncle Sylvester's second wife. As she pierced my ears, she predicted that I would be a big star one day.

"I think you have something," he told me. "Come to Hitsville U.S.A. for an audition. You were real good."

I was flabbergasted. When I arrived at this heaven of a nightspot, I never dreamed it would happen for me on that very evening. In the past I had only known smaller clubs—and some terrible facilities. I had learned several of the tricks of this business, like how to change clothes without exposing oneself to the entire band, comedians, dancers (shake, tap, or softshoe), jugglers, or whomever else I was booked with. All of my shows of the past were variety shows, reminiscent of vaudeville. I had worked with groups of girls along the "chitlin' circuit," as we lovingly described our stomping grounds. Here I was working for the first time at this world-famous place where all of the big stars played. Astonished, I kept repeating to myself: "I've just been discovered!"

I must say I acted real cool as I put his business card in my bosom, as I said "thanks" and "bye" and promised to take him up on his offer. But after I closed the dressing room door behind me, my heart was racing. I jumped up and down and let out a squeal of joy and thanked God! I was going to Hitsville U.S.A.!

My friend Emory came by to pick me up and drive me home. He was a kind man who would sometimes help me get to and fro, since I didn't have a car. I couldn't tell him fast enough of my good fortune. He didn't exactly share my enthusiasm, but he told me in his quiet way that he was happy for me. We had known each other for about a year, and he had seen me get excited about things in the past, only to be let down in the end. "I know I can pass the audition. It's gonna be a piece of cake!" I exclaimed.

Cautiously, he wished me good luck.

I made the decision to quit my job at City Wide Cleaners as we rode home. I had been there for two years and didn't see any growth opportunities for me in the dry-cleaning business. Besides, I had always prayed to be a singer like Lena Horne and Dinah Washington—those special ladies who sang their hearts out.

Emory and I frantically rushed home, for there was no way I could disobey my father's strict midnight curfew. I had been contemplating moving out of my parents' house. Daddy repeated over and over again, "If you can't make it to my house by midnight, then don't come in at all." He was dead serious about enforcing this rule, so I never took it personally. But even Cinderella was late sometimes.

I had briefly moved out when I turned nineteen, but that was a disaster. After a bout with pneumonia living in my tiny kitchenette apartment on Holbrook and John R. Streets, I returned home to get my strength back. I gave every cent of my money that I could spare from my meager earnings to my parents. Even when I moonlighted on the weekends, I only cleared about forty bucks after deductions. There was always some debt—the telephone, light, gas, or water bill—that Dad's salary from the City Water Board didn't quite cover. I rarely had anything left for myself except transportation fare and a limited fast-food budget. I knew in my heart that taking this A&R director's offer wouldn't be too much of a gamble. I was convinced that it would be a giant step for me.

I said good night to Emory, giving him a peck on his cheek, and left him there in the car. I tiptoed up the front stairs trying not to wake anyone or turn on any lights until I made it up the stairs to my room. I hurriedly prepared for bed, but sleep didn't come easily. I lay there and dreamed about my big day at Hitsville U.S.A. tomorrow.

It was then that it dawned on me that Motown was the new company that the Miracles recorded for. They had just hit it big with "Shop Around." Motown's girl group the Marvelettes were on the way to Number One with "Please Mr. Postman," and Motown's singer Barrett Strong became a star with the song "Money." Now I was *really* excited about tomorrow.

I also thought about the Del-Phis. Fred and Katie Brown and Pops Larkins, our former managers, had taken us as far as they could, and Checkmate Records didn't promote us, so we had wandered. I thought about how we would sing a lot of songs that had double leads like "The Night Time Is the Right Time" by Ray Charles and the Raeletts. I also thought about how versatile the Del-Phis were. Gloria Jean Williamson and I would alternate lead-singing chores on songs of our own liking. Finally I drifted off into my dreams about tomorrow.

I slept lightly and was wide awake at daybreak. When it was the proper time to stir, and as I cleared my stuff out of the bathroom, I listened to my siblings rushing about making their usual morning commotion: "Hey, did you go to sleep in there?" "Come out of that bathroom!" "It's my turn! I'll tell Daddy."

Amid all of the activity, I made it downstairs to talk to Momma and Daddy, to tell them of my good fortune, what I planned to do, and ask their opinion. They listened to me tell them of my "lucky break" while they went about their morning chores.

While she was cooking in that never-measure-anything way of hers, Momma advised me to do the best you can at whatever you do, and ask God to lead and guide you.

Daddy, who was usually optimistic, was slow to give his approval. He did, however, give me directions for the route on the Grand-Belt bus that would take me directly there. His directions, as usual, were foolproof. I set off for Motown.

As I crossed West Grand Boulevard and found 2648, the first thing I saw was a carved wooden sign with blue letters spelling out the words HITSVILLE U.S.A. With the exception of the sign, it looked like any other house in the neighborhood. Somehow I wasn't disappointed that it was not a big ten-story office building. I walked up the stairs and opened the front door. There on the floor of the front hallway sat a big Doberman pinscher that was chained just enough away to allow me to enter the door. It wasn't a large reception area.

The president of the company, Berry Gordy, had an office on one side of the receptionist's booth. In the booth was a four-line telephone switchboard.

Rebecca Giles, who is still Berry Gordy's private secretary, referred me to the receptionist. She then went back to typing away at lightning speed. There was also a beautiful girl there named Dee Dee, who buzzed me in. She placed a call to Mr. Stevenson, and on the other end of the line he replied, "Who? . . . Send her back."

I stepped through the door and found myself in front of an office no larger than a walk-in closet. There sat the same bright young man whom I had met the night before. He looked at me with a perplexed expression and asked, "What are you doing here?"

I felt the blood rush to my face as I answered sheepishly, "You asked me here. Remember last night? You gave me this card . . ." I said, extending it.

"I expected you to take it and call me for an audition," he explained in a huffy tone. "We hold auditions every third Thursday of each month. I should have told you," William said as he answered the ringing telephone.

Disappointed beyond belief, I was just putting the card in my handbag when he ordered, "Answer this phone. I'll be right back." With that, he left me in the small closet-sized, windowless office. The telephone started to ring again before he could get away, but he left without answering it.

So I picked up the phone. "Hello, A&R department, Mr. Stevenson's office, may I help you?" I asked in my most businesslike manner.

A voice on the line asked, "What?", and I repeated my spiel.

"Where's Mickey?" the woman on the other end asked.

I said automatically, "Who is Mickey?" Then I explained, "This is the A&R department."

She informed me that Mr. Stevenson was also referred to as Mickey. She told me that she was Louise of the finance department. I in turn informed her that he was not in and had promised to be right back.

There were several other calls from other offices, and each inquiry prompted an explanation as to just who I was, and drew the same astonished reaction that they "didn't know there was an A&R secretary." Each time, I proudly announced, "There is one now!" I was being brave—not knowing just how long this was going to continue.

Finally, during a brief pause from the ringing of the loud bell, a man slightly taller and heavier than Mr. Stevenson suddenly strolled in and casually asked, "What are you doing here, and where's Mickey?"

Well, I had already gotten quite used to saying, "He stepped out for a moment saying he would be right back." This man seemed distracted, and appeared to be only half listening to what I was saying. He started humming, shaking his combed wavy hair and causing a few locks to fall down in his face. Then he started playing on the piano, all this time not telling me who he was.

The phone rang again, and someone asked for Clarence Paul. When I repeated the name, this man took the phone call. Then it dawned on me that this was Clarence Paul, the famous singer. He had recorded some fine R&B hits several years ago. He was neatly dressed in expensive clothes and as well kept as William. But before I could thoroughly check him out, another guy came in and nonchalantly put a note on the spindle file of the desk before me. This time I recognized André Williams of "Bacon Fat" fame. I thought to myself, This place sure is full of talented men!

After a couple more phone calls, the door swung open again. There stood drummer Benny Benjamin and bass player James Jamerson.

"Where's Mickey?" they asked abruptly.

"Do you mean Mr. Stevenson?" I asked.

"Yeah, Mickey. Where is he?" said Benny.

I started to answer, and James Jamerson pushed the door open even wider and demanded, "Where is he?"

I got nervous because I didn't really know anything about what was going on. "I just know that he said he'd be right back," I explained.

James had such a serious, mean expression that it prompted me to ask questions.

"Can I help you?" I asked them with newly assumed authority.

Benny and James both asked "Who are you?" almost in unison.

I answered in a detached voice, "The A&R secretary." Little did I know that this would come to be.

"You call Mickey wherever he is, and tell him we ain't recordin' another session until he pays us our money," James said.

Then Benny added, "We cut two songs a few days ago, and we were promised to be paid before this date. We want our bread, or we ain't cuttin' shit!"

Together they got louder and meaner. Shaking, I tried to keep my composure, and started fingering the crudely scribbled notes that had been put on the spikelike spindle file I found on the cluttered desk.

As I leafed through telephone numbers, cleaning bills, and personal notes, there was a sheet of paper there that proved them right. It showed that they had indeed played on a session and had recorded two songs, but the paperwork had not been properly done. I let them know right away of my discovery. With that, Benny said, "Call Louise, she can make our checks out."

I found the number posted near the phone for the finance department, and nervously phoned her. She answered, and I said, "This is the A&R department calling, and I need to know the procedure to get the musicians their money. It was owed to them for a session they played on a couple of days ago."

"Who is this?" she asked.

And I said, "Martha Reeves. We spoke earlier. Mr. Stevenson asked me to answer the phone until he got back, but these guys are angry and refuse to record until they get paid. They seem to think that you can help."

She asked me, "Where's Mickey?"

"Mr. Stevenson told me he'd be right back."

"Who are the musicians?"

I asked James to speak to her, because he was the calmer of the two at this time. I handed him the phone. Louise obviously had dealt with him before, under similar circumstances. There were sixteen men in and out of that small office—making music, rehearsing, writing, recording, contacting players and singers, discovering talent, and making notes and putting them on spindles, but no secretary to handle it all.

The demands of these men were a friendly but obvious act of rebellion. Wouldn't you raise hell if you were recording every day for $15 or $20 a song and your compensation was always late? I certainly understood their anger. After I gave the phone to Jamerson, Louise assured him she would cut their checks and have them ready as soon as they completed the session. I obviously came there at a good time, for instead of feeling bad about not calling first, I felt like a hero when the session went on as scheduled.

The song they were cutting on that particular session was a production of Clarence Paul's. It was Hattie Little's "Your Love Is So Wonderful." It was nearly done when Mr. Stevenson returned: I handed Mickey the stack of telephone messages I had taken. As he arrived, songwriters Robert Bateman and Freddie Gorman were in the middle of a heavy discussion. Freddie was dressed in a mailman's uniform because he was a mailman and aspiring songwriter. His most famous song was "Please Mr. Postman."

Mickey quickly thanked me for the messages, and without missing a beat, informed me that there was the unfinished task of calling the musicians and performers for an upcoming session later that week. Then he handed me a list and a directory of names and phone numbers, and requested that I call to inform them of the time and place they were to record. Here I had planned to leave the moment he came back, but somehow I had inadvertently gotten into the mix.

At the end of the day, around six, I was thanked by the producers for all of my help and was offered a ride home by one of them. Clarence Paul, who turned out to be a swell person, drove me home in his Cadillac. I asked him in to meet my parents, which he graciously did. He then asked me to come back the next morning.

That's how I became the first A&R secretary at Motown. I immediately became fond of William Stevenson, or Mickey, as I grew to call him. He was the one who personally gathered together all of the top musicians as well as the winners of the local amateur contests and brought them to the Motown label. He had once been a member of a group called the Mellowtones, along with Carl, Stan, and Joe. He was tops in the field and everybody listened when he spoke. I was excited just to be working for him.

Mr. Gordy knew what he was doing when he hired Mickey. Although Berry received the glory of Motown's success, it was Mickey who was the company's true unsung hero.

After three weeks of answering phones, scheduling auditions, and communicating with musicians and artists on the label, I still hadn't been paid a cent. My father finally said to me, "You'd better get some of that man's money or you won't be going back to his company. You ain't gettin' any more of mine!"

I had quit my paying job at the cleaners and had gone to Hitsville U.S.A. hoping to become a singer, but ended up with a payless job instead. But I knew that if a chance to sing arose at Motown, I'd be right there to seize it. The very next day I approached Mickey, repeating exactly what my father had warned, and he agreed. I kind of had him over a barrel, because in my three weeks there, I had totally organized all of the paperwork in the A&R department. Since I was the only one who knew where everything was, he wouldn't be able to find anything if I left.

After a few memos, he obtained a $35–a–week salary for me. I'm proud of the fact that my father rewarded me with a '57 Chevrolet for doing as I was told and demanding a salary.

During the whole time I was a secretary at Motown, Mary Wilson, Florence Ballard, and Diane Ross seemed to be around every afternoon. They were so eager to get involved in recording that they sang background on several Mary Wells sessions to get a foot in the door. At the time, they just appeared to be popular and attractive girls that everyone seemed to know. Earlier that year they had signed with Motown, and by then they had been renamed the Supremes. Their second single, "Buttered Popcorn," had just been released, with Flo singing lead.

The Marvelettes were the top girl group at the time, and their first hit, "Please Mr. Postman," was on its way to Number 1. They were just returning from a triumphant tour of Holland when I started at Motown. While on tour, they were photographed in full Dutch attire–including wooden shoes. They looked like my paper dolls that I lovingly kept in a box as a child.

Gladys Horton of the Marvelettes laughed uproariously when I introduced myself to her on the phone.

"Is this Gladys Horton?" I had asked.

"Yes," she replied.

"Hi, this is Martha Reeves, secretary of the A&R department."

Her response was, "Ha, ha, ha! Who did you say you are!? When did Mickey get a secretary? Girl, I want to meet you! OK?"

"Mr. Stevenson wants you and the girls here for a session at two o'clock," I replied, trying to keep my businesslike composure.

She finally calmed down and assured me, "OK, I'll be there."

I liked all four of the Marvelettes at our first gathering. You can't find a heart bigger than Gladys Horton's.

My salary those first few months at Motown was enhanced with session work at extra pay. All of the Motown artists participated in the various recordings according to the producers' creativity, and whoever happened to be present to lend a hand–or a voice–did so. As I got more and more involved in my work, I was asked to leave the desk, join producers in the studio, clap my hands to the beat of tracks for four or six takes on some songs, and then stomp on the wooden floors or sing background parts when harmonies were being added. Five dollars per session went a long way back then, and it seemed like a lot for doing something I enjoyed so much. Watching the creative process at Motown was endlessly fascinating–there was so much energy there day and night.

When I first met Mr. Gordy, the owner of Motown Records, I said to myself, It's about time! I had worked for his company for several weeks and had seen him come and go into the studio, working with staff writers outside of the "beehive," the A&R department where I hung out. His eyes were what I panned in on. Those beautiful, large, penetrating, soul-shaking eyes.

The afternoon he walked up to me in the A&R department, I turned and I saw this handsome man, with his hair combed out in beautifully styled finger waves. He was smartly dressed. Evidently, he had been in a session, because he had a hint of perspiration on his brow, his tie was loosened around his neck, and he had removed his jacket.

"Where's this girl that Mickey claims has taken over his office here at my company?" he asked.

Although I had never been introduced to him, I knew instantly that he was the mysterious but famous Berry Gordy. Almost everybody called him by both names–first and last. I also knew that he was a "Jr.," because "Pops" Sr. was a regular visitor to the studio.

I couldn't say anything at first. Berry wasn't smiling, so when he suddenly appeared, I was a bit startled and frightened. He had never bothered to introduce himself until after I was put on the payroll. I guess he wanted to meet and know all of his employees. When we met, I knew that I had found a lifelong friend.

He then sort of laughed at me–not to offend, but to reassure me that I was a welcome asset to his company. He commended me on the job I had done organizing the A&R department. He then told me to keep up the good work.

I worshipped Berry Gordy for the creative dreams that he had made come true. I had never before seen an operation like Motown Records, or a man like the one responsible for all of this music. I was in awe. I also never in my wildest dreams thought that I could be his woman, for he was adorable. Since I was acquainted with his first wife, Thelma, and his three children, Berry III, Terry, and Joy, I didn't think I was his type. He and Thelma were now divorced, and he had become estranged from his second wife, Raynoma, while dating Margaret, his current girlfriend. His women were always dynamite ladies who were treated like queens, and I looked at him with eyes of devotion.

I had met his ex-wife Thelma before I came to Motown. She owned her own record company, Thelma Records, and in the past she had let us–the Del-Phis–rehearse in her studio. We had also sung backup on sessions for some of her artists. How ironic it was to be here at her husband's company.

Berry Gordy ran a tight ship. I marveled at the amount of music that was produced in his house. There was never any drinking or horsing around, and I never smelled alcohol or knew of any drugs in the establishment. People suddenly became very businesslike whenever Berry showed up to check out his facility and the activities that transpired.

He was neither short nor tall, and I never had to look up to him, or down. As I got to know him, I grew fond of hearing him talk, for I always learned something about music or songwriting. He would always listen intently and give sound advice. In time he helped me develop common business sense, and allowed me to become part of his plan to make Motown the biggest and the best.

I was aware of several white men who had something to do with this operation: Barney Ales, Irv Beagle, Ralph Seltzer, and Sidney Novak. But I wasn't certain of their roles in the company. I was convinced that Berry Gordy was the sole owner of Hitsville's Motown, and his regal manner supported this assumption.

When I arrived at Motown in 1961, Marvin Gaye was a drummer on the list of musicians that we used for recording dates. My job was to make sure the sessions happened. Marvin always answered the phone and called you "baby." He had a reputation for being late, so if I needed him there at three in the afternoon, for instance, I would tell him to be there at one.

By 1962 Marvin was not only signed to his own Motown recording contract, but he was also dating Berry's sister, Anna. He had recorded "Mr. Sandman," a beautiful ballad, and Motown's house background singers, the Andantes, did a beautiful job of backing him. When I first met him, he fancied himself as a ballad singer in the Nat "King" Cole style. His first albums, like *The Soulful Mood of Marvin Gaye*, featured his versions of pop standards such as "My Funny Valentine" and "The Days of Wine and Roses."

One day in July of 1962, Marvin had a session lined up. He was going to begin to record his first R&B album, and I had to book the background singers. After calling the Andantes, I discovered that they were scheduled to be in Chicago on that date, so I had to replace them. I couldn't let Mr. Stevenson down, so I called other names on the list. One way or another I had to supply him with the players he needed. Since that day's casting call was for singers, I got this brilliant idea to call Rosalind Ashford, Annette Beard, and Gloria Jean Williamson–the Del-Phis.

One by one I called them and tried to convince them that we could do this session. They weren't too pleased with earning only $5 per "side," but I let them know that everyone was paid that same amount to sing background. Rosalind had graduated from high school in June of '61 and was working a part-time job, but she agreed to show up for me. She then called Annette and Gloria, and talked them into it. We planned to meet in studio A to do our thing. It was so good to see them again and sing with them. Although we still talked on the phone from time to time, I had missed them those ten months we had been apart.

William Stevenson and Marvin Gaye had written a song called "Stubborn Kind of Fellow," and Mickey, the producer, wanted us to collectively come up with background parts. There were only four tracks in the studio at that time, and we stood slightly behind Marvin, inspiring him and backing him to the fevered pitch expressed in his vocals. All five of us were on one microphone. This was his first big hit, and the beginning of a good relationship for us.

We traveled in the beginning as Marvin & the Vandellas, until "Come and Get These Memories" hit the charts. We would sing our show and then run and change clothes to sing behind Marvin.

I've been asked time and time again what it was like to sing behind Marvin Gaye. All of the girls used to follow him around because he was so cute, but he didn't really pay attention to any of them. In a recent conversation that I had with Mary Wilson, she said,

"He was never interested in any of us, because to him we were just a bunch of lovestruck little girls." Nobody could really ever see what Marvin was up to. He'd come in and smoke a corncob pipe. He just did his sessions and left. He didn't reach Number One until he recorded that first string of hits with us backing him.

One day in September 1962, while I was busy typing, Mickey appeared at the door of the office, urgently saying, "Hey Martha, come on in the studio and sing this song until the union man leaves."

I asked him, "What song? What is going on? What's the rush?" I stopped what I was doing and followed him as he explained that the union man was at the front desk.

"Come on down in the studio and I'll teach it to you," he said to me as we rushed down the stairs to within the range of the micro-phone.

It seemed that for the past two years Berry Gordy had recorded all Motown's instrumental tracks at will, until the musicians' union began to pay unexpected and frequent visits. He had been warned that there should be a singer present on the microphone when recordings were being made or Motown would be fined, according to a new union ruling.

Mickey quickly had me stand in on a song being recorded for Mary Wells, "I'll Have to Let Him Go." I had been patiently waiting for my big break in the recording studio, so instead of taking it lightly, I imagined that this song was mine and sang it as best I could. Upon hearing it, Berry Gordy proclaimed, "She sounds good on this song, let's release it on her."

Having impressed everyone with the great job we had done behind Marvin Gaye, suddenly Mickey was curious as to whether my group had solo recording potential. A couple of days later, Mickey had me assemble Gloria, Annette, and Rosalind in the studio. He wanted to record a couple of songs with us to see what the Del-Phis sounded like. With Berry producing and Gloria singing lead vocals, we recorded Mr. Gordy's composition, "You'll Never Cherish a Love So True ('Til You Lose It)." With Brian Holland and Lamont Dozier producing, and Gloria on lead, we also recorded our first version of "There He Is (at My Door)."

When the recordings were done, Berry Gordy heard the pressed results and came into my office with a request for me to call the other three girls. He was going to give us a chance on his label. I nearly jumped for joy, but kept my cool until he was out of sight. Then I let out a big "Yahoo!"

He asked us to sign contracts, and I typed our names in the spaces provided in the standard forms. But when it came time to put our signatures on the contracts, Gloria decided not to sign. When it came right down to it, Gloria had made up her mind that she didn't want a career in show business after all because she had just landed a job with the city of Detroit. City jobs were hard to get–you had to go to school and take tests. Once you got a city job, you knew that you had a job for life. There was also a good retirement plan with the city, which was a far cry from show business where you didn't know what kind of future was in store for you. Besides, she had two children, and she had no real desire to travel out of town and be away from them.

This logic was exactly the opposite of my way of thinking. When the subject of contracts was first brought up, I never gave it a second thought. I totally trusted Berry Gordy. I admired him so, and was grateful for our big break.

After Gloria left, Berry called Annette, Rosalind, and me into his office to see who wanted to stay in the group and who wanted to leave–our first official meeting with Mr. Gordy as a group.

"Listen, we've got this record here. We know one of your members has quit. Are the three of you going to stay together?"

Annette and Rosalind both said that they liked the idea of recording and were willing to consider it.

My reaction was a definite "yes! yes! yes! yes! yes!"

Berry decided that the already pressed single of "You'll Never Cherish a Love So True ('Til You Lose It)" would be released with Gloria's lead vocal on it, under the group name the Vels.

The contract that he was offering us was as a new trio, with me singing lead on "I'll Have to Let Him Go." That's how I became the designated lead vocalist of the group.

I sat there and envisioned my group, the former Del-Phis, and the possibility of our making it there at Motown among all of these other megastars. I felt that we could hold our own, and I was especially confident since Mr. Gordy obviously felt that we were talented enough to become one of his creations. He told the three of us to make up a name to replace "Del-Phis." Since that name was a part of another deal, he advised us that it might cause legal problems in the future.

We only had fifteen minutes to pick a name, or be called "the Tillies" or "the Pansies," or some corny name in jest. As Berry prompted us to hurry, I waited, thought, and as the minutes seemed to fly by, I came up with a collection of words.

Della Reese had inspired me when I saw her at New Liberty Baptist Church, and my soul was blessed. She had sung the most beautiful rendition of "Amazing Grace," and then the next day I saw her singing "Don't You Know" on network television. In my mind, she could do it all—church and popular music. She was also one of Mr. Gordy's associates from his Flame Show Bar days. She was one of Detroit's finest, and one of the most beautiful performers when she was on stage. I felt that the association with her name would bring us luck, so I decided to go for it. The "Della" in Vandellas comes from her name.

As for the "Van," I lived in my parents' house, which is still our home, near Van Dyke Street. It would always identify us with Detroit, for it's a street that goes from east to west and connects you to north and south as it curves and winds through the heart of my neighborhood. So the name Vandellas was derived more or less right on the spot. It had a certain ring to it.

With that, Martha & the Vandellas were born! Our first single was the song "I'll Have to Let Him Go," which was originally slated for Mary Wells. The flip side featured us singing a song that I wrote and Mickey polished entitled "My Baby Won't Come Back." We lived through our first release as quietly as possible. It only sold about four copies, and we each bought one!

Despite our modest sales, I had a new group and a recording contract. I was part of Motown Records, and I couldn't have been more elated. I was on the threshold of the most exciting part of my life. I was determined that Martha & the Vandellas would go all the way to the top. I dared to dream of big things for us, and step-by-step I was about to see my dreams turned into reality.

CHAPTER 3

The Motown Revue

THE WAYS OF LOVE

The ways of love
    I thought I knew
So misinformed
    Till I found you
One magic day
    And our eyes met
You've made my best
    Get better yet

I've needed love
    An eternity
You've changed my dreams
    To reality
Put a mixed-up child
    In a woman's place
Added sugar and spice
    To my uncertain taste

You're sensational
    Yes you are
The answered prayer that
    Heaven sent to me
You're sensational
    Yes you are
Love is life's reward
    It's got to be

Signing a contract with Motown represented the beginning of a whole new world for me. When I was singing under the name of Martha LaVaille, my heart's desire was to be as moving and soul-stirring a jazz singer as Billie Holiday, Dinah Washington, Ella Fitzgerald, Sarah Vaughan, J. P. Morgan, Morgana King, and Carmen McRae. I had always wanted to become a jazz singer.

Momma had loved Billie Holiday's music so much when she was growing up that she wore camellias in her hair like her singing idol. She encouraged me as a child to pursue my dreams. "Never sing a song unless you mean it from your heart," she would tell me.

I always tried to put all of my emotions into my songs when I was starting out in the talent contests around Detroit. I took that same advice when I began recording at Motown. I wanted songs that I could believe in and put my heart into. For the most part, that was exactly what I would be given.

By hiring me as his secretary, Mickey Stevenson had been responsible for my first Motown recording session, my recording contract, and the beginning of my professional singing career. Martha & the Vandellas' next major recording, "Come and Get These Memories," would not be released as a single until the following February. It was a beautiful song, written and produced by Brian Holland, Lamont Dozier, and Eddie Holland. We were the first girl group to sing a composition written by this brilliant trio of Holland–Dozier–Holland. Once we added the song to our stage act, audiences immediately responded to it. I really tried to put myself into my performance whenever I sang it, and it always drew thunderous applause.

The song itself is about a brokenhearted girl giving back to her boyfriend all of the mementos of their love–gone–bad. On stage I would use a large teddy bear as a prop. I sang a line about giving back the stuffed animal that had been won at the state fair. When I came to that line, someone would hand me the teddy bear from the wings. Then I would throw it back when I would reach the line telling the boyfriend to come and get it.

According to Berry's eldest sister, Esther Gordy, when Berry heard our recording of "Come and Get These Memories," he exclaimed, "that's the sound I've been looking for. That's 'the Motown Sound'! " The song had a steady beat, great background harmony parts, horns, catchy lyrics, and a story line that everyone could identify with. I knew instantly that it would be a hit. I've always thought that the song really shows off the great harmonies that Rosalind and Annette and I had in the very beginning.

During our rise to success, we girls would hang out together. In my '57 Chevy I'd pick up Mary Wilson and Diane Ross, and we'd go to the Twenty Grand and dance with the fellas all night. A couple of years younger than I, they were cute and had been a fixture at Motown for quite some time.

One of my most exciting times from this era came during a show at the Michigan State Fair in Detroit. This was the first time that we met the Beach Boys. They had just released their first single, "Surfin' Safari." I was impressed by how nice and friendly they were. I was even more excited by how well we were received singing our new but still unreleased song, "Come and Get These Memories." Then we stood backstage singing on a mike and watching the girls go wild over Marvin Gaye doing "Stubborn Kind of Fellow." It was such a great day for us, and I really felt that we were on the threshold of stardom.

The next project we recorded with Marvin Gaye was "Hitch Hike," and after its success, we did a third single together, "Pride and Joy." It prompted an album by Marvin that featured us on every cut of the "A" side of it, and in a photo on the back of the cover. Entitled *That Stubborn Kinda' Fellow*, it was released in January 1963. Without an album of our own, and still amid our "Marvin Gaye & the Vandellas" phase, we were thrilled just to be featured on that album.

Years later a writer would claim on one of Marvin's *Greatest Hits* albums that I was trying to steal his glory by singing out so clearly. My voice does stick out on those cuts, but nobody could steal Marvin Gaye's glory. I loved him so, and all I had done was sing my best. I think that the statement in the liner notes was just an aside to the reader. I always admired Marvin, and even though he was guarded with his emotions, he knew that he had a friend in me.

Prior to the album's release, we traveled around with Marvin promoting the "Stubborn Kind of Fellow" single. In October 1962, we went with him to Philadelphia to sing background on that song on Dick Clark's TV show, "American Bandstand." We also got to sing "Come and Get These Memories," and became the first act to get an encore on his show because of the overwhelming applause. I thought the encore version of the song would be cut out of the show, but when I watched the broadcast, Dick Clark had obviously given the go-ahead.

The marketing strategy behind "Come and Get These Memories" was for us to perform the song everywhere we could. After Motown finally released the single, it would have instant recognition among listeners and would become a hit. Ultimately the plan paid off, and the song launched our career.

The amazing thing for me was the speed with which I went from being a secretary in the A&R department to a recording artist—all within the same company. As a secretary at this bustling record company, a typical day might begin with plans for upcoming recording sessions and might end up with providing hand claps and singing background vocals on someone's new hit record. There was never a dull moment at Motown, because one or more of the many writer/producer/singers were there till all hours. There were fifteen or more on staff—all enterprising hopefuls, playing the piano, making out schedule sheets, and going through the creative process that goes into making music. Although I reported for duty as a secretary promptly every morning, I definitely felt more like a singer than I had at City Wide Cleaners! Now, from an artist's standpoint, Motown was much more than just an office to come to. It became even more of an exciting place where magic was created.

One of the most dramatic star-making events was about to take place at Motown that fall of '62, and I was about to be swept up in it. From the end of October to mid-December, the company was going to launch "the Motown Revue" (sometimes referred to as "the Motor Town Revue" and "Motor City Tour" as well). It was an ingenious promotion that put us all on the map.

With a twelve-piece band, we were to set off on a three-month tour of America—with just three nights in a motel bed. We virtually lived on that one bus, and we always had to sit up because there wasn't enough room for anybody to stretch out. Only the Miracles rode in a car, because they could afford one.

Before I knew it, it was time to board the bus. Shortly beforehand, we had taken a group photo in the back of studio A. I was confident that I had remembered to bring everything that I would be needing. I had some shabby pieces of luggage—certainly nothing to impress anybody. With the exception of my summers spent in Alabama as a child, I had never traveled extensively before, and neither had many of the other players.

We were ready to depart Hitsville U.S.A., and all of the artists, musicians, tour managers, chaperons, and executives from ITMI (Motown's management company) were scurrying around taking care of last-minute details. I was uneasy—and anxious—about leaving. When the bus arrived, it had the words MOTOR CITY TOUR painted on the side in huge letters. I finally was able to sit back in the seat that I chose near the front door on the right.

The men in our group were all consoling their wives and trying to appear sorry to leave them, but the words "can't hardly wait!" were screamed in muffled tones. This was our first cross-country pilgrimage, and we were all hopeful that we could pull it off.

The fact that we were to travel for three months and perform ninety-four "one-nighters" was hard to imagine. Even more unbelievable was all of the young talent that was aboard the bus that day. The show included Mary Wells, the Contours, the Supremes, twelve-year-old "Little" Stevie Wonder, Singin' Sammy Ward, the Miracles (including Smokey Robinson and his wife Claudette), the Marvelettes, Marvin Gaye, Martha & the Vandellas, the Temptations (they were singing backup for Mary Wells before David Ruffin joined the group), Bill Murray (the emcee), and Choker Campbell and His Show of Stars Band. Thomas "Beans" Bowles and Berry Gordy were the brains behind this unbelievable tour, and Mr. Bowles would be traveling with us. "Beans" was also an accomplished flutist and saxophone player. His solos can be heard on Marvin's "Hitch Hike" and later on "(Love is Like a) Heat Wave."

Three girls from secretarial school replaced me as the secretary of the A&R department. Hosanna, Dorothy, and Elaine were glad to get their new jobs at Hitsville U.S.A., but I could see in their faces that they would have gladly exchanged places with us and gone on that crowded bus.

The entire staff was there for the big send–off. All of the women wanted to accompany Smokey, Marvin, Bobby, and Sammy, and all the men were hugging and kissing Claudette Robinson and Mary Wells. No matter what they said, we were still going.

I had just turned twenty–one that summer, and Annette and Rosalind were both twenty. The Marvelettes were all only eighteen, and so were Diane Ross and Mary Wilson. Mary Wells and Florence Ballard were nineteen. In other words, we were "young adults." Berry was concerned about how the guys were going to behave–virtually living on a bus with us for three months. To minimize any possibility of misconduct, he assigned a chaperon to keep an eye on all of us. Mrs. Morrison was a large woman with a strict, authoritarian attitude. While on tour she would lecture us about how we girls shouldn't mar this tour by "becoming intimate" with the boys.

Before we left, Berry assembled all of the guys and warned them that he had better not get any reports about them "fooling around" with the women on the tour. He then took all of us girls aside and told us that he wanted us to act like ladies, and jokingly warned us to especially stay away from the Contours, because they were "trouble."

Berry gave us a great pep talk: "You're not only representing Motown Records," he said, "you're representing all of Detroit."

As the bus pulled away, real tears were falling. My dreams were just beginning to come true, and I was approaching the big time. I remember praying: "Lord, let us be good, but most of all, keep us free from hurt, harm, and danger."

The plan behind the Motown Revue was to send all of the label's biggest recording stars and young hopefuls out on the road to promote our latest recordings, turn those recordings into hits, and return as "stars."

Everyone on the tour was busily promoting one new recording or another. Mary Wells's "You Beat Me to the Punch" was still on the charts, and "Two Lovers" was released while we were on the road. They both became Top Ten pop hits for her, and each went to Number 1 on the R&B chart. The Contours had their song "Do You Love Me" out, and it hit Number 3 on the pop chart during the tour. Like us, the Supremes were still trying to get a hit. Their last single had only reached Number 95 on the charts that August, but "Let Me Go the Right Way" was released on the tour. Stevie Wonder was also hitless at the time. His first single, "I Call It Pretty Music (but Old People Call It the Blues)," had come out in August. The Miracles launched their song "You've Really Got a Hold on Me" during the tour, and it went all the way to Number 1 on the R&B chart. Marvin Gaye was enjoying his first taste of success with "Stubborn Kind of Fellow."

FRIDAY, OCTOBER 26: WASHINGTON, D.C.,
THE HOWARD THEATER

The first stop on the tour was especially exciting–going to our nation's capital. This was the first time that I had ever seen the White House or any of the impressive monuments in the District of Columbia. The bus stopped temporarily at the theater to drop off some equipment. James Brown was just closing his week's stay, and the place was packed solid and jumping. I had never seen him live. Wow! The "Godfather of Soul" singing "Please, Please, Please" with the Famous Flames and Bobby Byrd: They were cooking! We didn't get to stay long, but I was knocked out by what I saw on stage. Knowing that we were going to follow James Brown on that very same stage made me even more excited and determined to do an impressive show there.

It was then that I began to realize how important it was for a singer to have a record played nationally on the radio. In each city we went to, we had loving and adoring fans waiting to greet us. We had record-breaking attendances, and encores galore.

Washington, D.C., was also Marvin Gaye's hometown, which made this stop special. Since we were his backup singing group, he invited us to come home with him and meet his parents, Rev. and Mrs. Gaye, and his younger brother, Frankie. They showed us a real good time. The home-cooked dinner was delectable, and his family was very gracious. What a perfect way to start the tour!

FRIDAY, NOVEMBER 2: BOSTON, MASS., THE FRANKLIN THEATER;
SATURDAY, NOVEMBER 3: NEW HAVEN, CONN.,
NEW HAVEN ARENA;
SUNDAY, NOVEMBER 4: BUFFALO, N.Y.,
MEMORIAL AUDITORIUM;
MONDAY, NOVEMBER 5: RALEIGH, N.C.,
RALEIGH CITY AUDITORIUM;
TUESDAY, NOVEMBER 6: CHARLESTON, S.C., THE COUNTY HALL;
WEDNESDAY, NOVEMBER 7: AUGUSTA, GA., THE COUNTRY CLUB;
THURSDAY, NOVEMBER 8: SAVANNAH, GA., BAMBOO
RANCH CLUB.

We had a great show in Savannah. We were very well received, and were running right on schedule. The minute the show was over, we had to board the bus and ride on to the next engagement. It had become a routine now.

One afternoon, just after I sat down in my usual seat, Mary Wells and Marvin Gaye walked up the steps to the bus. As they passed the front window, I heard what sounded like gunshots. Terrified, I dove to the floor between the seats for cover.

Mary Wells, observing me, started laughing. She pointed at me and said, "Look at Martha, down on the floor! Girl, those are fire-crackers! Look at her, y'all!"

I was so embarrassed, but she kept it going, laughing and taunting me. Completely humiliated, I stood up and brushed myself off. I could have sworn those were gunshots that I heard!

Later, in Birmingham, Alabama, the bus eased into a parking spot in front of the next venue. The driver got off of the bus to stretch his legs and to have a look around. He returned before we could all collect our belongings and get off. He had an odd look on his face as he declared a near-fatal incident: He had just dug two bullets out of the top of THE MOTOR CITY REVUE sign on the front of our bus. We had been mistaken for Freedom Riders and had indeed been intentionally fired upon. They had shattered the glass with the third bullet. I at least got a chance to say "I told you so!" to Mary Wells.

FRIDAY, NOVEMBER 9: BIRMINGHAM, ALA.,
NATIONAL GUARD ARMORY;
SATURDAY, NOVEMBER 10: COLUMBUS, GA., CITY AUDITORIUM;
SUNDAY, NOVEMBER 11: ATLANTA, GA., MAGNOLIA BALLROOM;
MONDAY, NOVEMBER 12: MOBILE, ALA.,
FORT WHITING AUDITORIUM;
TUESDAY, NOVEMBER 13, NEW ORLEANS, LA.,
STATE FAIR GROUNDS;
WEDNESDAY, NOVEMBER 14: JACKSON, MISS.,
COLLEGE PARK AUDITORIUM.

En route to Jackson, we had to pass through a small town I recall as being Lynchburg, Mississippi. There we saw a tree in the fork in the road, which was famous for miles around as the "hanging tree." Although the tree was alive, there was not a leaf on it. Legend said that no leaves had grown on it for twenty or more years.

We stopped at a gas station—a bus full of people of color, and all I can remember is having to go to the restroom *real* bad. On this trip we all had to wait until the bus driver decided to stop. There was shouting and some sort of commotion, and I stood up. I was just waking up from a nap, and as I walked to the front of the bus, I saw an old white man in a blue denim jumper suit holding a double-barreled shotgun, pointing at the door. He growled, "Don't you niggers step one foot off that bus, or I'll blow your asses to kingdom come!"

Someone said, "We only want to use the bathroom . . ."

"Don't you niggers come off that bus!" the man yelled even louder. "Now ride on out of here!"

After years of never being able to block that episode out of my memory, one day I found myself reminiscing with Joe Billingslea of the Contours. He was able to tell me details about that confrontation I had either slept through or was never clear about. "Me and Bobby

Rogers," Joe explained, "Sylvester, Billy Gordon, Billy, Hubert, Bobby from the band, and one other musician had gotten off the bus and told the owner we had to use the bathroom. He said, 'What?!' They repeated, 'We want to use the bathroom.' He said, 'Y'all niggers better get out of here.' And somebody asked, 'Who you calling nigger?' Then Bobby said, 'Yeah, man, I'm Bobby Rogers of the Miracles.' That's when the man grabbed his shotgun and followed us back to the bus. Just then two cars of Mississippi state policemen rode up and asked, 'What's the problem, Bob?' as they stepped out of their cars with pistols in hand. Bob said, 'These niggers are trying to get into my station and take it over.' Clutching his shotgun, he wasn't afraid. Then the troopers asked Junior Gunther, our tour manager, who he was, and who were these 'stars' on that bus? After a bit of explaining, we were told to remain on the bus, as Junior joined us. They escorted us out of town. There we were, riding behind the police cars, totally scared—with Bob's final words echoing in our ears: 'You niggers better not come back, either.' "

In Jackson we stayed in a hotel for the first time in over two and a half weeks! Usually on these tours, all of the groups would be separated once the rooms were assigned. For the girls, the breakdown was something like: one Supreme/one Marvelette, Mary Wells/one Marvelette, one Vandella/one Marvelette—but this time, this particular hotel could accommodate all four Marvelettes in one large room. Happy to be all together in one room, the Marvelettes threw a big party that nearly got us all in trouble.

For the maximum use of room space, even Smokey Robinson's wife, Claudette, stayed with the other girls. When I recently asked how she felt about not getting to share a room with her husband, she replied, "It was fun to 'change up' sometimes and bunk with the girls. We were young, and rest was much more important at that time!" That was what this trip was all about: all of us binding together as a team, willing to make personal sacrifices to make the tour work.

That night I shared a double room with Mary Wilson, and after dinner we did exactly what we were told: We retired early, for we had a long journey in the morning. As soon as we drifted off to sleep, we heard a frantic knock on the door, and as we woke up, the door flew open, the security chain breaking loudly. Mary and I, scared out of our wits, sat up in bed, our hair in rollers and head rags. There in the doorway stood Mr. Thomas "Beans" Bowles, with flashlight in hand, turning the beam from one face to the other, searching the room.

"Okay, where are the men?"

I answered him sharply: "Yeah, that's what we want to know! Where *are* they?"

Mary and I had a good laugh on that one. We were able to fall back asleep and disregard the broken chain. There were whispers buzzing around the hotel lobby and on the bus the next morning about the "room raid." The Marvelettes had had an unchaperoned card game in their room and invited in some of the male singers. This was, of course, strictly forbidden. They were later caught having a party—in their pajamas! Well, at least two permanent relationships came out of this tour, and assumably from that party. It wasn't long after the tour that Wanda Young of the Marvelettes married Bobby Rogers of the Miracles, and Georgeanna Tillman of the Marvelettes married Billy Gordon, lead singer of the Contours. I never did find out what card game they were playing. And me? I was thrilled to actually sleep in a bed. I couldn't have cared less who ended up with whom that night!

THURSDAY, NOVEMBER 15: SPARTANBURG, S.C.,
MEMORIAL AUDITORIUM;
FRIDAY, NOVEMBER 16: DURHAM, N.C., THE CITY ARMORY;
SATURDAY, NOVEMBER 17, COLUMBIA, S.C.,
THE TOWNSHIP AUDITORIUM.

At this point on the tour it was shaping up to be great fun. Living this closely on the bus made for some personality conflicts, but a lot of camaraderie, fun, and practical jokes as well. Stevie Wonder was one of the master pranksters. On several occasions while parked somewhere, twelve-year-old Stevie would yell out the window to sexy female fans who were passing by: "Hey, you with the red sweater on! You with the long hair, come here! I got something to say to you privately!" Well, the startled girl would look around and see Stevie with his dark glasses on.

"Are you talking to me?" she would finally inquire. We'd be look-ing on, just killing ourselves trying to suppress our laughter.

"Yeah, I really like that pretty gold necklace that you're wearing," Stevie would continue.

Well, by now the girl would be fit to be tied. We all knew that Stevie had no way of knowing what she was wearing or how she looked, yet he was a master at pulling off these gags with a straight face. Obviously someone would coach Stevie at every turn, telling him minute details about what was going on around us as a way to hilariously amaze unsuspecting onlookers.

Stevie also had a tutor, Ted Hull, who traveled with him, which is why he was allowed to miss so much school. Stevie and Ted kept us laughing all the time. Ted was only partially sighted as well, and the two of them would trade hysterical anecdotes about their attempts to get from one place to another.

SUNDAY, NOVEMBER 18: WASHINGTON, D.C.,
THE CAPITOL ARENA;
MONDAY, NOVEMBER 19: *DAY OFF;*
TUESDAY, NOVEMBER 20: GREENVILLE, S.C., CIVIC AUDITORIUM;
WEDNESDAY, NOVEMBER 21: TAMPA, FLA., THE PALLADIUM;
WEDNESDAY, NOVEMBER 21: BRADENTON, FLA., THE PALMS;
THURSDAY, NOVEMBER 22: JACKSONVILLE, FLA., THE ARMORY.

During this leg of the tour, "Beans" Bowles and his driver, Eddie Edwards, set out in a car before the bus left. They usually did this to scout out the next venue ahead of our arrival. Having stayed up very late the night before, Eddie fell asleep at the wheel and smashed into the back of a semi van. He was instantly killed on impact, and Beans, although in critical condition, survived. We were staying at a hotel in Tampa, and there was a telegram stating that Esther Edwards was on her way down. This was our one true tragedy on the tour.

This was also my first Thanksgiving away from home, and the first time in a long time that I wasn't with my family. But we had a big spread of Thanksgiving food on beautifully decorated buffet tables. It was pleasant having a turkey dinner, but dining in a conference room at a hotel with the general public didn't seem like the kind of Thanksgiving I was used to. I was glad that we at least had a chance to wish each other happy Thanksgiving and not feel so homesick. This was one of those occasions when all of us at Motown felt like a real family.

FRIDAY, NOVEMBER 23: MACON, GA., AUDITORIUM;
SATURDAY, NOVEMBER 24: DAYTONA BEACH, FLA.,
NATIONAL GUARD ARMORY;
SUNDAY, NOVEMBER 25: MIAMI, FLA., HARLEM SQUARE.

The ladies were all experiencing the dreaded humidity of Florida for the first time, and all of our wigs reacted adversely. As everyone's hair went limp, we realized that we were not ready for Florida. Last week's "room raid" prompted a surprise visit from the president himself–Berry Gordy. He came to, as he put it, "check you out."

All of us were gathered together and given a stern lecture. While I had worked as A&R secretary, I had gotten to know Mr. Gordy quite well and knew him to be serious most of the time. Now, however, he was clearly beyond "serious," and all the way to "angry." When he was upset, he had a way of turning his head sideways and one of his eyes would oddly gleam. He stared us all down for a long time before he began slowly speaking. He told us that he had heard how great our shows had been and was pleased about that. But he had been informed about several recent activities that had him upset.

Not only had the Marvelettes' card party infuriated him, but he appeared disappointed as well. "This is a big company, going places," he emphasized, "and big plans are in the works. You all can't be messing around doing the things I've heard about. I have spoken earlier to the individuals involved, who had actually been caught in the act. I warned them, and now I'm warning *all* of you. If this kind of wild behavior takes place again, I will end the tour and bring you all back home, and you will *never* go out on the road again!"

He scared us all. We were totally cooled out for two or three days after he left. Nobody dared to step out of line. After that reprimand from Mr. Gordy himself, we were more careful and quieter when we got together–even after "ditching" our chaperons!

MONDAY, NOVEMBER 26: ORLANDO, FLA., A SKATING RINK;
TUESDAY, NOVEMBER 27: TALLAHASSIE, FLA., THE FIELD HOUSE;
WEDNESDAY, NOVEMBER 28; CHERAW, S.C.;
THURSDAY, NOVEMBER 29: CHARLOTTE, N.C., LONG HIGH
SCHOOL GYMNATORIUM;
FRIDAY, NOVEMBER 30: LOUISVILLE, KY., NEW PARK CENTER.

As we parked the bus in Louisville, through the open door came a mountain of a man who had to bend down to enter. He sat down near the front and began talking loudly. He began telling everybody that we all had the wrong names. He told us that he had once been known as Cassius Clay but had found Allah and was about to become Muhammad Ali. We instantly recognized him, since he had just won a championship title from Archie Moore. He was good-looking and very cocky. He kept saying that he was "the Greatest," over and over again. By the time the evening was over, he had convinced us that he indeed was.

I was amazed at how truly handsome he really was. He bragged about how "pretty" he was and that was why nobody could hit him in the face. He and "Little" Stevie Wonder remained alone talking on the bus, long after we had gone in. We finally had to go and get Stevie so that he might dress and make his show time.

SATURDAY, DECEMBER 1: MEMPHIS, TENN.,
MEMORIAL AUDITORIUM.

We were really looking forward to playing Elvis Presley's hometown of Memphis. We were startled to find that we had a "split" audience: One side of the audience was "white only," and one side was "black only." I had never seen this kind of segregation before in which a theater was arranged with one stage and two separate seating areas. We walked out onstage and the band was positioned in the corner. We were instructed to sing all of the songs twice: once in one direction, and the same song about-face. When you turned to face the other half of the crowd, you brought your microphone around with you. Of course, our songs sounded the same no matter where we looked. Although we couldn't see any faces, I thought it was friendlier on the black side. After the show, we stayed over and were joined by fellow Detroiter Little Willie John. We were invited to meet him at a club where he was singing. We all had a ball that night, and for a moment it was almost like being at home. We were caught up in the magic of his music–the stuff we had grown up on.

SUNDAY, DECEMBER 2: NASHVILLE, TENN.,
THE CITY AUDITORIUM;
MONDAY, DECEMBER 3: PENSACOLA, FLA.,
FAIRGROUND COLISEUM;
TUESDAY, DECEMBER 4: *DAY OFF*;
WEDNESDAY, DECEMBER 5: RICHMOND, VA.,
THE MOSQUE AUDITORIUM;
THURSDAY, DECEMBER 6: *DAY OFF*;
FRIDAY, DECEMBER 7–THURSDAY, DECEMBER 16: NEW YORK
CITY, THE APOLLO THEATRE.

We pulled into New York and registered at the Theresa Hotel. This was my first trip ever to Manhattan, and I was really fascinated seeing the tallest buildings I had ever encountered. Harlem was the most crowded ghetto of my worst nightmare! It smelled of urine, and the men and women–who either stood around or joylessly walked by like zombies–were checking us out as we left the bus. They were strange-looking and unfriendly, and we heard comments like "Detroit niggers" and "singing motherf——ers." But then it became "There's Smokey Robinson. Hey, Smokey!" and "Look, there's Mary Wells!" It was soon transformed into sounds of love.

When we arrived at the world–famous Apollo Theatre, I couldn't believe what a glorious dump it had become through years of use and obviously a minimal amount of upkeep. *This* was *the* Apollo?! I was appalled by the condition it was in.

We were met by Mr. Spain, the doorman, who said in an unfriendly tone, "Who *are* you motherf——ers? What y'all wont?" Fortunately, we had a spokesperson, Booker Bradshaw, to deal with him, and after a brief introduction all of us singers were led up some dark stairs to five floors of tiny, filthy dressing rooms. The rooms were littered with traces of the many, many performers who had been there before us: on the walls, on the seats, on the mirrors, and in the restrooms. This would be home for seven days, and by the end of the engagement, we had been taken by the spell of this famous old theater.

At the Apollo "the half hour was always 'in,'" which in show business terms meant that you couldn't leave the theater during intermission. For seven days we performed six shows a day, starting at 12:00 noon and ending at 1:00 A.M. The order of the show dictated where you dressed. Since the Vandellas opened the show, we had the smallest of two dressing rooms on the fourth level. The fifth-floor dressing rooms had cots, and the Contours and the Temptations were given those rooms. You needed a cot after that long climb! The attendants cleaned up, mopped, and changed the cot sheets once a week, but it was still grungy back there. Still, we loved it.

As Rosalind, Annette, and I watched the band breaking their instruments down and moving them up from the basement to the stage, we kept reminding each other of where we were.

"I can't believe we're really here!" Annette said.

"But it's so *funky*," Rosalind deadpanned. "I can't believe how run-down it is!"

"Yeah," I agreed, "but we're at 'the world-famous *Apollo!*' So, girls, it looks like we're stars now!"

Our show there consisted of singing one number, our soon-to-be-released hit "Come and Get These Memories." After that, we did our background number with Marvin. Then we waited for the finale, which featured everybody back onstage to join the Miracles on "Shop Around." We repeated this six times a day, seven days a week.

FRIDAY, DECEMBER 17: PITTSBURGH, PA.

This was the last date on the tour, and by the time we returned home, we were all superstars! Or, at least that's what we all felt like. Careers had been launched, relationships had developed, competitions began, and audiences were thrilled. After this sink-or-swim tour, we all emerged swimmingly.

Mary Wells, the Miracles, Marvin Gaye, the Marvelettes, and the

Contours all ended up with new hit records being launched. To top it off, this "all-star" revue was captured on two albums: The first was *Recorded Live at the Apollo: The Motor Town Revue, Vol. 1.* The Vandellas and I were included the following year on *Recorded Live: The Motor Town Revue, Vol. 2.*

When we returned to Detroit, the highlight of the holiday season was Motown's annual Christmas party. After surviving our first Motown Revue, we enjoyed a truly festive time.

In the first couple months after Christmas, the Vandellas and I completed work on our debut album, also entitled *Come and Get These Memories.* The front of the album cover didn't have a picture of us on it, but it had a photo of the infamous teddy bear, several 45-rpm singles, and a stack of love letters—all of the things we sang about in the title cut of the album. The group's photo was on the back cover. Unfortunately, it was a photo that I have never liked. We had a makeup job by Charlie Aikens, and he added little moles—"beauty marks"—on our faces, a common touch in those days. He had rolled up balls of glue and painted them black after sticking them on the exact same spot on one of our cheeks. It made me ill to see it.

Our first album reflected the kind of music that was popular during that era. It included our cover versions of a couple of popular hits like Little Anthony & the Imperials' "Tears on My Pillow," Andy Williams's "Can't Get Used to Losing You," and a new version of "There He Is (at My Door)" on which I sang lead.

The *Come and Get These Memories* album was not very successful on the charts when it was released, but when the title song became our first Top 40 pop hit we sold an awful lot of singles. (Original copies of our *Come and Get These Memories* LP are now considered collector's items. The last one I saw in a record shop was priced at several hundred dollars.)

In 1963 James Brown headlined a tour that also featured the Drifters and Marvin Gaye. As Marvin's background singers, we were booked with our own spot in the show as well. Also on the bill were the Crystals, Doris Troy, Inez and Charlie Foxx, and Jimmy Reed. On that tour, we were all in for some good times. This was an eight-week tour, and James only played the biggest and the best venues in the country, so we were proud to be on "the Godfather's" tour.

The Drifters had one of the most ever-changing lineups in the music business. Although the group once included Clyde McPhatter and Ben E. King, the group I met in 1963 on the James Brown tour was my favorite. Abdul was the guitarist for the Drifters, and one of the finest gentlemen on the road. In 1961 Rudy Lewis had become the group's lead singer. He was extremely talented and a good friend to us. Johnny Moore had the lead voice, and he made the steps look good because he was so smooth. Gino was the group's "ladies' man." You couldn't wish for a nicer group to work with—always excellent, and definite crowd pleasers. Johnny Moore and Charlie Thomas were my favorite members of the Drifters.

I had been ill the first couple of weeks of the tour and hired a masseur named Mr. Perry Fuller to drive me from town to town in his big Lincoln. We would travel as my health allowed. Sometimes we'd be the first to arrive at the different stops, traveling at our leisure. Mr. Fuller gave me a sightseeing tour of the countryside that I will never forget, even stopping at his relatives' houses in the South along the way for good home-cooked meals.

He once stopped in the hills of Tennessee near Lookout Mountain and parked his car. We didn't get out, but he told me to put the window down just as this huge bear approached the car looking for food. Whenever I see Perry, he still chides me about how loudly I screamed, "Lord have mercy, Mr. Fuller—a *bear!*" He made what could have been a difficult tour a joy and a delight.

Abdul, the Drifters' guitar player, was an older gentleman. He was handsome and had a mystique about him—behind that knowing smile of his. He had the ability to make the Drifters' songs sound better than the recordings. It was the special touch he added on that hollow-box Gibson guitar that he treasured.

At the large arenas we played, all of the ladies would share the same dressing room. Doris Troy was the first woman I remember wearing different-colored wigs: blond, purple, and even royal blue on one occasion! Inez and Charlie Foxx had just recorded their hit "Mockingbird." When I first saw them, I thought they were one of the handsomest couples I had ever seen, and they wore beautiful matching costumes. I was thrilled to hear that they were sister and brother, because I had a crush on Charlie. But, to my disappointment, he was married.

One evening, Charlie Thomas came into the dressing room with

Abdul to prove to Dee Dee Kinnebrew of the Crystals that he could hypnotize her. I was a nonbeliever as well, and exclaimed, "I want to see this!" He proceeded to wave this necklace on a chain in front of her eyes, talking softly and slowly.

I still thought it was a put-on when she started chasing the "butterflies" that he told her were fluttering about her face. I became throughly convinced of its reality when he put a match to the point of a large safety pin and pierced her cheek with the sterilized point. Dee Dee registered no reaction to pain and suffered no loss of blood. Then he brought her back from the hypnotic state, and she couldn't remember anything. She only said, "See, I told you that you can't hypnotize me!" We all had a good laugh, and I have believed in mind over matter ever since!

Just like the Motown Revue, we would perform our songs and then sing backup to Marvin Gaye. It gave us the opportunity to see another side of show business. Marvin was *hot*, and women went wild for him.

Although opposites in stature, style, and taste, James and Marvin had a running competition. Every night before the show, James would send one of his spies to see what color suit Marvin had on that evening. He would then have the assistant go into his trailer filled with racks of suits and get one the same color as Marvin's, only more elaborate and detailed. The Godfather of Soul was not about to be outdone on his own tour! If Marvin did his set in a red tuxedo, James would close his show in an even brighter flame-red tux. If Marvin wore a white tuxedo that night, James would come out in a fancier white one. I marveled at the vanity of those two peacocks—and James Brown's determination to "top the bill," no matter what!

He didn't have a thing to worry about, though—he more than held his own. Since we all used his band, I can say that they were great playing behind us. However, they were programmed to really put the "fire" behind James's songs, which was exactly what he expected. I have seen him turn around in midsong and hold up fingers indicating the number of "fines" to be levied against individual players who made a mistake or missed a cue for a note they had promised to give him after he commanded them to "hit me, band!" That is a phrase that Mr. Brown himself invented.

The original group–Martha, Rosalind, and Annette–in our first publicity photo in 1962. We didn't wear wigs yet, but our gloves glowed in purple light when we sang "come on and get it." (*Michael Ochs Archives*)

Rosalind, Annette, and Martha with our teddy bear, which we used as a prop on our song "Come and Get These Memories." (*Michael Ochs Archives*)

The Motown Revue at the Apollo Theatre in Harlem. We played to standing–room–only audiences, with lines around the block, and magnificent shows. (*Michael Ochs Archives*)

Rosalind, Betty, and Martha backstage with Marvin Gaye in England, as Marvin & the Vandellas. (*Michael Ochs Archives*)

Martha, Annette, and Rosalind in our green satin and gold lamé costumes created by Helen Duncan. Our hair was designed and styled by Betty Bullock.
(*Photo by James J. Kriegsmann/Michael Ochs Archives*)

Annette, Rosalind, and Martha singing with Choker Campbell's twelve-piece band. (*Michael Ochs Archives*)

Rosalind, Annette, and Martha–the original cast and the original sound of Martha & the Vandellas. We first met each other in 1958. (*Photo by James J. Kriegsmann/Martha Reeves Collection*)

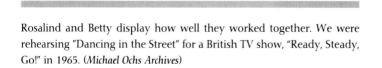

Rosalind and Betty display how well they worked together. We were rehearsing "Dancing in the Street" for a British TV show, "Ready, Steady, Go!" in 1965. (*Michael Ochs Archives*)

Singing a duet with Dusty Springfield on her "Sound of Motown" TV special.
(*Martha Reeves Collection*)

Rosalind, Martha, and Betty in 1965. We were "ridin' high," and Betty was a welcome addition to the Vandellas.
(*Photo by James J. Kriegsmann/Joseph Shillair Collection*)

Annette, Martha, Dick Clark, and Rosalind on our first appearance on "American Bandstand" in 1963. Our performance of "Come and Get These Memories" received an encore.
(*Martha Reeves Collection*)

In our infamous pants outfits on the Murray the K Show at the Brooklyn Fox. As Marvin does "Hitch Hike," we dance with Little Anthony & the Imperials, the Animals, the Ronettes, the Temptations, the Supremes, and twelve great musicians. (*Michael Ochs Archives*)

Rosalind, Martha, and Betty on the record sleeve of one of our singles in Holland.
(*Joseph Shillair Collection*)

Rosalind, Betty, and Martha on the cover of *Jet* magazine. We wore metallic stretch jumpsuits with one chiffon leg, an outfit designed by Helen Duncan. The story appeared during our performance at the Trip on Sunset Strip in Los Angeles.
(*Courtesy of Johnson Publications/Martha Reeves Collection*)

Rosalind, Betty, and Martha during a photo shoot for the album cover of *Watchout!* at the offices of EMI Records in London, 1965. (*Joseph Shillair Collection*)

Rosalind, Martha, and Betty in our gowns from Saks Fifth Avenue. (*Photo by James J. Kriegsmann/Michael Ochs Archives*)

Rosalind, Betty, and Martha in an advertisement for our hit "Jimmy Mack" in 1967.
(*Martha Reeves Collection*)

Murray the K produced the first action video of Motown music for his television special, "It's What's Happening, Baby." A 1965 Mustang was built from start to finish in twenty minutes–with us in it! We would get in and out of the car until it was driven off the assembly line by Murray himself.
(*Michael Ochs Archives*)

James was the highlight of the show, and we always stood in the wings when he would sing "Please, Please, Please." James Brown's finales were always elaborate. His trademark routine would find him feigning exhaustion, only to be draped in a series of colored capes as if he were Caesar being offered the crown. Finally, he would revive and launch into his dramatic closing number. He was so theatrical! It was exciting to see him night after night, because the crowds loved it so. We thought he would injure himself some nights when he fell to his knees on the hard surface of the stage time and time again. I was so impressed with him, and found him to be an expert performer and the undisputed "king of rhythms." James Brown deserves to know that he is still loved and appreciated for being "the hardest-working man in show business!"

It is still a happy time for me every time I get into the recording studio. When I first had the chance to enter into that fantasy world of songwriter/producers and make a song come alive, I was thrilled by the process. I cherish the time I get to enter that secluded studio space, dim the lights, place earphones on my ears, pour my heart and soul onto the tracks, and hear the magic that God performs through me. After rehearsing and dreaming on a song, you count the seconds until your own time comes to create. At those enchanted moments, the song envelops your spirit. It's between you and and the microphone. There's a special reward for my soul when I have connected with a writer's lyrics and feelings, and we both agree and feel good about what develops.

Martha & the Vandellas' first record, "I'll Have to Let Him Go," didn't go very far. But thanks to the groundwork we laid by singing onstage and on television right after its release, "Come and Get These Memories" was debuting on many of the national radio stations. Week by week we heard good reports from Berry's sister, Loucye Gordy Wakefield. She was a good friend of mine who worked in the sales department at Motown, and she would quote me the latest chart figures from *Billboard, Cashbox,* and *Record World.*

It's still an experience hearing myself singing on the radio. Every time I hear one of my songs, I'm taken back to the moment and the feelings I have expressed, how I had to work at overcoming the uneasiness and nervous tension, and the different sounds blended

together to compose our works of art. "Come and Get These Memories" is a song that I liked the minute I heard it. It was great to know
that the public agreed.

"Come and Get These Memories" hit Number 29 on the pop chart
and Number 9 on the R&B chart. With Holland–Dozier–Holland producing, we had truly come up with a winning formula. In the spring
of 1963 we went into the studio and recorded another hit by that
songwriting trio, a new single entitled "(Love Is Like a) Heat Wave."
When the song became an instant radio smash, it hit Number 4 on
the pop chart and Number 1 on the R&B chart. We had finally
arrived!

Here we had our first Number 1 single and no album to go with
it, so we recorded one—in one night! That's how fast we had to produce our second album, *Heat Wave*. We couldn't lose the momentum
that the single had created. At the time, we were on the road, but we
flew in to Detroit from Baltimore after doing five shows that day. We
got in around midnight and went right into studio A. We did "My
Boyfriend's Back," "Wait 'Til My Bobby Gets Home," "Just One Look,"
"Danke Schoen," "If I Had a Hammer," "Hello Stranger," "Mockingbird," "Then He Kissed Me," and "More" (the theme from *Mondo Cane*.)
We recorded everyone else's hits because it was the trend of record
companies at the time to cover all of the top songs of the day.

We recorded that whole album and did backup vocals for two
Marvin Gaye songs, including "Hurt So Bad." We flew back to Baltimore the next morning and performed on four shows as well as
doing backgrounds for Marvin. We all had to get shots for our throats
because we were suffering from extreme vocal overuse. I'm not complaining; I'm just marveling at what we accomplished. If I were that
age again and the circumstances were the same, I'd gladly do it all
again. You do stupid, dangerous things when you're really in love.
You find yourself swept up in it, and you don't stop for a minute to
think about any of the possible consequences. You say to yourself,
"Go get it, girl," and you never look back!

CHAPTER 4

Heat Wave

HALF LOVED

I feel half loved
Half understood
Until you take the bad
And turn it into good

I've gotten a lot of different meanings
From the things you've said to me
There's a reason for you in my life
And without a doubt I love you

When you're gone, I miss you
I don't listen to what people say
They can think anything they want to
Your love shows me the way

Everybody's got somewhere to run to
When the going gets tough
You've got to stand and let it be known
When you've had enough

You need someone to talk to
And especially in times like these
Let me set your heart at ease
Give me love that will not tease
And take my emotions
For pure, true devotions

In 1963 things really took off for us in a big way. Not only did we become an overnight sensation with "(Love Is Like a) Heat Wave," but Holland–Dozier–Holland also gave us a brilliant follow-up record with "Quicksand." It had even more of a driving beat than "Heat Wave," but I felt that "Quicksand" and our next song, "Live Wire," were released too soon, one after another. Just as "Quicksand" entered Number 8 on the pop chart and Number 1 on the R&B chart, "Live Wire" was released.

With three hits and our first two albums out on the market, we were kept busy promoting them with television appearances, interviews, and tours. I was thrilled and excited by all of the activity and attention that was suddenly lavished on us by Motown and by the public.

Annette and Rosalind and I found ourselves booked at the Apollo Theatre not once, but twice, that year. It was becoming one of our favorite places to perform. It was true what people said about that theater: If you can make it at the Apollo, you'll make it anywhere. We met a lot of friends there. In time even gruff–speaking Mr. Spain, who had greeted the Motown Revue so rudely on our first visit, became a friend. He would do a lot of special things for us over the years.

Our first experience at the Apollo with the Motown Revue in 1962 had been so wonderfully eventful that it was a good way to be broken in. Honi Coles, who was the Apollo's stage manager, met us in the wings of the theater that first night and told us, "You'd better be good. If they don't like you, they'll throw wine bottles and stuff at you! It ain't too late for you little Hastings Street girls to go on back to Detroit where you belong!"

He frightened Annette, Rosalind, and me so badly until we almost changed our minds about going onstage. After our first fright, Honi turned out to be every performer's best friend. With repeated visits to the Apollo, we discovered from Vivian Reed, whom he managed, that his bark was worse than his bite, and I stopped taking him so literally.

Honi was such a handsome man. He was so tall that he towered over us. He was like an all-knowing wizard. He was wise in the ways of the world, and when he spoke, you knew he was right. He was also a convincing performer and very charming. Honi was one-half of the Coles & Atkins dance team from vaudeville. Together they had traveled to Broadway and toured internationally with Pearl Bailey and Billy Eckstine. He was to experience a career resurgence in his later years. His former vaudeville partner, Cholly Atkins, would later join Motown as the company's choreographer.

The first two times the Motown Revue played the Apollo, the Vandellas had to open the show. No act likes to be the first on, because at the end of the show, no one remembers they were ever there until they see them in the finale. I would make myself feel better about the whole thing by telling myself, "The best act starts it all, to set the pace!"

Sometimes we girls would remain in perspiration-soaked clothes, standing in drafty wings waiting for the last curtain. Because of this, I often had bronchitis, and that would weaken me. A strong believer in the old saying "The show must go on," I never missed a performance. No normal life would require that amount of traveling, exposure to the elements with worn-out bodies, low resistance, unsuitable accommodations, or lack of sustenance. Yet we had become addicted to show business and gladly came back for more, time and time again.

When I first went to New York City to play at the Apollo, the city and Harlem represented a whole new world to me. Among the permanent fixtures at the Apollo were two little kids—not yet teenagers—who were always on hand to greet us. No trip to the Apollo was complete without seeing Ron Taylor and Connie Conley. They always seemed to be backstage talking to the performers, running errands, or watching after your belongings while you were onstage. They were both only eleven years old when I first met them.

Ron used to go to the store for his favorite performers. He'd take down their orders on a napkin, and had a reputation for being trusted with money. He'd always bring back the correct change. Fascinated by show business, he grew up to become one of the finest valets that a recording artist could hope for.

The 125th Street neighborhood that the Apollo is located in is–and always was–very treacherous. We were truly babes in the woods up there. People would break into the theater windows and take your last little dress right out of your dressing room! For mere pocket change, Ron and/or Connie would gladly watch over our belongings. People knew not to mess with Ron and Connie, and when we got off-stage, our things were right where we had left them.

There would always be a card game and gambling down in the basement of the theater because that's where all the guys would usually be between shows. Ron often found himself right in the middle of a game. Smokey Robinson, the Temptations, Marvin Gaye, and the Miracles were often among the players–whenever disapproving Berry Gordy wasn't looking, that is. Occasionally I ventured down there to see what was going on, but mostly I heard whoever lost the most money complaining bitterly.

When I recently asked Ron about the gambling, he recalled, "I have fleeced Smokey Robinson, I broke Marvin Gaye, I had Bobby Rogers owing me money. And the Temptations–I used to clean them out, especially Melvin Franklin. He did talk a good game though. He'd say, 'Yo man, win or lose, I'm in the game.' The hardest one to get to pay up was David Ruffin. David would not pay. He would say to me, 'First of all, you ain't had no business down here, and second of all, where'd you get the money to get in the game? I know them niggers staked you here to beat me, 'cause you're *good!*' And I'd tell him, 'Don't worry about that, just pay me!' Because I was a kid, they thought that they could take me, and they didn't think I had the kind of money I had. Obviously someone had given me the cash to beat one player or another."

The first time I spoke to Connie, I was out in the alley behind the theater. We had gone out in the back wanting to go to the store, but we didn't know which way to turn. When I asked her for directions, Connie politely said, "Where'd you want to go?"

I said, "I want to go grab something to eat. We're hungry. We need some food, and we've only got half an hour to get it."

Trying to be helpful, Connie said, "Come on, I'll show you where to go."

She walked slightly ahead of us in her little baby-girl cotton dress like she wasn't scared of anything. She looked like she knew everybody on the street. People would walk past us and say, "Hey Connie!" and they spoke to her with a lot of respect. It wasn't like they were talking to a little girl. She knew where she was going, and she was always all right on the streets of Harlem. Connie showed us where we were going, and we were so grateful. She had a spirituality about her, and I felt that I had met a sister or my godchild.

Here I was in the big city, a young adult relying on two subteens to show me the ropes in Harlem! I felt like a slow little country bumpkin.

Every time we played the Apollo after that, as soon as our bus or car pulled up there, I'd look for Ron and Connie. There were also times when they would look out for me, especially if I became interested in some suave man who was handing me a line.

"Don't even like him, he ain't cool," Ron or Connie would say to me. They would usually be warning me about my fellow entertainers, too, because they knew them personally and I didn't. They also knew how green I was!

The Apollo was always an adventure, especially back then with Annette, Rosalind, and me in a little cubbyhole they called a dressing room. That was the worst. You also had to wait your turn to use the bathroom. The system for dressing rooms was that the "star" would be on the second floor in dressing room #1. Dressing rooms #2 and #3 were on the third floor and #4 was on the fourth. Being on the fifth floor in #5 meant that you must have opened the show. The fifth floor would often accommodate groups–or so they thought, but there wasn't enough room for everybody to take a nap. If one would lie down, someone had to sit up! You could end up sitting on the toilet if you really ran out of seats. Sometimes we would *stay* in those little rooms, too. We might go and work that whole week and only leave the theater once or twice because most of the time "the half would be in." You always had to save your energy. Five or six times a day you would get up onstage and do those two or three quick little songs, wait for the finale, and get very tired. But that was the fun of doing these shows. Thank God we didn't have to do forty-five-minute sets!

Sometimes we would walk several blocks back to the Theresa Hotel after the show. Again, it was great to have local friends like Ron and Connie to make us feel safe. Sometimes, while walking to the Apollo, we would feel right at home on 125th Street, and lovingly referred to Harlem as "the jungle."

One night at the Apollo I came to the teddy bear line in our song "Come and Get These Memories," and I saw a stranger on the side of the stage with a gigantic teddy bear. He brought it out on the stage and I didn't know how to react, because the bear was larger than me! I only weighed 107 pounds, and I didn't know what to do with this big ole thing. Somehow I managed to drag the teddy bear backstage with me when the song was done. He was adorable, and I managed to get him all the way back to Detroit, only to have someone take him out of my hands—never to see him again.

I'd so love to see that era come back. I really miss theaters and especially miss meeting the people. It seems like I don't meet people anymore and there is no way to communicate with an audience. But back then, with so many acts jammed into those crowded theaters, you couldn't help but become close to people. If we stayed some-where for a week, people might say, "Hey, come over for something to eat," . . . "Come by and just say, 'Hi, how'ya doing?' " . . . "Hey, we'll walk you around." . . . "Did you know that this place is open where you can get some decent food when you get off work?" Little things like that really helped out a lot.

The release of "(Love Is Like a) Heat Wave" heightened interest in our group, and the gigs started coming in. Our first trip to New York City in a car was with Berry Gordy. Earl, Berry's personal chauffeur, drove us in a long, green, roomy Cadillac. It appeared longer than it was because of the fishtail fins that year's model was known for. Berry's right-hand man, Billy Davis, didn't accompany us and we were disappointed. Billy had excellent taste and he was known for the gifts he bought that Berry gave us on occasion. Usually Billy and Earl saw to all of Mr. Gordy's needs. They were his constant companions. For this trip Billy stayed in Detroit to take care of all of Berry's personal concerns.

As we loaded up the car at Hitsville for the twelve-hour drive to New York, we felt that we were special, because for the first time we would have Berry–our "king"–all to ourselves. We three–Annette, Rosalind, and myself–sat in the back seat and slept on and off on each other's shoulders. Mostly we were too excited watching the scenery go by and looking out of the window for the long, dark tunnels on the Pennsylvania Turnpike. There we were with Berry Gordy and Earl, cruising in this big, luxurious Cadillac. Chauffeured in this car, I completely enjoyed the "star treatment."

At this point we had appeared at the Apollo with the Motown Revue on two other occasions. This week we were playing the Apollo as the only Motown act on the bill.

We felt as if we had moved up in the world this time because we stayed in midtown Manhattan. Only Harlem represented New York to us before this trip, staying at the Cecil Hotel and sometimes the Theresa. The three of us girls shared a twin room with a cot added, but we were thrilled to be at the President Hotel. It was across the street from Mama Leone's, the famous Italian restaurant that had long lines of people waiting to get in at all times of the afternoon and evening.

On this trip, we came to New York to perform and Berry had several business meetings. We had a week with him there, and he would take us along with him sometimes. This always made us feel special.

Still fearing "the big city," we didn't dare walk on our own to the nearby shops. The second evening we were New York, though, we decided to venture out. We were hungry and had $5 apiece allotted for food. Rosalind, Annette, and I decided to walk together and scout to see what $5 could buy us. As big a place as New York is, who should see us walking about but Berry's sister, Gwen, and his ex-wife, Raynoma Gordy.

They instantly placed a call to Berry and accused us of "tricking on Broadway." I understand that they were on their way to a fortune teller's reading. Hmmm, they may have tried to *read* our situation, only they were fantasizing. The minute we returned from our brief walk and a hot dog purchased from a street vendor, the telephone rang. It was Mr. Gordy himself.

"You can't be streetwalkers!" he said, lecturing me on the phone. "Don't you know better than to go wandering around on your own in Times Square? You will be recognized as Motown stars, and you aren't to be confused with prostitutes!"

At first our feelings were hurt, and we felt really bad to have been misunderstood. But once we thought about it, we girls had a good laugh. How could anyone confuse us with streetwalkers? The "ladies of the night" on Broadway were *much* sharper than we were, and always the flashiest dressers in the entire area. From Detroit's House of Beauty on John R. to the bar at the Twenty Grand, we had *always* tried to look as good as "the ho's." After that embarrassing episode in New York City, though, we didn't dare walk outside of the hotel again without permission. Besides, we were very shabbily dressed in jeans and leather jackets.

One day Berry announced that we were going with him to a business meeting at a Chinese restaurant. We were so excited to go anywhere with our hero! We sat at the table, with him at the head of it. He introduced us to his distinguished guests: a few disc jockeys, some publishers and their wives—altogether about ten people including the three of us. He insisted on ordering for us, since we had never been to a Chinese restaurant and could not read the menu. We hadn't a clue as to what egg drop or egg rolls or moo goo gai pan or chop suey would be. He was pleased when the food was served. He set it out, and before I could finish my cup of egg drop soup, he dipped what he called an egg roll in some yellow mustard-looking stuff. Handing it to me, he told me to taste it.

Well, I trusted him. I knew he had good taste, so I bit into a mouthful of his egg roll. As I began to chew it, my ears stopped up, my eyes teared, and I felt that I had been poisoned! I wouldn't spit it out—I couldn't swallow it because it was so hot with the taste of peppers, so I got up and ran to the restroom. I was choking, coughing, and rushing to get relief. After I wiped my tears and washed my mouth out, I returned to the seat that I had made such a hasty departure from. All I could remember was everyone's laughter as I left, and when I returned again, I was horrified and embarrassed by this cruel joke that he had played on me.

Mr. Gordy apologized, saying he thought I knew about Chinese mustard, so I managed a humble smile as I tried to find the humor

that had amused everyone—even the Vandellas. I had been introduced to a substance that I avoid even today because of my first
experience. Mr. Gordy made it up to me by buying all three of us
teddy bears—the biggest he could find—from a sidewalk vendor. With
the three teddy bears, we slept even better on the return trip. We also
had a real good show, and I felt confident that we had made him
very proud. We had accomplished a lot of good things in New York
City—or the "Green Apple," as I call it.

It was so wonderful being part of Berry Gordy's dream. Berry's
dream was to make all of us famous. He would get one group started
and then shift his attentions to the next artist. He discovered, nurtured, and supported all of us during the best years of his life. He was
sharp, very clever, witty, and quicker than average. He was also very
smooth on his feet. Maybe that is what his past boxing experience
contributed to the total man that he is. He could ballroom and bop
so-o-o good, and whenever we danced together, we would draw a circle of people. He's even a great jitterbugger. Berry and I got a chance
to dance at company parties or whenever he would go along on sock
hops. Once in a while we would linger and dance with everyone else,
and I would love every minute we could capture on the dance floor,
especially a waxed one. We would slide and give Fred Astaire and
Ginger Rogers a run for their money.

When I first started with the company, just before I had my own
car, Berry would drive me home after work. We would linger for
hours in the car in front of my parents' house after work, discussing
all sorts of things.

I've always wondered just why it was that I started wanting to
please him and gain his approval. Was it his magnetic personality or
was it the great recordings I was now blessed with? I admired him
immensely, and would cling to his words as he spoke about the
future plans he had for Motown. What was especially fascinating for
me was to hear firsthand of his dreams that had become reality. In an
astonishingly short period of time, Berry Gordy and his creation,
Motown Records, really arrived on the international music scene.

We would have long conversations and he talked to me, spirit to
spirit, telling me things that I never shared with anyone else. I was in
awe as I listened to him project his plans for Motown Records' magnificent future. I couldn't imagine half of the pictures he painted with

profound words when we were one-on-one, because his dreams were so elaborately detailed.

I guess I'm trying to justify my love and adoration for Berry, but I have very limited experiences with men of his caliber. I especially appreciate the time spent with him just talking. I interjected my opinions as well, but mostly I listened to him when he would share his hopes and dreams. I would already be in a trance after hearing all of that heavenly music–the result of this army of music makers and the flowing of creative juices that manufactured the Motown Sound. So listening to eloquent Berry was the frosting on the cake.

Berry Gordy was well liked, and he had dedicated friends who believed in him and supported his every idea. It was as if they knew he was blessed. Several of his friends worked for him on a steady basis, and there were even company meetings where we would sing a company song written by William "Smokey" Robinson. That was the "all for one and one for all" kind of atmosphere that existed at Motown back then.

At Hitsville U.S.A. there were opportunities for creative people in all areas. There were several remarkable women who worked at Motown as well. Fran Heard headed the tape library. Faye Hale and Berry's sisters, Esther, Anna, Loucye, and Gwen, all held positions. My biggest inspiration while recording for Motown was Loucye. I loved Loucye, and I would take advantage of my frequent visits to her office. Motown was expanding by leaps and bounds, which became obvious as renovations on the newly purchased house next door were progressing. Loucye would graciously welcome me when I visited her office in the new building, and she would fill me in on what was transpiring within the company. There would be many labels under Motown's roof. In addition to Motown, there was also Soul, Tamla, Mojazz, and my label, Gordy, and we dominated the charts for years.

As for Berry's sisters, they were all sophisticated and elegant. We used to make jokes about the fact that Esther, Anna, and Gwen would only speak to you if you currently had a hit on the record charts. At least that's one of the things we jokingly accused them of. The oldest sister, Esther, was the wife of Congressman George Edwards, and her grace made me always imagine a crown on her head. She was always there to assist in this "family" company. Anna was tall and always dressed with the best of taste. She'd appear only on special occasions and had the facade of being "kept," yet she was a former record company owner (Anna Records). The baby sister, Gwen, was a great sport, and she was so cute I imagined her an avid tennis player. She bounced on her toes, glided as she walked, and always wore the warmest of smiles. Gwen was always charming and fashionable, and she had become a grand lady married to Motown producer Harvey Fuqua. He was a former member of the singing group the Moonglows.

Berry Gordy himself couldn't sing a note, but he could determine in a few seconds if a song had potential, if a singer had any talent, or what changes were needed, and his opinion was always well taken. He would assign certain projects to his employees, and if they followed his directions accordingly, the results would be in the good taste and standards he sought. If an artist needed a new hit and no one could create one to suit his taste, Berry would get busy and make a Number 1 record to show everybody how it was done.

Whenever Motown was called "a family operation," the reference to family was accurate. His parents, "Mom" and "Pops" Gordy, as we lovingly called them, treated us all as their own. And we saw them often. Pops was head of construction and was always busy cleaning, painting, and fixing up the foundation of that building–and each additional one–as Berry expanded his operation. They would both dress up and look so distinguished as they appeared at our openings, sending flowers, telegrams, and wishing us luck.

"Momma Bertha" was a sweet woman of few words, smiling at all times like the devoted parent I know she was. She was so proud of all of these brilliant people. Iris Gordy, the daughter of Berry's oldest brother, Fuller, was head of quality control at Motown. She and Billie Jean Brown had the task of choosing the next records to be released. I didn't envy them their job, because they pleased and/or displeased everyone with their decisions. In my first months at Motown, I saw meetings take place where local clergymen, disc jockeys, educators, politicians, and famous doctors and lawyers all met to listen to potential new releases and express their opinions.

Mr. Gordy, who had once worked on a Ford Motor Company assembly line, was popular with everyday people. His former associates were among hundreds who now supported him in his efforts. A lot of the nightlife crowd were his personal friends as well, since as a young man he had once been the regular piano player at the Flame Show Bar. Gwen and Anna held the positions of coat-check girl and camera girl, respectively, and dressed for their parts. I was too young to go in there at the time, but I remember peeking in once or twice through the side door, only to be chased away. On a couple of occasions I was able to catch a fleeting glance of Sarah Vaughan, Billy Eckstine, Della Reese, Arthur "Red" Prysock, Miles Davis—just some of the greats who had graced that stage.

It was while at the Flame Show Bar that Berry began writing songs, and along with Billy Davis (under the pen name of Tyran Carlo), he wrote a string of hit singles for Jackie Wilson. Among them were "Reet Petite (the Finest Girl You Ever Want to Meet)," "To Be Loved," "Lonely Teardrops," and "That's Why (I Love You So)." In 1959 he borrowed $800 and started what was to become Motown Records. The first hit he produced was Barrett Strong's "Money," and soon he was on his way. The Motown empire had all been built from his imagination and dreams.

Berry was very spiritual, and had visions far beyond any of our imaginations. He was a fountain of information and future plans for his company, which was becoming bigger and bigger before our very eyes. The phone lines grew from four to eight to sixteen in no time. It wasn't long before Berry finally had to move all of his personal belongings to his new condominium, because Hitsville U.S.A. and the house next door became filled up with tapes and equipment. Michael McClain, our chief engineer, had upgraded the board to make it an eight-track recording machine. I was amazed how a new addition was added every day, and how technicians were introduced and joined the operation. I can smile about being used by a blind date to get an engineering position. My date charmed me for a couple of months, and did finally become an engineer at the company. I never felt any animosity toward him, because who could blame him? Everyone wanted to be a part of this remarkable organization.

With newfound success came changes. Martha & the Vandellas had just gotten started, we had excellent chart action, we had our sights on hitting the elusive "Number 1 with a bullet." Engagements were pouring in, so we were constantly on the move. Annette got married as soon as she finished high school in 1963. Not long after–

ward she complained that she was experiencing problem pregnancies. She had a tubal pregnancy, so her doctor recommended that she
stay home. This prompted her to want to leave the rigorous pace of
the road. After we heard her say, "I'm sorry, but I have to stay off my
feet, stay at home, and take care of myself and my husband," I knew
there was going to be trouble. All of a sudden, Rosalind and I were
left hanging. "Now what am I going to do with a hit record and only
one Vandella?" I asked myself.

Motown had just signed a group of girls named the Velvelettes.
Then, right before recording their hits "Really Saying Something" and
"Needle in a Haystack," the original members had a huge disagree-
ment and broke up. When they got back together, there were
replacements in the group. It happened all of the time.

I met Betty Kelly at Hitsville one day, and she let me overhear her
saying to someone else that she was no longer in the Velvelettes. I
asked her if she was interested in being a Vandella and told her that
one of the girls had just quit and we had several shows scheduled.
She said that she didn't even know if she wanted to stay in Detroit or
move back home to Kalamazoo. She didn't want to stay where she
was because the house she was staying in was so overcrowded. So I
invited her to stay at my house until she made enough money to get
her own place. She thought for a moment and then said to me,
"You've got yourself a new Vandella!" With that, Betty officially
joined the group and we began teaching her all of our routines.

I needed a new Vandella, and Betty needed a job and a place to
stay, so we decided that by having her join the group, we could help
each other out. She didn't much like wearing someone else's shoes
that weren't even her size, and Annette's dresses turned out to be too
tight. We quickly changed and altered everything to accommodate
Betty. We didn't make any official press statement about our new
member, nor did we try to hide the fact. We simply went on with
Betty in Annette's place in the act and on new recordings.

Some people noticed, but some didn't until I pointed out the
change myself. There were those who accused me of trying to replace
Annette with an exact look-alike. Although Betty and Annette had
similar personal styles, I didn't think they looked anything alike. As a
matter of record, I never had to go looking for a replacement for
Annette. It all happened so fast that no shows were canceled or

missed. Everything was in good, divine order. "Ask and you shall receive," says the Bible, and in December of 1963, the minute I realized that I was in need of a new Vandella, Betty appeared instantly!

She went on to stay with the group for six years. She is featured in most of our publicity shots, and we were also videotaped constantly while she was a member. Annette had been with me to launch the group, but it was Betty who is seen in most of our photos and footage from our glory days. Betty was a great sport, and she very quickly adapted to being a part of the act. In addition, she was able to adjust to our rigorous schedule, which was just growing more hectic by the minute!

CHAPTER 5

Dancing in the Street

ALL THE WAY FOR LOVE

The matters of the world teach you to smile
And then you frown
You love being up
Because you know what it is to be down
Your guardian angel keeps right on watching
Over you
Let's keep our hearts wide open
And we'll stay in tune
Pressing it, obsessing it
Learning it, earning it
Let's go all the way for love

We laugh at fears
That are behind us
Things that we now have overcome
Automatically we won our battles
Never knowing how it was done
Let's remember everything
All that we've gone through
By pressing it, obsessing it
Learning it, earning it
Let's go all the way for love

Let's learn to smile through it
There's no need to frown
Remember when we get up
What it was like being down
Our guardian angel is watching us
So let's stick to our tune
Let's find a way
To always be together
Give it a try, we won't be satisfied
Until we go all the way for love

In the early years of Motown–from 1959 to 1962–the company was mainly following trends and trying to fit into the music scene as it existed. But Berry Gordy was always looking for the distinctive musical sound that would distinguish his company and its stars from everyone else. In 1964 the musical era changed, and Berry's "formula" suddenly clicked. That year marked the debut of the Beatles and the British Invasion, TV shows like "Shindig," *and* the official arrival of the Motown Sound.

For Motown the year kicked off with the Temptations' first big hit, "The Way You Do the Things You Do" (Number 11). Their former singing partner, Mary Wells, had her biggest seller, "My Guy," which became a huge Number 1 success for her. Marvin Gaye had "You're a Wonderful One" (Number 15), the Four Tops established themselves with "Baby I Need Your Loving" (Number 11), and the Marvelettes were singing about "Too Many Fish in The Sea" (Number 25). The Supremes scored with "Where Did Our Love Go," "Baby Love," and "Come See About Me."

Martha & the Vandellas had a smashing year as well. Our first two 1964 singles were "Live Wire" (Number 42) and "In My Lonely Room" (Number 44), released in March and May, respectively. In December I was at an office Christmas party at Hitsville U.S.A. Everyone was celebrating, and Brian Holland and Lamont Dozier came in the sales department and dragged me out of the party and right into the recording studio. They played me a demo tape of "Live Wire." I thought that they both had lost their minds when I heard it because the pace of the song was so fast. The intro was long and slow, but I didn't dispute their taste. The ballad "In My Lonely Room" was also a Holland-Dozier-Holland production. I was so emotionally touched by the lyrics that I cried when I recorded it.

Our next single became one of our crowning achievements: "Dancing in the Street." It became a huge Number 2 pop and R&B hit. *Billboard* magazine in the 1990s declared that song "one of the most consistently played dance records of all time."

When I first heard "Dancing in the Street," it was sung by Marvin Gaye. He had written it along with Ivy Hunter and Mickey Stevenson. When I heard Marvin's version it was sung in a male register. I thought it was a good song, but not really in my key. So they said, "OK, Martha, give it your treatment," and I came up with the melody. To be honest, I didn't like the song at first, but when I put myself into it and made it my own, it became the anthem of the decade. From the very beginning, no matter where it was played, everybody seemed to get up and dance to it. I still love the excitement and magic of it and the way people's eyes suddenly light up whenever I sing it.

I've always said that "Dancing in the Street" is Mickey Stevenson's greatest gift to me. Not only did he write it, but he produced it as well. Kim Weston always reminds me that the song was written in her attic because she was married to Mickey Stevenson at the time, and I always tease her that she let a good song get away—right out from under her own roof!

Credit for the creation of the Motown Sound wouldn't be complete without mentioning some of the wonderful musicians who actually played the music that would keep the world dancing to classic Motown for the rest of the century. They called themselves the Funk Brothers, and they were aptly named. It was these musicians who were responsible for all of the success of the singers at Motown, because it was their music that inspired us to sing our best with excitement.

The Funk Brothers were not only responsible for the Motown Sound, they were also some of the best jazz musicians in Detroit. They were all overweight and at first were nicknamed "the Greasies." (The heaviest member of the group was Earl Van Dyke, who tipped the scales at 280 pounds.) Finally, they all agreed to officially call themselves the Funk Brothers.

Berry Gordy and William Stevenson were clever enough to collect the finest players in town, put them on the payroll, and get them under contract. They were not allowed to record with anyone else during the high-rolling days of Motown, when hit after hit was being produced twenty-four hours a day. These arrangements were necessary when it became apparent that the Motown Sound was not in the actual room, but was more like a delicate recipe. It took the right combination of soul-filled artists to produce.

Uriel Jones smiles when he reflects on how together the Funk Brothers were as a unit. He recently told me, "We could play and not even look at one another." If one of them made a mistake, they would laugh and joke each other into shame and keep on playing, but most of their mistakes would be what the producers would take and elaborate on. They were a producer's dream. Some producers only needed to hum the tune to the musicians and they would transform it into pure magic. With Earl Van Dyke on keyboards, Robert White and Larry Vider or Eddie Willis on guitar, James Jamerson on bass, Jack Ashford on vibes and tambourine, and Benny Benjamin on drums, the music soared—and it was all because these musicians were geniuses at their best.

Uriel came on the scene when Earl felt Benny's health was slipping away and he needed an optional drummer. Joe Hunter was on hand as the optional keyboard player. These were some mighty big shoes to fill. When I told him that I wanted to know more about Benny, Uriel ranted and raved about how "Benny Benjamin was the cat" and nobody could capture the style and speed he executed. He was part Spanish and had hung out with Latins, so he knew those rhythms. This Latin flavor was apparent on his pickups and drum rolls. He utilized timbals, which were placed just above his snare drum. The unfortunate fact was that Benny was a heavy drug addict, something that befalls a lot of talented people. He always had to be shaken, dusted off, and nurtured to be effective.

When I had been the A&R secretary, I knew when I spoke to Benny what actions were necessary to get him into the recording studio for sessions—if he could be reached by phone at all. His landlady would accept calls for him in her home and try to assist us when we needed him. When he was on his own, he would arrive usually all fired up with excuses like, "I was sitting on my porch talking with my girlfriend and her man came up and shot at me. He just creased my face." To explain the open and bloody lesions on his face, the result of drug abuse, he'd say: "My woman attacked me with a can opener. I just left Receiving Hospital." But as long as he could still sit and play the drums, it would be an acceptable excuse.

We were always glad just to see that Benny was alive. Even in his altered state, we were amazed that he was able to sit on that drum stool, knocking out session after session. Each and every song he played on had its own identity, groove, and the necessary ingredients to make a hit. They were played uniquely as only Benny could. We knew his heart, and he was a special guy. We always had difficulty finding players who could interpret or imitate the recorded style while performing live onstage. After my first confrontation with him—my first day of work—Benny affectionately called me "Mamacita." That was also his greeting to any other females that he addressed. In the studio we all would watch and marvel as he presented us with his miracle drum licks. We were all sad when he departed this earth at the age of thirty-nine.

There were over a hundred musicians registered on the comprised list, but only a few were allowed to travel with us. Then there were certain players who could only be spared for special concerts. Mary Wells had the pleasure of having Benny travel with her in her first year at Motown, but found it increasingly difficult to deal with his problems. After that, he was restricted to the home base in Detroit.

The evidence of the artistry of the Funk Brothers can still be found on Motown's recorded masterpieces from the 1960s. It is a sound captured on record: music and emotions that are only imitated, never duplicated.

At one glace at a lead sheet, or after hearing the chord progressions of proposed lyrics, James Jamerson would invent bass lines that were totally unique. He was the only bass player that the Motown producers wanted to use. He was also most peculiar about his drink, preferring a Greek brandy named Matoski, with four *X*'s on it. He would keep a bottle in his car and made frequent visits outside after one or two tries at a song. Sometimes, while the other musicians rehearsed to get their parts right, he would excuse himself and head for his car. On one occasion the other musicians played a trick on him and hid his liquor. He thought someone had stolen it and walked around cursing, calling everybody in the general area names until one of them delivered his drink safely back into his possession.

James was quick to pick up on any new song. He was always the first to come up with something fresh and jazzy. What might take the others maybe thirty minutes, James would have planned out in seconds.

He took the time to show us Vandellas "sevenths" and "elevenths," musical chord structures that would be needed to sing songs with three-part harmonies. He had an upright piano on which he drilled us for about an hour and a half per song.

James was a family man, and his lovely wife Anne and their two children lived in a house on Vinewood. It was a special treat one time to be invited over to his house for dinner. Anne was gracious when her husband showed up with Martha and her Vandellas as surprise dinner guests. James, being from the South, loved rice, which we had with hot dogs and pork and beans. At first I thought we had intruded, but Anne was so sweet and kind. It made me realize how only a housewife and mother could take but a few dollars, stretch it, and somehow make it work. James talked a lot about music, and that evening we were filled with good food and wonderful knowledge.

The producers would never spare James for tour dates, so he could never travel with us. He was needed in the studio to keep the records coming. Uriel told me of the time that they were slipping out to record for Wingate at Golden World before it was purchased by Berry Gordy, and were all caught. He said, "When Mickey Stevenson asked us had we been recording for anyone else, we told him no. Then he pulled out some pictures of me with my drum cases and the rest of us leaving. They had detectives watching us, and we had to pay a $300 fine if caught. We couldn't deny the allegations, and paid up without any further conversation." Those musicians were one of the main reasons why our records from this period still sound as exciting as when they were brand-new. Motown was truly an extraordinary place back then.

Major Lance's big 1963 sensation "Monkey Time" had hit the Top Ten at a time when black people had gotten over the stigma of being referred to as "apes." Everyone especially liked the way he did his monkey dance to his hit recording. The dance itself was characterized by upward and downward swinging arm movements with knees slightly bent. In fact, the dance called "the monkey" became so hot so fast that Holland–Dozier–Holland instantly wrote the song "Mickey's Monkey" (a tribute to Mr. Stevenson) to capitalize on it. Smokey Robinson & the Miracles also took their monkey song to Number 8 on the charts a couple of weeks later.

Major Lance was overwhelmed with the success of his record and the reaction it drew when he performed it. Audiences loved the song and his stage routine so much, in fact, that several times his fans got out of control in their response. The fans can sometimes "geek" you and get carried away. While performing in Chicago, his hometown, he stepped too close to the edge of the stage one night. Standing in the wings, I saw fans grab him by the ankles and pull him off the stage and into the crowd. He was tall–about five feet eleven–and weighed all of 150 pounds, but it took five of us to get him back from the fans grabbing and tearing at him.

He was pretty shaken up by that incident. He looked scared and bewildered once he was back on his feet. He straightened his hair and checked his diamond ring to see that it was still intact. Unfortunately, he lost his cuff links, tie clip, and watch, which his fans grabbed as souvenirs of the star. He had tried to placate the crowd by throwing a handkerchief he had mopped his brow with, but some guy down front tossed it back. The watch was another story.

After a successful week of performing as a troupe, we used to have fun with each other during the final show. We called this "burying the show." On the last night of our engagement together, I went into Major Lance's dressing room while he was onstage and put on one of his suits. We usually took practical jokes like this lightly–all in fun. But this time the suit I chose was one of his best costumes, and he didn't think this was funny at all. I had made my entrance while he was performing, and doing my best Major Lance imitation, I looked like him and tried to move like him for a few bars of his song. Then I hurried and put his suit back in his dressing room, just like I found it.

He got even. During "(Love Is Like a) Heat Wave," he came out onstage wearing a dress that he had borrowed from some girl on the show. He got between Rosalind and Betty and made our routine look terrible. Oh well, I thought. Turnabout is fair play. The audience loved our acting up, and their uproarious applause for our onstage antics made for an easy way to say good-bye and close out the festivities.

As Motown became more and more popular and we recording artists became music stars and representatives of our generation, Berry Gordy wanted to make sure that we would become refined ladies and gentlemen who could fit into any echelon of society with ease. In our first days at Motown, all the girls were chaperoned, and watched constantly. To put the final polish on our character and manners, Motown put us through extensive training. In order to do this, Berry set up his own "finishing school" of sorts, called the artist development department. We were not being groomed to be one-hit wonders; we were being readied for distinguished lifelong careers and proper manners to serve us wherever we went.

All of us were tutored whenever we weren't performing. The minute we got back to Detroit, we were taken into Motown's studios and taught modeling as well as choreography. We were taught music theory. We were taught manners. We were even taught the proper way to eat, just in case we should ever be in the presence of the Queen of England or the President of the United States. We were coached about what fork to use, what knife to use, and how to practice polite etiquette in any situation. I'm glad they did it, because it prepared us for later on, traveling abroad and being involved in a lot of different circumstances. In a way, being at Motown in the 1960s was like attending a university and our major was personal development. I didn't appreciate it half as much at the time as I do now.

Beginning in 1964, Berry hired four instructors at Hitsville U.S.A. to teach the performers. He hired Maxine Powell to teach etiquette and Cholly Atkins to teach choreography and movement, while Maurice King taught us stage routines that he and his assistant Johnny Allen came up with.

It was Mrs. Powell's job to "refine" us for stardom. Mr. Atkins was famous for the high stepping he taught Gladys Knight & the Pips, and Mr. King was the best musical director, arranger, and saxophonist in town. Mr. Allen was always there with Mr. King writing and arranging—and polishing all of us for the "big time."

Maurice King had formerly managed Gladys Knight & the Pips when Gladys was at the tender age of five. It was evident that this group would one day become Motown artists. We all knew these singers from Atlanta and had worked together internationally years before their arrival at Hitsville. We loved and admired Red, Ed, Bubba and sweet Gladys.

I looked forward to every class with a hunger for knowledge and a thirst for success. Among them all, Mrs. Powell was special. She worked with small groups of six to eight of us—men and women—and let me tell you, she turned this tomboy around! I needed instruction, and so did all of the rest of us, whether we were receptive to her or not.

Berry Gordy's eldest sister, Esther Edwards, exemplified elegance. It was she who suggested to her brother that we could all benefit from the wonderful program that Mrs. Powell could offer—and she was right. Mrs. Powell would always capture our attention with an opening lecture, sometimes by repeating previous directions. But she would always take care to drive the message home and show us the light of possibility—future designs on our lives, and the promise of success. I took all of my lessons home, like so many other things that I learned, and drilled my four little sisters, giving them the same instructions that I had received. I even imitated Mrs. Powell's gestures. I think that all of us have benefited because of it.

"Posture is the key. If you stand up with your shoulders back and your chin in the right position, you can give an image to anyone looking at you that you are confident, have self-esteem, and that you are well balanced." This is just one example of the things Maxine Powell instilled in me in her classes, and I apply her teachings in everything I undertake. The Supremes, the Temptations, and Marvin Gaye were all among her pupils as well. Motown is often compared to film studios like MGM, which traditionally groomed mere actors into stars. With us, the effect was the same. An element of dignity was added to our every move.

Mrs. Powell would tell us, "When you walk into a room, everyone should notice you. You should make a statement: 'I have arrived!' should be on your face."

In one session Mrs. Powell pointedly said, "You are not the most beautiful women or the best singers in the world, but each of you is talented. Like flowers in the garden, I will help each one of you to grow and bloom. Charm and grace will take you all over the world.

When I 'finish' you, you will be able to wine and dine and know how to carry yourselves in the presence of kings and queens. We want to do away with rude, loud, and boisterous personalities and become the prettiest ladies that we can be. If you pay attention, I will help you. What you are going to learn in my class is how to present yourselves at all times. You will learn poise and finesse. I will teach you to walk the proper way, I will show you the correct way to lift items, walk up stairs, and how to sit and stand. I will help develop your personalities to go along with your fame. My models, including Anna and Gwen Gordy, and all of my students have achieved great success, and represent class in all walks of life, the thirty years that I have been teaching."

Mrs. Powell spent her youth in Chicago studying drama, intending to become an actress. Although she loved character parts, her voice was a bit too high, and it didn't help that she sometimes stumbled over big words. She happened to visit Detroit for a weekend, and had stayed at the Gotham Hotel near Orchestra Hall. From a manicurist position she eventually launched a finishing school and modeling agency. From there she joined Motown.

The one specific class that sticks out in my mind was the day when she called on Gwen, who had graciously offered to let us crowd into her luxurious home in Detroit. Gwen proceeded to model, pose, and demonstrate the routine that she had mastered to perfection. She proceeded to walk, sit, lie on the floor or couch, and strut her stuff with ease, giving us an idea of how good we could look if we carried ourselves right and had control of every movement of our bodies and minds. She sat on stools and in a variety of different lounging positions, and we all enjoyed learning that session.

Anna always had an air of sophistication about her, and I loved to see her in hats. She could really coordinate her attire, and always looked as if she stepped out of the *Vogue* magazine pages. She and Marvin Gaye made a nice-looking couple, and both were the products of Mrs. Powell's charm school. All of the Gordy family seemed to be refined, handsome, well-dressed people, with Berry leading them all. Their cousin, Gwen Joyce, assisted Mrs. Powell, too, so we were constantly encouraged in our development.

In 1964 Mary Wells, the Motown roster's acknowledged top female star, renounced the contract that she had signed as a minor.

As soon as she reached her twenty-first birthday, she suddenly quit Motown, and was able to do so because of that little technicality. Mary's husband, Herman Griffin, was the one who really convinced her to leave. He was certain that Mary was such a big star that she could negotiate a better deal elsewhere. Berry was in shock when he discovered that her old contract actually allowed her to do so, and he was terribly hurt.

Mr. Gordy was a little changed after that. He was amazed that after all of his fatherly attention and guidance, Mary Wells would just walk away. He then had every one of our contracts revised, and made each artist re-sign with the company. This in turn added two more years to the existing eight-year contract I signed in 1962. No one else would ever walk away from Berry as Mary did right after the huge success of "My Guy."

She then signed with 20th Century Records and recorded several hits like "Ain't It the Truth" (1964) and "Use Your Head" (1965). Unfortunately, she never repeated the kind of success she had at Motown. We all watched Mary's career momentum vanish. She became an example to us of how treacherous the record business could be away from the winner's circle at Motown.

The Vandellas and I were busier than ever with concert performances across the country. We always had favorite venues to play. While the Apollo Theatre was always a highlight in Manhattan, just across the East River was another New York institution: the Brooklyn Fox. This is where we had the opportunity to work and become friends with so many of our costars in the rhythm-and-blues and pop-rock circuit, including the Shangri-Las and Patti LaBelle & the Blue-Belles.

In September of 1964 we rode to New York in station wagons driven by various road managers. Ours was Gene Shelby, one of my best friends at the company. All of these managers were handpicked and interviewed by Mrs. Esther Edwards, Thomas "Beans" Bowles, or Berry Gordy himself, just to make sure that we were in responsible hands and were protected while away from home.

We checked into the Hotel President that day, and left immediately to report to the theater at 9:00 A.M. It was truly an exciting time, for there was already a line of anxious music lovers around the corner ready for the doors to open. They stood behind the police barricades, which were needed to keep the fans from attacking their idols.

This was our third time playing the Brooklyn Fox, and we were all very fond of the host/promoter Murray Kaufman, better known as Murray the K. He worked us hard, but was right beside us, organizing, changing, announcing, and enjoying some of the best theatre productions ever dreamed of. He would invent these great openings and themes for group presentations, and hired performers that you admired and wanted to get to know. You would cooperate with Murray the K, and you'd find yourselves acting like children together, falling down, rolling around, carrying signs, playing "musical stools," dancing and laughing, learning the fundamentals of performing and everything involved in the making of shows that the crowds rallied to and loved. This show was a true "rock-and-roll extravaganza," and it was thrilling and electric from beginning to end.

The show lineup was of brilliant design, and we were glad to be a part of this winner. During the opening skit we all marched out onstage carrying signs on sticks. The signs had other performers' names on them, and they would also be announced on an offstage microphone. Then we all ran up the stairs and changed into our costumes. There were three floors of dressing rooms and only one staircase, so you ran past each other and worked like bees—four shows a day, sometimes five, depending on the lines outside. This was in mid-September, and school had started for the fall semester. But that didn't matter; we had a grand turnout.

Our first time there in 1963 had already given us the opportunity to perform and enjoy getting to know Gerry & the Pacemakers, Little Eva, Gary U.S. Bonds, and Bill Medley of the Righteous Brothers. Brooklyn natives Little Anthony & the Imperials were also there, and my special relationship with Sammy Strain sticks out above the rest. He was kind enough to check on us constantly, making sure that we knew all that there was to know to stay on schedule. This was a fast-paced show, and it was each performer's responsibility to keep up. Sammy was an angel to watch out for us and keep us informed of our cues. There were a couple of stage managers, but they took their orders from Murray and saw that his wishes were honored—pronto!

It was about the third day of our ten-day September 1964 stint, and one of Murray's runners, named Jay, knocked at the dressing room door. We had just come offstage after opening and singing

"Come and Get These Memories" and our new hit "Dancing in the Street." It felt good to relax and await the finale. There was always one immediately after the designated star had finished his or her last song, and a signal would be given.

"Martha, here, come with me for a minute," said Jay. "Murray wants to see you."

I got moving quickly, but in my mind I was wondering why I had been singled out.

Questioning the move, I promptly followed Jay to the office just behind stage, next to where the star's dressing room was. Murray sat facing a mirror.

"Martha, I need you to do me a favor. You don't have to. I just think you can handle this situation, and don't worry, we'll back you up," he said.

I asked him cautiously, "What is it? Anything for you, Murray."

"One of our English acts is homesick and upset. We need someone to go and talk to her, be her friend. England is a long way from here, and we want our friends to feel at home, so I thought, if you will, you could go in and be her friend, spend some time with her."

It didn't sound like a difficult thing to do, so I agreed and asked, "Where is she?" No one answered me.

I followed Jay once more to the second floor, where there were four dressing rooms. He led me to the one on the left at the end. The door was closed, and behind it we could hear someone yelling and breaking glass. At that point, I was starting to change my mind. As I turned around to make my exit, I saw other acts standing in their doorways laughing at me.

I turned to face the door again as Jay called out, "Dusty, open the door. There is someone here to see you."

The sound of things shattering up against the wall stopped for a moment, and all was still. I knew who it was by then. I had long wanted to meet this beautiful girl from England. She was a big star and added flavor to this lineup, making the show an international one. Her first American hit, "Wishin' and Hopin'," had just made the American Top Ten charts around the same time as "Dancing in the Street."

He repeated, "Dusty Springfield, open the door, honey. Martha Reeves is here to see you," and she slowly opened the door, just enough to see out of it. We could see that she had been crying and her makeup was a mess, with black streams of mascara running down both of her cheeks. Once the door was partially opened, Jay sort of stuck his foot in the door, and we started in. He placed his hand on my shoulder, nudging me gently into the room.

The room was a mess. In the center of it I saw a cardboard box full of broken cups and saucers, a few dessert plates yet intact. She obviously had been throwing some of these upside the wall. I said, "Hey girl, what's going on here? What's got you so upset?" With that, Jay backed out of the room, closing us up in there together.

She tried to talk, but was full of despair, so I started to kick some of the broken glass around on the floor, making it seem like fun to hear the noise of dismantled china. "This one is real pretty, do you mind if I keep it?" I said.

She took a tissue, dabbed her eyes, and said in a lovely accent, "Do what you like, I don't care."

I was glad she finally spoke to me, and after awhile, she started revealing the source of her despair. She told me that Vic Billings, her manager, did not come with her to the theater and she was alone among strangers. Frustrated, she had gone to a local thrift shop and purchased this china to vent her anger. It was a tradition of her people, she said, that when they felt anxiety they couldn't contain, they broke things until their feelings changed.

She finally stopped crying, and seemed to feel better. As I started to pick up some of the larger broken pieces, she waved her hand for me to stop, and I sat down at the dressing table near her as she repaired her makeup. While she wiped away the mascara tears, we chatted, and her attitude brightened like clouds parting after a storm.

We became good friends right away. With her makeup redone and a new friend in tow, we walked out onstage hand in hand for that show's finale. I realized then how sensitive she was behind that tough barrier she put up when she was not in familiar or friendly surroundings.

When we arrived at the theater for the next seven days, my concern was to go and check on my girl Dusty to see if she was in the right spirit, and if not, we'd talk until she felt better.

One night when I asked her if there was anything she wanted, she asked for me to send out for a bottle of vodka. We were both over twenty-one, but I personally wasn't much of a drinker. But she spoke so calmly when she requested it that I gladly complied with her wishes. She was perfectly happy having a cocktail in her dressing room after that. For the rest of the Brooklyn Fox engagement, she was just fine, and I had fun with my new friend.

Years later I found out that Dusty developed a drinking problem. It was a longtime friend, Lesley Gore, who informed me that it was I who had introduced Dusty to her first drink of alcohol. I was horrified. I prayed immediately that if I was guilty of turning her into an alcoholic, it was not my design. I didn't drink any of it with her, and God, please forgive any harm I caused. Those were not my intentions.

With newfound fame, success, and acclaim came new pressures. The innocent days of all those Motown acts cheering each other on was sometimes replaced with competitiveness. We haven't always had an easy road. There have been times when we have had petty arguments and rivalries. If Motown was a "family," then disagreements and fights between siblings were to be expected. We've certainly had more than a little sassing out at times.

My one and only fight with a Motown act–the Supremes–was regrettably publicized by someone who happened to be sitting by the door at the time. Even worse, this person only saw and heard enough to get it all wrong in a book written in anger. Being loved is great until some misunderstanding turns it into hatred. We loved it at Motown, and it is eternal. Nothing can destroy it or take any of the glory away from it. However, this engagement at the Brooklyn Fox was the site of one of the major "sassing out" sessions. I'm glad to have the chance to tell it just as I remember it happening.

Murray the K met us on the second floor in a large room with chairs enough to seat all of the stars side by side around the walls. On this show, the opening was to be done in street clothes. The girls were told to wear pants, because when the curtains opened, we would all be lying on the floor. As the music and announcements were made, we were to get up, dance a certain routine that we were quickly shown, and told to remember how we were placed. "Let's go. Oi vay!" Murray would exclaim in Yiddish.

Marvin Gaye, who we still backed up offstage, decided not to take part, and was excused. But among the Shangri-Las, the Supremes, the Searchers, the Ronettes, and Jay & the Americans, we had fun acting out and opening the show with excitement and a bang. We had our own style of pants, having looked high and low for these two-piece metallic black costumes that were easy to care for and ideal for theater work.

I was finishing the opening act and was told by one of the stage managers that if the Supremes weren't back in time for their spot, we would have to go on early. So Rosalind, Betty, and I climbed the steps to the dressing room on the third floor and put on our favorite stretch outfits. As we stood around waiting to see if we would be needed early, Diane Ross, Mary Wilson, and Florence Ballard strutted past us, dressed in newly purchased frocks that were the *exact same outfits* that we had on! We had worn them for a couple of the shows earlier that week! It was evident that they had copied our idea and our outfits, only theirs were in silver.

I yelled, "You bought the same outfits! We're wearing ours this show! How dare you!" Just then Rosalind grabbed my arm to keep me from grabbing Diane, who curtly answered, "So what?" in a catty tone. She was not at all sorry about the incident, and she knew exactly what she had done.

I just exploded. "You wait until you come off that stage!" I yelled as the Supremes were announced to sing "Where Did Our Love Go," their only song at the time. Well, we knew where *we* had to go: back upstairs to change into something else. We were three acts down in the regular schedule, so we would surely be seen as copycats later on. We ran back up to put on our gold stretch pants and sequined tops, glad to have something else ready at such short notice.

All the while I was fuming. "Wait till I get my hands on her!" I threatened as we changed clothes.

"I can't believe her nerve," said Betty.

"Where does she get off copying our outfits?" Rosalind complained.

It was wonderful being on a label with so many talented acts, but to dress totally alike was taking this "family" thing one step too far. Especially since we didn't work together all the time now, I felt they could have waited until after this gig was over to wear their pants. The worst part of it was that the Supremes went on before us, and we still had to sing behind Marvin Gaye right after our performance. When we got back downstairs, we were all winded and out of breath from running up and down the stairs–all because of the Supremes' inconsiderate copycat antics. I was becoming madder and madder by the moment.

When we sang the last note of "Hitch Hike" with Marvin and the curtain had rested on the floor on the front of the stage, I sprang into action. I immediately headed in the opposite direction, wanting to finish the fight started by Diane's smart–mouthed comment. Singing always soothed me, so I had calmed down somewhat. I spotted Diane in the public telephone booth located at the entrance of the back-stage door, and she had this big grin on her face. As she beckoned to me from the slightly opened door, I rushed toward her, thinking that the phone booth was a fine enough place for us to get on with it!

When I got there ready to do battle, she thrust the receiver in my face and stepped out, giving me plenty of room. "Hello!" I snapped into the phone–and to my amazement it was Berry Gordy on the other end of the line. Diane was probably the only one of us who could call him up at any time like that. He infuriated me even more when he asked, "What's the problem, Martha Rose?" I hated when anybody would address me by my first and middle names! Berry knew this and his chuckle indicated that he didn't think this was a serious, earthshaking confrontation.

I was really bent out of shape, but the respect and high regard I had for our company president left me speechless, and I became embarrassed that such a trivial matter had been brought to his atten-tion. Diane had already told him what for, and all I did was hold the phone just as I had decided to hold my tongue. It was obvious that the Supremes were "his girls" and could do no wrong in his eyes.

I just listened as he continued: "I know that Diane and them just went out and bought some outfits just like yours. They promise not to wear them anymore while they are there at the Fox. I don't want you girls fighting. You are all from the same company, and you should all get along. They are truly sorry. Don't be mad at them. Diane admits they made a mistake."

All I could say was "Uh–huh" . . . "oh yeah" . . . "OK" and finally "bye." I was so mad, hurt, and frustrated when I handed the phone back to her, and she simply closed the phone booth door to finish her conversation privately. Besides having to swallow my unvented anger, I had to shake off my feelings of uneasiness and go on with the next show.

I felt true abandonment from my hero for the first time. It was as if our entire group had been put out to pasture. We didn't have any more problems with costumes or anything else after that. Diane and I found enough space to avoid each other until our tension eased, and we were back to the show business at hand.

Lead singers not only do the majority of the work, sing all of the songs, and offer most of the opinions, but their personalities are generally singled out and taken as the general attitude of the unit. I could tell that Diane had the fortitude, charisma, and boldness that one needs to compete and succeed. If anybody could succeed, I knew she would do it.

The "family" feeling had now grown dim, and from here on it would be every group for itself and God for us all. Diane had stolen onstage ad-libs from everybody. Even when her improvisation of others' cooing and ooing style had nothing to do with her song, she'd still get away with it. One example that comes to mind—and one we thought the jest of all times—was her singing "Let Me Go the Right Way" and adding the ad-libbed "shake it, shake it baby." This little touch was added after she heard us use it behind the Isley Brothers' "Twist and Shout," which we sang in our original act along with the big hit we had at that time, "Come and Get These Memories."

Our last 1964 single, "Wild One," was written and produced by Mickey Stevenson and Ivy Jo Hunter. The Shangri-Las had a hit with "Leader of the Pack" earlier that year, and I always felt that "Wild One" was our ode to the bikers. I really thought that it was going to become as big a hit as "Dancing in the Street," but it didn't get the kind of push it needed. I just knew that song should have hit Number 1. It did, however, hit Number 34 on the pop charts in January 1965.

It was early that same month when I got a call. It was from Dusty Springfield in England, and she informed me that her record company, Phillips, had awarded her four tickets to the annual Carnival in Rio. She asked me to go along. She said, "Do you *really* want to see people dancing in the street? Well, join Tom, my brother, Madelyn Bell, and me for a holiday." There were no gigs on the books during that week, so I accepted her offer for mid-February.

We met in New York City at La Guardia Airport. We had both traveled from cold climates and had on big bulky sweaters that we wished we could pull off. We flew together on three different planes and boarded, slept, disembarked, filled out papers, showed our passports, and ignored the stares as we enjoyed each other's company.

We finally landed in the land of the samba. Rio de Janeiro was more than I imagined, and it was a welcome change from where I had just been. It was hard to realize that freshly fallen snow now covered the East Coast of North America in a midwinter storm. Only hours away I was basking in a tropical climate.

I really liked the strip that ran from one end of the beach to the other. You could walk from Ipanema to Copacabana. From every point that we traveled, we could see the large statue of Christ on Corcovado with the arms extended. Sugarloaf Mountain was off in the distance and looked just like a big sleeping bear. It was thrilling just being there. We met up with Tom and Madelyn and had a wonderful week, going to parade after parade and seeing some of the grandest costumes I had ever dreamed I'd see. And the music was nonstop. Up and down the strip there was one band after another. Conga rhythms were heard each time they came and danced by, everybody joining in the parade of colorfully dressed natives and tourists with the same festive spirit.

This was an incredibly fascinating time in my life. I had new friends from all over the world and this was my first trip where I was at leisure–and I had Dusty to thank for it.

CHAPTER 6

Nowhere to Run

WHAT DO YOU DO WITH A LOVE AFFAIR?

What do you do with our love affair
That is about to end?
What can it be when two lovers vow
To suddenly just be friends?

After a lifetime of getting along
Make it through earthquakes
Together and strong
Began fighting over right and wrong

What do you do with a love affair
That definitely has to end?
What were our reasons, what was said
That we should ever begin?

So, I'll fold the arms that used to fit
I'll seal these lips that used to kiss
Just open your eyes
Love never existed

We'll learn to let our lives go on
Throw ole' yesterday away
Let our hearts love freely
As tomorrow gives, one more day

While I was enjoying Rio de Janeiro, our next big hit single was released. Another Holland–Dozier–Holland classic, "Nowhere to Run" became one of our most memorable songs. The tracks had been recorded several months earlier, but we hadn't yet put our vocals on it. Motown held on to it until we could come off the road long enough to finish it. Since we needed new product immediately, we had been rushed into the studio with Brian Holland and Lamont Dozier, who were the producers. I considered it one of the jewels "left in the can" from our early work with them.

I loved the lyrics the moment I heard them. One of the reasons that I so strongly identified with the song in that session was because of the pace, urgency, and pressure under which it was recorded. We had worked so hard on the road and were not given a moment to rest, so it seemed like it was I who had nowhere to run and nowhere to hide!

The song soared up into the Top Ten, hitting Number 5 on the R&B chart, and Number 8 on the pop chart. In addition, it became one of the first three Motown singles released in Great Britain under the label's new British imprint, Tamla/Motown Records U.K. In England the song reached Number 25.

Marvin Gaye, Kim Weston, the Marvelettes, Mary Wells, the Supremes, the Temptations, and Martha & the Vandellas were the forerunners of artists who were part of an exchange system that the U.S. and the U.K. were establishing at the time. In order for American artists to perform in Europe, the same number of artists and players had to discover the fans of the United States. When Motown singer Kim Weston went to England, the Rolling Stones came to America. When we were invited there, the Beatles came here.

Only months before, in November, Martha & the Vandellas had flown to London to promote the single "Dancing in the Street" on the television shows "Ready Steady Go!" and "Thank Your Lucky Stars." The song had reached Number 28 in U.K. This success gave us a foot in the door to launch our own 1965 "American invasion" of the British Isles. While there, on November 5, Dusty invited us to her flat for a party and to view the Guy Fawkes Day fireworks.

Dusty was by now a huge sensation in England. She had begun her career as one-third of the group the Springfields with her brother Tom and a friend. In 1964 she launched a solo career, and was so successful that by 1965 she was offered her own English television special on ITV, produced by the innovative Vicki Wickham. Vicki, who later transformed Patti LaBelle & the Blue-Belles into LaBelle, was one of the first TV producers to recognize the impact that Motown was about to have on the British record charts.

It was Dusty's idea to invite me and my group to England to be her special guest stars. What a fantastic idea, and what a lovely compliment from my new friend! Besides, Berry Gordy was already planning for a Motown Revue tour of England from March 20 to April 10. So this TV special was the frosting on the cake for our European kickoff. What this TV special finally did for us in England was comparable to what the Beatles' appearance on "Ed Sullivan" had done for them in America a year earlier.

Our Motown Revue British tour featured not only Martha & the Vandellas, but also the Miracles, the Temptations, Stevie Wonder, and the Supremes. We opened the twenty-one-day, twice-nightly tour at Finsbury Park in Astoria, London, on March 20, and concluded it on April 12 at the Guildhall in Portsmouth.

When our excited group arrived at Heathrow Airport in London, huge crowds were waiting there to meet us with banners waving—thanks to the Motown Appreciation Society started by Dave Goden. There were hundreds of well-wishers, and we were almost buried alive with bouquet after bouquet of fresh flowers. In this chilly climate, we were met with warm hugs and kisses.

A parade was held in our honor to announce our arrival in the

U.K. Bundled up in winter coats, we rode in open–roof cars through the beautiful streets of London amid the glaring flashbulbs of a sea of cameras. Several streets were blocked off to allow our motorcade to pass. I was stunned by the enthusiasm of all of our adoring fans. They shouted words of encouragement and approval. It felt like homecoming, only we were the kings and queens!

For our concert tour the majority of the Motown entourage rode across the lush green English countryside, from one venue to the next, in rented buses. No problem. I was thrilled just to be there. And this was luxury compared to the 1962 Motown Revue tour. I should have seen the handwriting on the wall when Berry Gordy hired a chauffeured stretch limousine for himself and the Supremes. This was the trip where we all saw for ourselves that Berry had even bigger plans for the Supremes.

I was still in my "there's room at the top for all of us" frame of mind, so *c'est la vie.* I was having too much fun with my own circle of friends. I became chummy with British tour assistants John Reid and Michael Aldred, and my pal Dusty would pop in and out of the towns we played as her schedule allowed, and we had a great time. She would drive her American Cadillac with right–hand steering, and we'd go off on shopping and sightseeing expeditions of our own.

So far, the trip was a sheer treat. In addition to Dusty, John and Michael were great friends who made us feel at home. They assisted us in every way they could, everyone was nice, and the reaction of the audiences was real ecstatic for us American newcomers. John even introduced us to Elton John, who in 1965 was in a band called Bluesology, and they backed up several touring American R&B stars like Major Lance and Patti LaBelle & the Blue–Belles. I learned on that trip that the British really do know how to party!

I always looked forward to Dusty's visits. She was my devoted friend, and it made me feel special and loved to have a close friend like her. On one of her visits, she had been working in a different town and was not booked in our hotel. She was having problems in her personal life at the time that made her cry. We had a heart-to-heart talk, but I couldn't get her to go into it. She had been having trouble sleeping, although she was exhausted. She was so relaxed after tea service in my room that she curled up and went to sleep fully dressed, just like the baby doll that she was. She looked so peaceful, so I just let her sleep, and I covered her with a comforter like any friend would.

The next morning Mickey Stevenson came knocking at my door to tell me of some changes in the show scheduling for the day. As Mickey was standing in the doorway talking to me about some alterations in the show's lineup, he looked past me and spotted Dusty as she lay there with one of her big legs stuck out from under the comforter—fishnet stockings and all. For the rest of the day, all the men on the show kidded and teased me, as though something odd had transpired. I was amazed at just how others regarded our friendship, but I couldn't have cared less what anyone thought.

When we arrived back in London, we were all having a wonderful time. One night after a very successful performance, the Vandellas and the Supremes were grouped together and treated to a show featuring the legendary sensation Eartha Kitt. At the dazzling nightclub the Top Hat, the atmosphere was one of sheer excitement. Just being there in the audience filled me with dreams of one day performing on that same London stage.

I was proud to be an American in the company of five other beautiful young women—Betty Kelly, Rosalind Ashford, Florence Ballard, Mary Wilson, and Diane Ross—right down front in the best seats to witness our idol. It was a dream—come—true event.

Eartha was superb, at her best, looking and sounding great. With each selection she grew more and more intriguing. She boldly and expertly captured and held the audience's attention. She had us eating out of her hand, totally mesmerized by her every move. After one of her breathtaking numbers, she stood behind a screen with a pinpoint spotlight illuminating just her face, and changed clothes with an alluring expression—using her eyes to full effect. When the lights came up she had executed a dramatic complete wardrobe change. She ended her next song lying on an exotic cat-skin rug, purring the lyrics to "Santa Baby (Hurry Down the Chimney Tonight)." She wooed everybody, and ending her show in a frenzy, she received several curtain calls and standing ovations. I stood and yelled, clapping so loudly until someone touched my arm to calm me down, for I was overcome.

I was even more elated when she agreed to receive us fellow performers after the show. After watching her perform her act with cat-like precision, I felt that the six of us were mere novices. I was so anxious to tell her how great she was, how much more beautiful she was in person, and how well her show was put together. Her song interpretations were magic, as well as her smooth costume and mood changes.

We were so thrilled when we were ushered backstage and into her dressing room. An assistant swung the door open and we entered the inner sanctum of this glamorous star. There she sat at her dressing table, looking every inch a "diva" in full command. She was making some minor repairs to her eye makeup and was uninterrupted by the entrance of us wanna-bes.

Before anyone could say hello, Diane stepped ahead of us all and blurted out, "Eartha, a lot of people tell me that I look like you."

Well, after that you could have heard a pin drop. Eartha said not one word in reply. In the icy silence we were all suddenly nervous and uncomfortable.

Eartha didn't miss a beat, though. Without saying anything, she scooped up her makeup and deposited it into her evening bag. She snapped it shut, stood up, and turned to our group of dumbfounded girls. She just stood there–staring first at Diane and then looking over the lot of us. As she draped her cheetah-skin coat about her shoulders, she exited saying, "I'm not *half* as beautiful as you."

Eartha left us all standing there with our mouths agape and bewildered. I was deeply disappointed not being given the chance to tell her how much I loved her show. Quietly, we left.

In our first years as Motown artists, we witnessed the execution of Berry Gordy's master plan. I had always listened intently to his descriptions of his dreams when I first came to Motown, and I watched in amazement as I saw those dreams grow to full realization. Since I too was a part of this dream, I never questioned his directions or his motives–until this trip to England.

Dusty's TV special became "Dusty Springfield Presents: The Sound of Motown," because she had expressed publicly that she loved the music of Detroit. However, Berry had the concept changed to also encompass the rest of the acts on the tour as well as Martha & the Vandellas. I was all right with this arrangement, and I still had the big production number duet with Dusty in the show. At first I didn't mind that my label-mates joined me as well.

Dusty allowed me to sing a duet with her on her big hit "Wishin' and Hopin' " with the Vandellas singing background. I could see Diane in the wings eating her heart out because she hadn't been chosen to do it. On another number we also sang backup for Dusty.

As the show progressed, Berry took command, and some of the shots he called displeased me. I sensed that he was being "Supreme-minded" again. This special was to be produced by Vicki and Dusty, yet Berry was insisting that several changes be made to accommodate his wishes. I took offense when Berry began moving acts around until the Supremes were in a costarring position.

The Supremes didn't even know Dusty, but suddenly they were incorporating a cover version of Sam Cooke's arrangement of "Shake" to supply them material for an additional spot.

This rearrangement especially rubbed me the wrong way since their records were just starting to sell in England. Martha & the Vandellas, on the other hand, had toured England once before and we were well known. If anything, we should have gotten the extra number. Then Berry took the Supremes shopping for new red dresses for their new spot in the show. We had to wear what we brought.

In the middle of the show's taping, Berry took me aside to explain to me that the Supremes—"his girls"—were on the top rung of the ladder and that my group was on the lower one. I was in shock. I felt totally betrayed and powerless. I still tried to do a good job as I watched them made up, groomed, and put in the costar position on the show. Here we had just toured England with Georgie Fame, and after being personally invited by our host, we were pushed aside for Berry's new pet project. His plan was to make the Supremes known in England by placing them ahead of the rest of us.

Ron White of the Miracles saw me backstage with my mouth stuck out in disbelief. With sobering honesty he looked me in the eyes and said to me, "We all get a turn at the top. You had your turn." I appreciated his directness, and after telling me this, he was helpful in putting it all in perspective. Although the remark didn't lessen my hurt feelings, I now clearly saw what was happening to me.

My face was broken, along with my heart. My disappointment showed clearly on my face and in my voice. As we lined up for the finale, I was directed by the producers to a spot where the camera did not reach. Standing off to the sidelines for the finale, I must have looked real ugly because I was so sad and hurt. When the show was broadcast in England on April 21, I wouldn't even be seen on the show's grand finale. Whenever I view that special on videotape, to this day I feel the same betrayal of having been overlooked.

From London we went on to Paris. Not only did we appear at the Olympia, we recorded a live album while there: "The Motor Town Revue in Paris." I was really under the weather during that engagement. Because of stress and exhaustion, I had become physically sick. It was probably psychosomatic from being pushed around, and put down the ladder in London.

April in Paris seemed so perfect, and yet it wasn't. That night in the City of Lights, I was sent out first to open the show. I remember clearly that opening song, "If I Had a Hammer." We also sang "Dancing in the Street" and "Nowhere to Run," which were on the same album. I would have liked to have taken a real hammer and beat off that heavy feeling I carried there because of my sadness over Berry's preference for his new girl group.

After the show I retired to my room and got a good night's sleep. This was the first time I ever slept in down coverings. Lying in that big bed I replayed my rationalizations and my hurt feelings over and over in my head, thinking: "I should have realized that they were special to him. They were there before I arrived at Hitsville. It took a lot of concentrated effort to bring them up to the status where they have finally arrived."

To justify it I kept telling myself, "In order to become number one, there must be a number two." This was the beginning of my developing a second-rate position and attitude. I never really felt that we were "happening" after that, or that we would ever be respected artists around Berry or any of the Motown acts. In press articles we were described as "raunchy," "grating," and other abrasive adjectives that I never accepted or took seriously.

After this American Invasion—on my spirit!—I began to accept being the opening act on the shows and then suddenly having to take a backseat. We were groomed differently, and I watched from the sidelines as my fellow singers started to pull off in different directions. Although I tried to keep a stiff upper lip, I cried in the privacy of my room because of all the heartbreaking letdowns and putdowns I had to endure.

From that point on, I began to put on this hard, cool outer appearance whenever we performed on the same show with the Supremes. This was about the time when Berry and Diane's personal closeness became apparent to everyone. He was now her man only.

It wasn't all just about me and my feelings–it affected all of us at Motown. But the guys reacted differently. It seemed to me that Smokey didn't mind because he was a man, and he had established his reputation to such a degree that he knew where he stood. He was the star of every show, and everybody knew it. He and the Miracles closed every show, and at the finale we all did the monkey onstage to "Mickey's Monkey" together.

The Temptations were glad to have their brand–new Number 1 hit, "My Girl." The lead vocalist on that song was David Ruffin, their latest addition to the group. Along with Paul Williams, Eddie Kendricks, Melvin Franklin, and Otis Williams, the Temptations always stole the show. They were smooth, tall, and handsome, and when they sang it was reminiscent of the harmonies of the Dixie Hummingbirds and the Soul Stirrers–gospel music's greatest groups.

Stevie Wonder was still enjoying the success that came to him when he hit Number 1 with "Fingertips, Part 2," a record that he had created onstage in Chicago. Because of his expert musicianship, his great vocal ability, and Clarence Paul, his constant companion, absolutely no one wanted to follow him onstage.

Here I was in Paris, and I was feeling blue. Everything seemed to be unraveling before my very eyes. Even our sound had changed somehow. Ever since Annette left the group, I discovered that I was missing our original harmony. I had come to rely upon it onstage. I was convinced that, for whatever reason, Rosalind could never really blend her voice with anyone except the Del–Phis. Betty was a hard worker, and I knew that in time everything was going to work out fine. I had personally groomed her for the group, accepted the change, and worked with it.

Life on the road wasn't always easy, especially for us girls. Annette had left my group because of her problem pregnancies, and on this tour Claudette Robinson of the Miracles was absent for the same reason. We all understood that periods and pregnancies some-times made show business impossible.

Our records were being played constantly and people were

responding to us universally. If I could just have shaken off the effects of this brainwashing and smiled through all the behind-the-scenes skullduggery, it might have been fun filming our first English special and recording a live album in Paris. Instead I made myself ill, believing the things said to me personally by my longtime hero. Berry had changed on me, and used psychology to keep us all in line to do whatever he dreamed of doing. He was going to make the Supremes as big as he could—whatever it took.

When I brought my sad, sick, and worn-out body back to Detroit, I had threatened to find a job and get on with my life. I felt knocked out. I have threatened to quit show business a million times, and this was one of the first. I was disappointed and discouraged when I should have been happy for Diane, Mary, and Florence. They had many records in the past that didn't sell, and they had been sent home from some engagements because of lack of showmanship. They were finally getting rewarded for holding on and hanging in there, and trying everything possible to become established. Their song "Where Did Our Love Go" might have been a question to Diane from Smokey and Brian, for now it was Berry who would watch over them.

There was a time when I would never in my wildest dreams have imagined not being at Motown Records. I guessed—much later, of course—that Berry could imagine it easily. I worked real hard to please with my God-given talent and never ever thought of Motown as what it really was: a record company and a business.

It was Berry whom I worked for. I have compared my love for him as that of the devotion of a dedicated house slave for a master. I was just so happy because I was free to live my life my own way, and my spirit soared in my song.

We were all so young and anxious back then, trying so hard to be good and come up to the standards set by the participants of the Motown Sound. I was especially fascinated to see how from this point on, the Supremes would be pushed through the same regimentation and placed way out front in the spotlight.

It wasn't as if I didn't have my own moments of glory. In January of that year we had just been nominated for a "Best R&B Recording" Grammy for "(Love Is Like a) Heat Wave." I took personal delight in the fact that our records steadily sold, even without a big push.

I had a very active career that needed my attention. I may have felt sad and mistreated when I flew back across the Atlantic, but not discouraged. I continued to work and study my craft because I was determined. This latest snub ultimately made me stronger. I could plainly see that success was not going to be handed to me on a silver platter, and I began to work harder than ever before.

I don't know when I was being watched, but I always felt that I must have been, because the songs I was given to record always revealed my life and loves. Sometimes this would occur in the very time and space that they were written in and I sang them in. Now whenever I sang our hit "Come and Get These Memories," I sang it for Berry Gordy, because of the memories of what used to be–and how different things suddenly were now.

CHAPTER 7

Love Makes Me Do Foolish Things

I'M READY FOR YOU NOW

I'm ready for you now
I look forward to showing you how
Good our love can be,
Not that you have chosen me
I knew you as a child
So hold me for a while
And let our feelings come to life.
I've tested faith and emotions
Traveled byways and oceans
Seeking satisfaction
With good and bad reactions
Now we've settled down
After trying the almosts and maybes
Now I know I'm your baby
    And you're mine.

I'm still married to you
And although you're sleeping somewhere else
Your side of the bed goes untouched
I fix meals for two and it scares me to say
I'm looking for you to return any day.
Your smell's in the closet
Where some of your clothes hang,
For the life of me, I don't want to change it
Your hat's still on the rack
And although we called each other out,
You're not gone somewhere
Your shoes are under the bed
I could move them, but they remind me
Of the good times we had
And how secure I am just clinging to your picture

While we had been in Europe, our third album, *Dance Party*, was released. It was our first concept album, containing only upbeat, danceable songs and/or songs about dances. The majority of the songs were written and produced by Mickey Stevenson, along with Ivy Jo Hunter. With songs like "Dancing Slow," "Mobile Lil, the Dancing Witch," "Dance Party," and "Dancing in the Street," it was clearly a party record. We sang two dance numbers, "The Jerk" and "Mickey's Monkey," and we covered one of the Marvin Gaye hits we were on, "Hitch Hike," which also had its own dance moves.

On June 28, 1965, we were featured in Murray the K's ninety-minute CBS television special, "It's What's Happening, Baby." The show was a virtual who's who of the rock and pop world at the time. We were thrilled to have Martha & the Vandellas seen on the same program as Ray Charles, the Dave Clark Five, the Drifters, the Four Tops, Marvin Gaye, Herman's Hermits, Jan & Dean, Chuck Jackson, Tom Jones, Gary Lewis & the Playboys, Little Anthony & the Imperials, Johnny Mathis, Patti LaBelle & the Blue-Belles, the Righteous Brothers, the Temptations, the Supremes, and Dionne Warwick.

On this special, we virtually had our very first "music video." Not one to do static stage shows, Murray wanted to show off all of his guest stars as they had never been seen before. He came to Detroit to the Ford Motor Company and filmed Rosalind, Betty, and I riding in a 1965 Mustang, which was on the assembly line and was being built while we rode in it. There we were at seven o'clock in the morning, and those poor workers didn't have a clue what was going on. No one warned them that we were coming to film. We'd run through the lines, surprising the men and hearing their comments like, "What are these women doing here?" and "What's going on?" Welders, electricians, and assembly workers literally created the car around us. It was really outrageous. We were depicted running in and out of cars on the assembly line while we sang "Nowhere to Run." What a trip!

Our next several releases were all songs about unrequited love, like "You've Been in Love Too Long" and "Love (Makes Me Do Foolish Things)," or torchy jazz numbers like "My Baby Loves Me" and "What Am I Going to Do Without Your Love?"

The single featuring "You've Been in Love Too Long" on the "A" side and "Love (Makes Me Do Foolish Things)" on the "B" side is a perfect example of how Martha & the Vandellas often suffered from what I refer to as "split play." Most of our records had "A" and "B" sides that were equally as good. People would call up a radio DJ and request that both sides be played. In August 1965, when "You've Been in Love Too Long" was released, it went up the charts to Number 36 pop and Number 25 R&B. Instead of continuing to gain momentum, the "B" side started to chart as well to Number 70 pop and Number 20 R&B. Instead of having two Number 1 hits in a row, we were incorrectly tabulated because both sides were being promoted.

My two all-time favorite recordings were Holland-Dozier-Holland's "Love (Makes Me Do Foolish Things)" and Mickey Stevenson and Ivy Jo Hunter's "My Baby Loves Me." My dream was always to be a jazz singer and I was always hoping to record more jazz songs. "My Baby Loves Me" is real close to jazz, and so is "What Am I Going to Do Without Your Love?" There are actually no Vandellas on "My Baby Loves Me." We had the Andantes and the Four Tops singing behind me for that one just to achieve that sound, and it was pure jazz. It became one of my biggest hits: Number 22 pop and Number 3 R&B.

On this string of slow, heartbreaking love songs, I was often asked what my inspiration was in my singing. Well, let me tell you: Love has made me do some truly foolish things.

When I would stand in the recording booth pouring my heart out on songs like "My Baby Loves Me," my thoughts might wander back to my very first disappointing love affairs.

I can remember how heartbreaking it was when William, my first fiancé, let me find out that he had married someone else. I met William when I was thirteen. He was walking down the street in his U.S. Navy uniform, swinging those exaggerated tailored bell-bottoms. His cap was sitting on the back of his head, blocked and placed in his own style. I was sitting on the porch of our house on Riopelle and Leland, and I thought he was real tough-looking. I used to pretend he was the real Popeye, since I was as skinny as Olive Oyl–only seventy-five pounds soaking wet.

The street gangs were prominent during those hot summer days, and he had dared to walk down our street alone, as if he were challenging and daring anyone else to mess with him. He was actively winning boxing competitions in the military, so he strutted with that kind of authority.

We acted like sweethearts, courting each other by writing hundreds of letters between 1954 until 1958, the year he was to "make a woman out of me." I had burned for him with a consuming unrequited love. I had passed on our one opportunity to make love. I decided that if it was to be a brief moment in the backseat of a car, I'd rather not.

The next time I heard from him was during his next furlough. He married a childhood sweetheart who attended the same church. I was heartbroken.

Sitting on the porch another summer day while I was still a teenager, my next infatuation, Charles, came by on the back of a truck filled with straw. He and Little Joe were part of a group called the El-Moroccos. He could sure play some bongos. Little Joe played the maraca shakers, and they both wore brightly colored ruffled shirts, tied at the waist, with big round sombreros on their heads.

I heard their amplified music and walked to the curb to get a better look. It was love at first sight! I would experience some more of this puppy love–the kind that makes your toes sting and your fingers tingle. We flirted with each other, and I gave him my phone number. Charles started to call two or three times a day after that, and we became engaged. He was the friend who gave me Rosalind's number and led me to the Del-Phis.

He joined the army after graduating from Northeastern High School. I continued to write letters, waiting to see him on his furloughs, dreaming of our future together, waiting patiently, and putting the memories of that love affair away like an ostrich buries its head. We went "all the way" and we were to be married.

Unfortunately, Charles was away more than I had expected. He gave me a ring that he bought from a guy on the street while we were out shopping on Woodward Avenue. I lost sight of my dreams of living "happily ever after" after the world's largest piece of cut glass fell out of that ring. As I turned my concentration toward my singing career, he felt lost in the shuffle. He ended up marrying some woman in South Carolina who had four kids. Like the cheap glass in that ring, I was shattered. I thought we had it going for life.

Then there was that day when I was nineteen and my brother Thomas and I were out for a walk, as we often did. He and I were so close that we could discuss almost anything. He had snooped around in my belongings and found my diary. I had tried my best to hide it, but in that crowded household, privacy was a luxury.

He asked me as painlessly as he could, "Sis, do you think all of those guys that you have been with really loved you?"

I was stunned and speechless. I had made a list of the guys that I liked or names of those that liked me, or who I had slept with—being independent at that age. I politely told him, "It's none of your business!"

I didn't feel too pretty growing up, and I wasn't that popular. I considered his question flattery: How could I possibly have had that many involvements? Having a fond attraction for a lot of different guys, I considered his words and kept them in my thoughts.

Back then, my source of pre–adult "lovemaking" consisted of going to the Greystone Ballroom or the Madison Ballroom and dancing the night away. We would "ballroom," "social," "jitterbug," "huck-a-buck," and "Madison"–all of the popular dances of 1959. Some people thought that I was wild because I had so many dance partners, but that was their opinion. I knew the truth: I came here to dance, not to find love.

Some of the guys would hold you so tight, sway you, and make every muscle in your body tingle. There were a few who became lovers, but they were never interested in becoming dance partners for life. It was just a smooth dance together, then "good night, Gracie."

Most nights I would leave the Greystone and the Madison ballrooms satisfied to have my cute little hairdo flattened on one side from too much slow dancing. I would dance with one guy four or five records in a row and we'd never say a word to each other, never knew each other's name. We just loved dancing with each other.

When I started to sing professionally, my romantic songs kept me dreaming, causing me to sink into love much more than I desired, and I landed very hard when the bottom fell out. I should have had a safety net under me for some of the plunges I took. Why did I care so much, only to realize that all of this burning love was mainly in my imagination?

In love with the idea of being in love, it was as if I hadn't had enough pain or rejection. I got back into the game time and time again. Once my career began to take off, though, I started attracting married men in droves. I never took their flattery seriously, and I wasn't about to be labeled a home wrecker. I never really considered such charity as reality, and vehemently rejected their offers to leave their wives. I had already watched enough soap operas to be wise to those tired old lines I was being handed.

Standing there in a recording studio pouring all of my heart out on vinyl on songs like "My Baby Loves Me" and "Love (Makes Me Do Foolish Things)," I would be classified as a soul singer who had been made into a singing star. But in reality, it was my own soul crying out to be loved in return.

In March of 1966 we returned to England for a successful concert tour of our own, and that May *Martha & the Vandellas' Greatest Hits* album was released. It became our biggest-selling album and included several hits that weren't contained on our first three albums.

It was the height of the mod, groovy, Carnaby Street, a–go–go era in America, and we were right in the middle of it. I'll never forget our appearance on the TV show "Shindig." Dressed in skin–tight satin skirts, bugle–beaded tops, and spike heels, I was elevated on a plat-form six feet off the ground while singing "Nowhere to Run," and really *feeling* the lyrics.

Love has a way of finding one in the oddest places. We arrived in St. Louis, Missouri, and were set to play Kiel Auditorium the follow-ing night. The bus had to be parked out back, and I was bending down, digging in a trunk, separating some gowns so that I could leave the majority of them underneath the bus for the evening. Since we were to walk the rest of the way to the hotel, just a block across the street, I wanted to extract just the few dresses I needed.

I was nearly ready to sling the bag that I had prepared over my shoulder when I heard a man say, "Here, let me help you. You look like you need a hand." He startled me, making me jump. I looked up and nearly fell over, because before me stood an Adonis.

He reminded me of "the Big Boy" doll, only he was all man and real tall. I let him take the bag. He swept it up just as easily as he had swept me off my feet. What a way to go!

Calling me by name, he said, "How are you, Martha? My name is Wiley. Do you want to put this bag in my car and ride to the hotel?" He was so handsome that his plan was perfectly all right with me. When we got to the hotel, after some small talk and a promise of a call later, he departed after seeing me safely to my room.

From the moment I met him, he seemed to just take charge, as I always envisioned that the man should. I waited with bated breath until he called. Although he couldn't come back that night because his aunt was ill, he promised to have breakfast with me the next morning before our sound check.

I couldn't sleep all night, because this knight in shining armor had stolen my heart. The more I tried to go to sleep, the clearer his image would become in my closed eyelids.

I liked everything about him, which is just where I pictured myself–all about him! When the sun came up, I was just lying there, waiting on the day, watching the morning news, until the phone rang.

The first call was from Betty Kelly. She immediately asked me, "What are you talking so sexy for? What are you into?"

"Ain't nothin' happening, but it don't always have to be that way. I'm waiting on a call right now," I said. Then I proceeded to tell her all about Wiley. I learned long ago to let loved ones around you know what you're doing, and to check up on your entourage, too. Some guys try and pick up on us, and make the rounds from room to room and from group member to group member. You just have to make sure that everyone is OK. Just as there really is such a thing as jet lag, there are crazed groupies out there, too.

After hanging up from Betty's call, the phone rang again. It was

Wiley, and he was in the lobby. I asked him to come up, and he walked into my life. From that point on he showed up mysteriously everywhere I went. This on-again, off-again affair went on for nine months.

In June 1966 our new single "What Am I Going to Do Without Your Love?" hit Number 71 on the pop chart. Our next single, "I'm Ready for Love," sailed up to the Top Ten, scoring at Number 9 on the pop chart and Number 2 on the R&B. In the U.K., it went to Number 29. It was a song that Holland–Dozier–Holland had recorded with us earlier. In November of 1966 our *Watchout!* album was released and became our biggest-selling non-*Greatest Hits* album.

Another song that Holland–Dozier–Holland produced for us (which sat in the can for two years) was released and became our third million-seller. It was one of those songs about a specific guy, and we made that man's name a virtual legend: "Jimmy Mack." The record went to Number 10 on the pop chart, and on the R&B it went all the way to Number 1! (This song is where the rap term "mack daddy" came from.)

The "B" side of that single, another Holland–Dozier–Holland gem called "Third Finger, Left Hand," became one of our cult records. Unavailable on album until the CD era, the song became a favorite in Britain.

I always loved playing the clubs in Los Angeles like the Trip, and the Whiskey A–Go–Go. Whenever we played there, lots of Hollywood stars would come out to see us, and it was a guaranteed good time.

The Trip was aptly named, because it was just that magical! It was a trip to be on Sunset Boulevard. This was the first of many night-clubs we played in La-La-land. Long since gone, all that is left of the Trip now is our memories. That club was like a combination of Dis-neyland, Basin Street, Morocco, and Las Vegas all rolled into one. It was now early 1967 and we were host to wild, enthusiastic, sell-out crowds, even prompting Johnson Publications' *Jet* magazine to do a cover story on us entitled "Soul Children."

One night between shows on one of our busiest weekends, there was a heavy knock on the dressing room door. Our dressing room was downstairs with only one way in and one way out. Well, when that door opened, we got a big shock. In walked this big, tall, tanned handsome mountain of a man, accompanied by a fat, slightly bald friend.

The tall hunk was fussing with the lock of hair that had fallen in his eye, similar to the scene in a movie I had seen him in. He had to bend down slightly to enter the room where Betty, Rosalind, and I were gathered entertaining a few friends between shows. We all recognized this beautiful white man at once and squealed with excitement, "It's Robert Mitchum!"

He inspected the scene, looked at us, and said, "Where are the party girls?"

I was tripping, thinking that someone had purposely misled him to our door. We were hip, but we weren't exactly "party girls."

Gilbert Roland had become a special friend of ours, and on occasion had invited us to his home, where he served us at special gatherings of movie stars. My first thought was that maybe Gilbert had sent Robert Mitchum there just to thrill us. Mr. Roland had taken a liking to our music and showed us the glamour of Beverly Hills. But I was on the wrong track. Gilbert hadn't sent him at all.

"Big Daddy, my friend here," Robert Mitchum continued, pointing to his black companion, "told me that there were some party girls down here. Bring on the party girls!"

We were all silent for a moment, and I could see some temperatures begin to rise. Before Betty could say the words I saw forming on her lips, and as Rosalind swelled up developing an attitude, I jumped in saying, "Robert Mitchum! Wow, I never thought that I would ever meet you! I've seen all of your movies, and I just love you. You are my favorite!" As I spoke I grabbed his arm and pulled him down into the empty seat right next to me. I wanted to see him up close since he was so tall, and in that small room we were all suffering from neck strain looking up at him.

I started naming movies that I had seen on late-night television, calling him by the names of characters that had won him fame: the wicked preacher, the rugged soldier, etc. I even made him blush by telling him how sexy the cleft in his chin was, how romantic he was in love scenes, and that I was sincerely in awe of him and his presence.

I felt bad that his partner had steered him wrongly by thinking that we were swinging "party girls." However, I turned the uneasy mood in the room around, and I took advantage of the opportunity to praise him for his fine acting.

He was as cordial as any man could be who had been deceived. He had expected a wild time, and instead he found himself thrust in the midst of adoring, avid fans ranting and raving. After a clumsy apology for not having pictures of himself on hand, he obliged us with autographs and retreated hastily.

While we were booked at the Trip, I met a band called the Kinfolks, managed by Hosea Wilson. I "discovered" them and brought them to Motown. Eventually they became our touring musicians. David T. Walker was to me the finest man I had ever seen, with that guitar that he loved as he played. He was so talented he could hold a box in his hands and make it sing to him. Bass player Tracey Wright was suited just right to make the blend needed for our sound. Although he couldn't really read music and doubted at first that he could play our tunes, he set our charts on fire. Richard Waters was an excellent drummer and he had learned a lot from playing behind Etta James. She had taught him about starts and stops—all part of the art of accompanying a singer. Buzz Cooper has gotten to be one of the most talented people I have ever had the pleasure of working with.

Around that time, for some crazy reason, Wiley and I decided to get married. It was so sudden and impetuous that we were wed at the Chapel in Las Vegas. I wish I could remember the exact date, but I have done my best to erase this whole event from my memory. The look on his face when he said "I do" was so comical that I laughed when he uttered it.

Right afterward I had to leave for Great Britain, then on to Japan. I cried all the way to England. I was miserable. I missed my husband, having never had a honeymoon, and to top it all off, my period began. Maybe the Lord was trying to tell me something.

But once I returned from London, I would be a changed woman: In my absence I found that Wiley had not only moved into my house, he had moved in several of his freeloading relatives as well. This simply would never do. I should have at least made their acquaintance to give my approval before they moved in with me. I didn't know what to do.

The first matter at hand was an engagement at Detroit's riverside nightclub, the Roostertail. Not only were Martha & the Vandellas headlining, we were recording a live album there, too. I found it so hard to sing with Wiley at my first show after returning from abroad. The Roostertail was filled to the brim, and all I wanted to know was how on earth he ended up at that front-row table all by himself. He had the talent for communicating on any level, and obviously he had talked his way into the prime spot where I couldn't miss seeing him.

When you hear my *Martha & the Vandellas "Live"* album and I actually start to cry on the song "Love (Makes Me Do Foolish Things)," then get myself together and go on with the show, you're witnessing an instant emotional turnaround. Wiping away those onstage tears, that's when my healing came.

I didn't know what to do otherwise. Not long after that, and in my absence, Wiley and his relatives were removed from my house. We annulled our mistake of a marriage without any further communication.

What an adjustment to make. I had to forget I was ever married, just as quickly as I had gotten hitched. As though I hadn't had enough slick talkers in my life at that point, here I went and fell for his line. I guess I still hadn't learned the lesson: "Believe half of what you see, and some or none of what you hear." Or is it, "Believe *none* of what you hear, and half of what you see"? Whatever–it seemed that the word "gullible" must have been stamped on my forehead!

With all of this craziness going on in my life, someone had slipped me some LSD in a private discotheque without my knowing it: "windowpane" in my champagne! The next thing I knew, I was in a hospital bed. If I could have just taken a nice long vacation, it would have been heavenly. The recovery part is a blur. "If I could just direct all of this powerful energy within me into the right direction, I'll be all set," I thought to myself.

Rosalind and Betty were real good to be so patient with me until I calmed down and put both of my feet on solid ground again. I would lie awake at night devising plans and schemes. They found my behavior to be erratic, and they had done their best to understand how I could suddenly decide to get married, then just as suddenly decide to get a divorce. It was quite an adjustment for me as well.

I was relieved that the biggest price I payed for that mistaken marriage was to my lawyer for the annulment–plus the cost of the tranquilizers to calm me back down. They should have put a warning label on the box with me in mind: "*Caution!* Do not take if you intend to drive, sing, make sense, or attempt to get over the convulsion of pain caused by heartbreak."

After that episode, my relationship with Betty began to deteriorate very rapidly. For whatever reason, Betty clearly began to resent me. She would be sarcastic and sharp with me between shows. Onstage gestures that were once choreographed routines with swinging arm movements had now turned into what looked like karate moves. Instead of concentrating on my performance, I was distracted by her insolence.

Our friendship was becoming strained, and the anger that I began to feel toward her nearly spoiled one of my show business high points. We were on a local Philadelphia television show along with the gracious Sammy Davis Jr. I wanted so badly to be at my best when I met Sammy, but Betty chose that show to do everything she could to antagonize me.

The whole mess was further complicated when Betty started an affair with Tracey Wright and I began one with David Walker. Two girl group singers dating two members of the band! I was also aware of the fact that David already had a girlfriend named Cynthia, who lived in Los Angeles. When we would play there, she would show up at the gigs and I would eat my heart out with jealousy. Betty would hang this over my head for effect.

My problems with Betty continued to grow. It had gotten to the point where we barely spoke to each other. There was an icy limousine ride between the Latin Casino in Cherry Hill, New Jersey, into Philadelphia to appear on "The Mike Douglas Show." Wenny Brown, who was Florence Ballard's cousin, started an affair with David. I was so stunned by this news that I forgot the words to the song "Les Bicyclettes (de Versailles)" on national television. Wenny had been our hairdresser for a couple of years by now, and she and Betty had bonded together to mutually antagonize me. I'd had it with her, too. The two of them would share private jokes at my expense. It was during that limo ride that I decided to get rid of both Betty and Wenny. That was the last time I wanted her touching my hair!

Since I felt that the next development in our relationship was going to be violence, in June of 1967 I directly confronted Betty. I told her that I couldn't put up with her onstage sabotage and her offstage sarcasm. This had to end, and I informed her that it was time she did something else with her life. It was getting impossible to keep up the artificially happy outer appearances. She was already pregnant with Tracey Wright's baby, so everything was really getting complicated. She was very mad at me at the time, but years later we were to bury the hatchet. She actually thanked me for having fired her when I did. It seems that she had lost partial hearing in her left ear from standing so near the bass amplifier. "I might not have been able to hear my baby cry had I continued," she told me.

Well, here I was again, looking for a new Vandella. I didn't have to look far for this one, because I hired my own sister, Lois. Right after she had graduated from Eastern High School, she had come with me on the road for companionship. She helped me fill in the space between shows and travel. When we were both in Detroit, I shared my house on La Salle with her. Besides, we have always been close friends as well as sisters.

I was having trouble finding a replacement for Betty. Lois had rejected any invitations to sing professionally–until I was faced with a ten-day gig at the Fox Theater in Detroit and only had one Vandella! I begged her to *please* sing with Rosalind. Although she didn't take to my idea well, she finally went along with me. I didn't have to teach Lois our routines. She was already all too familiar with them. Still, Rosalind lent me very little assistance in working Lois into the act.

To my horror, Wenny and Betty both sat in the audience opening night, yelling rude things at my baby sister and trying to stop us from continuing without them. I could ignore my first antagonistic encounter, but it was a vicious and mean way to be treated–being harassed by people you knew personally, who were hiding in the darkness of an overcapacity crowd in your own hometown. I didn't acknowledge any of the venom being spat at us. Besides, I had the mike.

I was relieved when we were called back for an encore. Wenny and Betty rudely chose to make their exit in our spotlight, hoping to pull the people in their general area of the crowd with them. It back-fired when everybody did stand up–to give us a standing ovation!

That standing ovation was the final element that convinced Lois to continue as a Vandella. Applause is what everyone is after, and we had been rewarded. Lois put aside her personal plans so she could sing with me, and ended up being my longest-running Vandella to date. Ever since that night, she has shown love, dedication, and total perfection in her efforts.

This ten-day engagement was promoted by local DJ Robin Seymour. He used to have a TV show on CKLW called "Swingin' Time." Also on the bill were J. J. Barnes ("Baby Please Come Back Home"), Deon Jackson ("Love Makes the World Go Round"), and the Parliaments ("[I Wanna] Testify").

One night during this same engagement at the Fox, I was onstage singing "Dancing in the Street," when someone in the wings started waving their hands to get my attention. When the song was finished, I went over to the side of the stage to see what the commotion was all about. The stage manager grabbed me and told me what was transpiring around us.

With microphone in hand I went to center stage and, as calmly as possible, announced that widespread rioting had broken out and Detroit was on fire. A local dispute with the police had sparked the riots, and out-of-control mobs roamed the streets smashing store windows, looting, and setting fire to whole blocks of the city. I will never forget the kind of responsibility I felt to announce something like that and not start a stampede of people running for their lives!

We weren't about hang around to find out how this was going to end up. We quickly packed up our equipment immediately, and off we went to our next tour date in Newark, New Jersey. When riots broke out there, too, we headed south. It was a confusing and frightening time in America. It was especially startling for me to return to Detroit and see all of the destruction that the riots caused. To this day, there are still burned-out areas that have never been rebuilt or developed.

Throughout all of this drama and trauma, we remained active on the record charts. That fall the *Martha & the Vandellas "Live"* album was released, complete with my real tears on it. Although it says on the back of the cover that the album was recorded at the Twenty Grand, in actuality only part of it was. The rest of it was from the Roostertail.

In August of 1967, our next single, "Love Bug Leave My Heart Alone," was released. There had been a competing Detroit record company called Golden World Records. Motown bought them out, and with the acquisition came several talented songwriters, including Richard Morris and Sylvia Moy. I began working with them during this time.

We followed it up in October with the southern-style hit "Honey Chile." When I first met Sylvia she decided to write a song that was tailored for me. She caught wind of the fact that I was born in Alabama, the product of a southern upbringing. She wrote "Honey Chile" and filled it with a lot of southern anecdotes. It went to Number 11 pop and Number 5 R&B.

Beginning with "Honey Chile," my releases now carried the banner of Martha *Reeves &* the Vandellas. It was entirely a Motown decision. That same year, the Miracles became billed as Smokey Robinson *&* the Miracles, and the Supremes became Diana Ross *&* the Supremes. Sadly, in the case of the Supremes, the name change also marked the time when Florence Ballard was expelled from the Supremes. When the Supremes became a vehicle for Diane to launch her solo act, Florence had begun to rebel. She had such a strong and soulful lead singing voice, and it was a shame that few people ever heard it when she was in the group.

I always love seeing my fellow entertainers show up at any of our shows. Being in the business, it is wonderful to have the respect of your peers. However, these aren't always happy events. Back in February of 1968 we were booked at the Apollo Theatre, and who should show up but one of my teenage idols, Frankie Lymon. In 1956, when Frankie Lymon *&* the Teenagers' "Why Do Fools Fall in Love?" came out, we thought that this group's harmonies were the absolute ultimate. A star at the age of thirteen, Frankie became a prime example of how drugs could ruin your life.

He came backstage at the Apollo, all messed up, asking me for $2. He claimed that it was for cabfare to go downtown to pick up a royalty check at BMI. I knew he wasn't going to BMI for his royalties.

"Give me the money, I'll be right back," he begged.

I said, "No, uh-uh—I ain't got two dollars to give you." There was no way I was going to supply him with the money to buy what was to become his last hit. This was my first meeting with my idol, and there he stood—all messed up. The sad thing was that a week later he did find someone to finance his fatal dose. I was very distressed to hear of his death. Here was a brilliant singer who had thrown it all away on drugs.

Other celebrity encounters have shaped my habits. As a rule, you won't hear me singing very many cover versions of songs made popular by other artists. This is due to valuable lessons learned in close encounters of the strange kind. I was caught in San Francisco at a nightclub singing "You Don't Know How Glad I Am," a song beautifully recorded by my dear friend Nancy Wilson.

In the middle of the song, there was an audible commotion coming from the back of the club that rippled all the way through the room, traveling up front to where we were busy doing our thing. From out of the dimly lit room appeared the lovely Nancy herself.

My rhythm section had been making a poor attempt at playing this song, which I had just added to my list. Upon seeing her, I relinquished my microphone to Nancy and she took the song to the heights that only she could. I stood there dumbfounded as my band kicked in and played like the professionals I had hired them to be in the first place. After that, I was barely able to continue my act, angered by my "cats" for playing so well behind her and so lousy behind me.

Then, on another occasion at the Apollo, we were proudly doing a tribute to our own Aretha Franklin, Detroit's "Queen of Soul." It was an arrangement of Maurice King's featured on our *Live* album. "Respect" and "Do Right Woman" were combined in a way where we did bits and pieces of each song, and then on with our hits. Suddenly a parade proceeded up the aisle and backstage during our song, and it was perfectly timed.

We finished our show and returned to our second-floor dressing room. Shortly afterward, "the Queen" was led into the room. I saw her backup singers Margaret Branch, Carolyn Franklin, Brenda Franklin, and about seven or eight more members of her entourage gathered like a gang, ready for violence.

Aretha finally spoke, saying curtly: "I heard you have been singing my songs, Miss Martha."

I was waiting to hear her say more, maybe "Thanks for the tribute," or "Nice arrangement," but she was finished and remained solemn.

"Well, you won't hear that anymore," I replied. She appeared satisfied with this decision. I guess it bothered her to hear another singer doing her hits. I know the feeling.

She turned and walked out, with everyone following her except Carolyn, whom I was always in constant contact with and always greeted with open arms. She nervously tried to explain that her sister was truly upset that we were singing her songs.

I had only been following directions, doing material prepared for us in Motown's artist development department. Although the brilliantly designed arrangement was a definite showstopper and a fine work of art, we dropped it from our show and it wasn't missed. Besides, I still had several of my own new songs to sing.

CHAPTER 8

I Can't Dance to That Music You're Playin'

THINKING YOU WERE FOR REAL

The way that I met you
*   Is faint in my mind*
Yet I'm happy with all of my heart
With lips that tingle
*   From unforgettable kisses*
I sing your praises although we're apart

You put your shoes under my bed
*   Good thoughts inside my head*
Then let me know that it wouldn't last
Well, the piper wants his due
*   There will be some brand-new shoes*
And new thoughts of you in my past.

You should have played with baby dolls
*   While you were fresh and young*
To pull the legs off, pull out the hair
*   Grabbed a hammer and attacked that toy*
Screamed, yelled, and had your fun

You could have let out your frustrations
*   On something that could not think or feel*
I could have been spared some of this torture
*   Just for thinking you were for real.*

$\mathcal{The}$ golden era of Motown that I was part of was changing and evolving around me. With the Detroit riots, the Vietnam War, and the sexual revolution under way, the world was a different place, and the music that defined it had changed as well.

Motown was making all sorts of changes. They were growing and expanding, and signing new artists and producers. Gladys Knight & the Pips and Tammi Terrell began recording for the label in 1967, and the production team of Nickolas Ashford and Valerie Simpson started working at Hitsville U.S.A. There was also a girl named Rita Wright who was signed to the label. She recorded a couple of singles for Motown and was later to find fame as Stevie Wonder's first wife, with a singing career under the name Syreeta.

Our hit "Honey Chile" was our last big Top Ten single. Although we'd have four more years of chart hits and lots of Top Forty action, my relationship with Motown started unraveling in 1968. In April the company released another of our usual two-sided hits, "I Promise to Wait My Love" backed with the topical song "Forget Me Not." "Forget Me Not" was about a soldier sailing off to war, so it was particularly meaningful at the height of the Vietnam involvement. The song was written by Sylvia Moy for her brother, Melvin, who was going into the navy, and she dedicated it to him. This song hit home for me as well, because my own brother Melvin perished as a result of this war. Oddly enough, "Forget Me Not" was a mild hit in America, but it ended up hitting Number 11 in Great Britain.

Our *Ridin' High* album was released in June and was my sister Lois's first album cover. This LP had an interesting mix of songs on it, and was one of our most popular albums. On the cover of it I am wearing a top hat and a scarf, as though I were on horseback amid a fox hunt. For the most part it was produced by Motown newcomer Richard Morris. "I Promise to Wait My Love" was by Hank Crosby and Billie Jean Brown. That same year, I covered Lulu's "To Sir with Love" and Dionne Warwick's "I Say a Little Prayer." In addition to "Honey Chile" and "Forget Me Not," we also had chart hits with "Love Bug Leave My Heart Alone," "I Promise to Wait My Love," and "(We've Got) Honey Love."

Also in 1967 we had two hits with songs that didn't appear on any of our albums until the CD era. These songs were "Sweet Darlin'," which Richard Morris had produced, and a song by Deke Richards and Debbie Dean called "I Can't Dance to That Music You're Playin'." The latter song was going to be Deke's first Motown production, and I was pleased to be honored with his debut on the label–until I heard the song that he intended for me to record.

I have always believed that no singer should record songs that he or she doesn't believe in. I try to be careful what material I sing, because whatever you sing or chant about, you become a part of. The minute that I read the lyrics of the song "I Can't Dance to That Music You're Playin'," I knew there were going to be problems, but I figured that some alterations could be made.

We started recording, and the song was shaping up very nicely. There was even a great point amid the recording where I hold a note and the saxophone hits the exact same note, as if my voice had blended into the sax. It was a very clever effect.

In the song, the singer is lamenting about her affair with a musician. Already I was up in arms by the inference to my own personal life, being that I was madly in love with David, my guitar player. In the song, the musician spends the night out supposedly playing a gig, although he left his saxophone home, and the woman singing lets him get away with his infidelity. I wanted nothing to do with a song in which the woman plays victim, and I especially didn't want anyone to think that I'm that kind of a woman. The further I got into the recording, the more the song bothered me. The theme of dating a musician, and one line about "changing" one's "prescription," went about two steps too close to home for me. Finally I came to a line in the song that I refused to sing.

At first I dealt with it rationally, saying, "Deke, I have a problem with these lyrics in the second verse," and I asked that they be altered.

The writers that I had worked with in the past always listened to me, and we had come up with some winners. I had input in every song I had ever recorded, tailoring it and making it mine. Brian Holland, Eddie Holland, Lamont Dozier, Sylvia Moy, Richard Morris, and Mickey Stevenson—all of the writer/producers—considered my input. I expected the same courtesy from Deke.

"No way!" Deke instantly proclaimed. I couldn't believe that he would say that to me. In my years of recording at Motown, it was never a dictatorship like the one I faced now with the producer of that song.

I had to leave the song unfinished, because he was set on keeping it just as it was and I refused to finish the session. In my absence they called Syreeta Wright into the studio and had her add her voice to the song. However, instead of sounding like me, she sounded just like Diane Ross! This really pissed me off. And then they had the nerve to release it. The song ended up charting at Number 42 pop and Number 24 R&B. I couldn't believe that they had done this to me. With a minor lyric change or two, I could have finished the recording session and the song should have been a million-seller for me.

This incident was one of the first that didn't sit well with Berry Gordy. After that, I had the reputation of being difficult to work with. My relationship with the company was rocky from that point forward.

I wasn't the only person who was having difficulties at Motown. The Temptations, who were amid a winning streak of Top Ten hits like "Beauty Is Only Skin Deep" and "I Wish It Would Rain," were having internal problems. David Ruffin's lifestyle varied from the routine the group had established. He wanted his own dressing room and a separate limousine.

As the lead singer of many of the group's biggest hits, David felt that he should have a larger share of the glory. After a big group meeting, David was informed in a document signed by his four singing partners (including a reluctant Eddie Kendricks) that he was no longer in the Temptations. In addition, they had gone and found a replacement for him in Dennis Edwards. David wasn't about to go along with this plan. A couple of times David showed up at Temptations concerts and jumped onstage in midperformance. Bodyguards had to drag him off. He would not accept the idea that he could be thrown out of the group like that.

I felt very bad when he showed up at a venue in Valley Forge, Pennsylvania, where Martha Reeves & the Vandellas were performing with the Temptations. David tried to get backstage. The management blocked off the area with wooden police sawhorses and yellow barrier tape, and the security guards had orders not to let him backstage. I watched as they told him that he didn't belong there. They had Dennis Edwards in the wings, ready to take his place.

I heard Eddie say to the rest of the Temptations, "Hey man, I'm going through this for this little bit of money? I won't be with you guys very much longer. I don't like what's going down."

Although the music scene continued to grow and stretch in different ways in the psychedelic era, we kept busy in the public eye. On September 15, 1968, we appeared on an NBC–TV show called "Soul," which costarred Lou Rawls, Redd Foxx, Slappy White, Nipsey Russell, Flip Wilson, and Richard Pryor. That fall our song "Sweet Darlin'" peaked at Number 80 pop and Number 45 R&B.

That same year, Marvin Gaye and Tammi Terrell racked up their third and fourth Top Ten singles, "Ain't Nothing Like the Real Thing" and "You're All I Need to Get By." Ever since the two had paired up, with Ashford and Simpson producing, it seemed that everything they touched turned into a hit. Their version of "Ain't No Mountain High Enough" was an instant classic. Tragically, in October, while performing onstage with Marvin, Tammi collapsed right in his arms. She was later diagnosed with a brain tumor.

Whenever somebody would ask me to say something nice about Tammi Terrell, I couldn't–except that she was a pretty girl who could sing. She could sing, and she played the piano as well. Tammi was a very talented girl, but everything she did was crazy, wild, and not right–at least, as long as she was around me. But I knew that she was young and far advanced for her years.

She and David Ruffin had had a stormy affair. On one occasion at the Apollo, we were on the bill with the Temptations. She came out onstage and told the audience that she was engaged to David and had a ring on her finger. David was so furious that he threatened to beat her up, for he was already married.

"He *did* beat her up," my friend Ron from the Apollo confirmed in a recent conversation. He also explained that "Tammi was a troubled person. I knew Tammi before she became 'Terrell.' I met her when she was still Tammi Montgomery. When I was out on the road with James Brown, she was out on the road with him, too. Neither one of us should have been out there, because we were both too young. She was James Brown's woman. That lie that they put out about David Ruffin hitting her in the head with that hammer, causing that brain injury to her head—trust me, that happened way before David Ruffin's time. I know for a fact."

Her illness saddened all of us and she wound up having ten separate brain operations to rectify the problem. After that, she tried valiantly to carry on. Once we were playing at the Latin Casino in Cherry Hill, New Jersey, and she came to see us. She was just barely able to hold her head up after all of the surgery. She had shown signs of recovery, determined to continue, but once she would attempt to record, her condition worsened. On Tammi and Marvin's third album together, *Easy* (1969), producers Nick Ashford and Valerie Simpson substituted Valerie's voice on some of the songs, never letting on that Tammi didn't succeed herself while singing in her deteriorated state of health.

As if I wasn't under enough pressure, Berry Gordy would on occasion attend my shows, sweeping into the venue with Diane Ross on his arm. They'd enter late and sit right down in front. Everyone in the audience would be aware of their presence. After the show, Gordy would come backstage and run down a list of criticisms about the show in general and my performance in particular. I, of course, had to suspect that several of those digs were initiated by his "date," with whom he had whispered back and forth during my show.

I was now working constantly, touring across the globe and playing to excited and enthusiastic crowds. Several of these individual gigs were memorable, especially when we played in cities where our performing peers lived. Playing at the Regal Theatre in Chicago was always a thrill because of the wonderful people who supported us and came to see us, including famous local residents like Curtis Mayfield & the Impressions. When they backed Jerry Butler, would they ever sound *good!* It was great just to be able to stand in the wings, sometimes to slip into the audience and watch the other acts. I loved Fontella Bass ("Rescue Me"), Barbara Acklin ("Love Makes a Woman"), Betty Everett ("The Shoop Shoop Song [It's in His Kiss]"), Shirley Ellis ("The Name Game")–I mean some *singing* women! In the Windy City we'd get to see and visit with the Dells, the Chi-Lites, Gene Chandler, Little Milton, Alvin Cash & the Crawlers, the Staple Singers, and the local disc jockeys like Purvis Spann, Al Perkins, and Jack the Rapper, who were on hand to promote and announce the shows.

We would play fifty straight days with one day off for travel between each major theater date, and we would rest on trains and boats and planes. We'd draw audiences of 500 to 4,000 people, who unlike today would mix and dance, and we'd all sing together. Today's style of audience is similar to watching television. People use their best discipline trying to sit real still and breathless as if at a symphony. Our music was meant to make you dance. On one occasion Smokey Robinson stopped his show when a security guard attacked a spectator who was happy with the music.

Smokey halted the music and, from the stage, said to the guard, "Let him alone, man. He's just having fun. Our music doesn't make violence–these are songs about love." For the remainder of the show, and those to follow, our crowds were allowed–even encouraged–to dance.

At the end of the day, after all this excitement, you'd finally stop for a minute, and your body said, "Hold it. Now I'll react to what you have inflicted on me." But when there's a gig scheduled and you've got to go somewhere in two or three days, and you can't go like this, you must. There's a signed contract. You seek professional help, and the doctor looks in your ears, nose, and throat. All you can tell him is that you just don't feel good. He sees it: You're all sung out, your ears have been blasted out by loud music, and your eyes are red from standing in the bright spotlights. Then he tries to work a miracle, he gives you "downers." Then to counteract the effects of the "downers," he gives you "uppers." It's just that easy to join the Valley of the Dolls club. Back then I had a charter membership.

At the height of all of this nonsense, my band up and quit on me, giving me two weeks' notice. According to a phone call from their manager, Hosea Wilson, they had an offer to record for Capitol

Records. With that, David, Buzz, Tracey, and Wayne (Richard's replacement) were gone. Very quickly I had to bid them all farewell. And so ended my affair with David, my guitar player.

Just as I replaced Betty with my sister Lois, I hired my brother Victor as my new drummer. I had originally purchased him a set of drums as a bribery gift for not dropping out of high school. He had become disillusioned and decided to quit. But before he had pulled the plug on his education, I said to him, "This is a mistake that is going to affect the rest of your life. I'll do anything in my power to convince you to graduate from high school. Isn't there anything I can buy you in exchange for a diploma?"

He looked at me and said three little words: "A drum set." I knew we had a deal. Learning to play them, he nearly drove the entire household crazy. My poor parents' nerves became rattled when he would practice for hours, at the most ungodly times of the day and night. I finally had to move him into my house to keep peace in the family. Self-taught in my basement, he quickly proved that he was very good at playing "the skins." He occasionally traveled with me, and when one of the opening acts was stuck for a drummer one night, I volunteered Victor.

Now I was suddenly stuck for a new drummer, and didn't know where I'd find one on such short notice. Then I suddenly recalled the pounding, bashing, and crashing of drums that had been emanating from the basement of my own house on LaSalle. Mulling the prospect over, I thought to myself, "Vic certainly knows my music backward and forward. Why not give him a try."

As he tells the story, "Sis, you took me from your basement to the Copacabana." That is literally how it happened.

We had an upcoming "return engagement" at New York's world-famous Copa. We had the pleasure of headlining at that ultimate nightclub a total of four times. In spite of all of the excitement and some talk of a mob clientele, the Copacabana was always colorful and one of the high points of my career.

I soon discovered that several of those wild stories about the Copa were indeed true. The place was run under Jules Podell's command. We saw well-trained maître d's and waiters in white, red, blue, and black tuxedos, with the colors indicating their level of authority and degree in the martial arts.

While booked there, I was thrilled to discover that Victor's drum playing was real close to what Benny Benjamin, Uriel Jones, and Richard "Pistol" Allen had recorded on our older hits. Victor dressed downstairs with the musicians–my rhythm section as well as the big house band. My musical director, Chris Greco, didn't like my brother's attitude, so after the gig he took all of my show tune arrangements–some that I am still trying to replace.

Victor gained insight as to how Jules Podell ran his nightclub, and still tells wild stories about the encounters he was subjected to. The dressing room for me and the Vandellas was upstairs, and we couldn't hear or see anything until we came into the show room. Therefore, I only marvel at what he tells me about just what went on. Thank God we were one of the favorites of Mr. Podell, who even thought to remember my birthday and for years sent me telegrams wherever I was. We were treated royally.

I had always dreamed of bringing my parents to New York City for one of our shows, and now that Lois was one of my Vandellas and Victor was playing drums, I could finally convince them to come and see what their children were doing.

I had arranged Ruby and E.J.'s flights so they could come to our last night at the Copa and fly back the next day. They had never flown before, so we met them at the airport. Dad kept complaining in the limousine ride from the airport to the hotel. "I wish I'd have driven my car from Detroit," he claimed. Mom then amused us by relating how Dad had argued with the gate attendant when they wouldn't let him carry his suitcase onto the plane with him. Daddy kept asking them where it was going. They had to convince him that it was safe in the baggage area, but only after he had given them some choice words. Daddy swore that after this round–trip he would never fly again, and that was a promise he kept.

We had registered at the Americana Hotel six days prior to their arrival, and because it was filled to capacity, we found a nice room across the street at the City Squire Hotel. My parents complained that the ninth floor was too high for them, but they survived. I gave them two hours to relax, and then Victor, Lois, and I went back to check in on them before our rehearsal at three o'clock. I should have explained to them about the chain on the door and the privacy sign, because when we returned, Mom had cursed the maid out for coming in with the passkey just as they had fallen asleep.

At the time I was so busy with my career that I was having trouble sleeping, so I began to take sleeping pills. The pills left me so zonked that in the morning (or afternoon) I took an "up" to counteract the "down" from the night before. And so the vicious circle of prescription pill-popping began innocently. I thought nothing of the traveling pharmacy full of doctor-prescribed "dolls" I had in my possession when I ushered my parents into my hotel.

I asked Mom and Dad to join me in my room, to see the difference in the hotel decor and to have a bite to eat. Dad wasn't impressed with the room. Suddenly he got all bent out of shape when he noticed the amount of pill bottles lined up on my windowsill. He sat down on the foot of my bed and put his face in his hands and began to cry silently.

I felt his pain instantly, and asked, "What's wrong Daddy. What is it?" He looked up at me through reddened eyes with tears running down his face. "You're taking all of those pills?!"

He had told us time and time again that God made us right when we were born, and we didn't need anything for the rest of our lives. Only if we were ill should we take medicine. But in show business I had learned to rely on pills. I tried to explain to him that the doctor had prescribed these tranquilizers and uppers only for when I needed them. I also explained my seven years of sleepless nights, and he consoled me, for I had started to cry by now.

He said, "When you work hard during the day and have your mind on straight, sleep will come. Sleep is earned." He should know because he had worked all of our lives. Mom didn't say anything until we had dried our tears. She also could attest to hard work being the right prescription for sleep, for I know twelve children had been a handful for her.

Yet I was so deeply entrenched in the Valley of the Dolls syndrome that I wasn't even aware of it. I guess the real purpose for my parents and I to be there in that time and space was to get me straightened out.

Daddy was a great role model by working diligently. I never meant to hurt anyone and thought this was the thing to do to keep up with the pace of my career, so I vowed to slowly wean myself off these legal drugs. I am not and have never been nervous. In fact, I have been told on many occasions that I have too much nerve. But such comments usually came only from onlookers who never got the chance to know me, who never spent any time with me. God uses us singers in a mighty way, and I'm grateful.

We had a limo at our disposal, but I needed to walk that experience off and so coaxed Mom to walk with me to do a little sightseeing, shopping, and looking for some help with my hair.

With Mom on my arm, I soon felt better. In fact, I felt like a million, for a large family makes you accept sharing your parents. Mom was so innocent and childlike. This was a special experience, because she rarely traveled, and while growing up, I never had her to myself. We held hands as we looked in windows, watched the sidewalk vendors, and the three–card monte players, had some roasted chestnuts, and went in and out of the shops that were on the way to Rockefeller Center.

Radio City Music Hall was exciting, but not as much as the skaters in the middle of the square who poured onto the rink as soon as the ice–roller had made his turns. It made patterns that were soon covered by the tracks of the scantily dressed twirlers. On the walk back to the hotel, we saw real serious bums lying about begging, not ambitious enough or too weak to stand. We stopped one more time at a men's store to purchase a fancy ruffled shirt to go with Dad's tuxedo that night, and we both hoped that he would wear it. We had the spirit of schoolgirls taking our brief walk around Manhattan.

I got dressed for the night early, and the three of us went to help our parents dress, only to get there and find them ready except for the cummerbund. Dad needed Victor's help fastening it. I noticed Dad's recent illness, caused by his ulcers, had made him thinner. He wasn't saying very much, and he must have been in a lot of pain. I noticed his lack of energy and that he walked much slower than before. I didn't dwell on it, though, thinking, "This too shall pass."

I put a little makeup on Mom, though she never needed very much. She has natural beauty that I have always admired. Mom has a dislike for limos, saying, "They remind me too much of funerals," but we got her to ride in it again anyway. Tonight Daddy looked very handsome in his dress clothes, and together they made a handsome couple. I was so excited to introduce them to Jules Podell and other staff members that I had gotten to know at this famed Copacabana in New York City. And I was so proud.

I was also blessed to get them a front table. The club was so crowded, the table was placed on the dance area, just in front of the band. I could see for myself how proud of their children they were, and of the entire show's presentation. Shecky Greene was the comedian who opened for this particular engagement in 1968. Shecky had made Mom laugh so, she was wiping tears from her eyes. Momma also laughed heartily when she heard our version of Bobbie Gentry's "Ode to Billie Joe," especially when Lois said "I don't want none" when I sang the line asking for the black–eyed peas to be passed around.

Daddy was angry after the show, having been presented with the check at the very end of it. It was a minor error on the part of the waiter. Although I made arrangements to have the check put on my tab, it gave Dad a glimpse of what the total cost was for an evening at the Copa. He complained for the rest of the trip about how he thought that it should be against the law for anyone to charge that much for food–and for drinks that had been watered down. I laughed as I helped them with their new cashmere coats bought just for this occasion, and led them to the waiting limo back to the hotel.

It was the spring of 1969 when we again headlined the Copa. *"Joe Mauro, Don Staiton, the World-Famous Copa Girls, and MARTHA REEVES & THE VANDELLAS,"* read the advertisement for the engagement. We made a good combination, and business boomed for Jules Podell. We had been assisted by Douglas Coudy, the stage director, and Al Foster's band was brilliantly conducted by Mr. Maurice King there at 10 East Sixtieth Street. We did two shows nightly: at 8:00 P.M. and 12:00 midnight, with three shows Fridays and Saturdays at 8:00 P.M., 11:00 P.M., and 2:00 A.M.

Only the really great performers were entitled to wear the Copa's symbol of success, and we did not take it lightly when the Nightclub Academy Award, the Laurel Wreath of Stardom, was presented to us. Just to be listed with greats like Jimmy Durante, Dean Martin, my idol Lena Horne, Joe E. Lewis, Johnny Mathis, Frank Sinatra, Danny Thomas, Tony Bennett, Peggy Lee, Sammy Davis Jr., Joey Bishop, Nat "King" Cole, Steve Lawrence and Eydie Gormé, Bobby Darin, Jerry

Lewis, Jimmy Roselli, Jerry Vale, and Connie Francis, among many others, made us feel that we had reached the big time. We were delighted to have finally arrived. Just to be placed in the same category of all those established stars was a true honor.

One Friday night, Lois, Rosalind, and I were backstage in our dressing room at the Copa between one of three shows. We were sitting around a seventeen-inch television killing time between sets when there was a knock at the door. "Come in," I said, glancing upward. Much to my surprise and delight, there stood Judy Garland! You could have knocked me over with a feather. Wide-eyed and excited, we sprang to our feet and invited her to come in and sit down. We couldn't have been more thrilled if the Yellow-Brick Road itself had unfolded before us.

That meeting with the real-life "Dorothy" brightened up my world in untold ways. I was doubly thrilled. Not only was I impressed to have this childhood idol of mine standing right in front of me, but I was also touched by the very idea that a figure of show business royalty would seek me out for a friendly visit.

This was just months before her "home going." Judy was so kind and gracious as she spoke words of encouragement and told us how she had truly enjoyed our show. She was tiny, with the face of a baby doll. Her eyes were full of wisdom, and although the ravages of alcohol and pills were now evident, she seemed as if she would be fine if she could go on a vacation somewhere far away from the pace of New York City and the discotheque where she invited us to join her after the show. The disco was Arthur's, which was managed by her fifth husband, Mickey Deans.

As she spoke with us, she would close her eyes slightly and answer some of our questions with a smile and a slightly bowed head. It was as if we amused her with our naïveté, but we were in seventh heaven. One of our First Ladies of Song had taken the time to tell us that she liked what we were doing and to keep up the good work. She stayed with us the full hour of our break, answering more questions and giving us sound advice while we kept everyone else at bay. How fragile and delicate she looked, and how we treasured the brief time that we spent with her.

That year there was suddenly a renewed interest in Martha & the Vandellas in England. "Dancing in the Street" was reissued, and thanks to a huge push from the radio show "Pick of the Pops," it hit Number 4. "Nowhere to Run" went to Number 42 there. In America we released the song "Taking My Love (and Leaving Me)," which was a Number 44 R&B hit, but only hit Number 102 on the pop chart. Where was the promotional support we used to have from Motown?

A horrible chain of events began in 1969. I watched a bubble–the product of my vivid imagination, I guess–burst right before my very eyes.

In 1969 things started to change. International Talent Management Incorporated (I.T.M.I.) was dissolved, taking away the personal management wing of Motown. All these years I hadn't questioned any of their decisions. In other words, for all of these years, Motown not only took care of all our finances, it also held all of the books and all of the control. When this happened, it prompted me to wonder about the security of my personal assets. Here I was performing at big–name establishments, having racked up several million dollars for the company selling our recordings. I began to question where all of this money was that I supposedly had–and its exact worth. I went to Berry Gordy Jr. and told him that I wanted an accounting of what finances we had acquired. For the first couple of years of my singing career, I had felt like one of the heroines in the movie melodramas I so loved to watch.

Now, after seven years of traveling the globe as a singing star, I began to wonder where the big money was that I was obviously earning. I had turned all of my financial affairs over to Motown. After carefully examining the contracts that Motown had me sign, although I was an international star, I was shocked to find that I was far from rich. I had signed contracts with Motown in 1962, 1964, and an addendum in 1968. The first royalty promised was a third of four percent, with The Vandellas and I sharing equally, and then in 1968 the addendum earned us six percent to split three ways. I had agreed to do all the lead singing, interviews, ad–libbing, improvising, planning, scheming, and debating for our group for eight (later twelve) years with no change or increase in my portion, though I was only given a third of the money earned.

It's true, most performers spend half of their earnings taking care of family members, which the public expects you to do when you sell a million records. You can't very well live in a castle while your kin is on the poor side of town and barely have food. Some want you to get to the top and rely on you making it for them, too.

I was reputed to be the first Motown artist to ask where the money was for the records I sold and earned on tours and live performances. Up until this moment I had believed all of the movies I saw in the fifties about heroes and lovers always finding a happy ending at the end of the melodramas they were lost in.

It was horrifying to learn that I sold my emotions on those songs of heartbreak that made me famous—and sold them cheap. In the end, I realized that I was truly a victim of the songs I had sung.

I confronted Berry Gordy Jr. He took his own personal time to tell me that I couldn't tell him how to run his company. I guess everyone else would back off and be quiet when he got angry, but I wouldn't back down. I think of all of those years I actually believed that I was becoming rich off of my highly visible career, like all of us signed to Motown Records, but in reality I had succeeded in making the company wealthy. I must have been a stepchild in this family company.

As if that blow wasn't enough, other things got worse. At this point, Rosalind was the only remaining original Vandella, and she went and got involved with the member of a male group, which opened up a whole can of worms. He insisted on traveling with us on every engagement. Lois, Rosalind, and I were all single, and suddenly we had this intruder with us—in no official capacity.

I nicknamed him "Cheap Ed." He wore pastel colors: His shirt, suit, shoes, hats, ties, and handkerchiefs were all light yellow, baby blue, or tan, and sometimes he would calm his attire down with all maroon, brown, or navy blue. It looked like we had a kept man or a gigolo among us.

Furthermore, "Cheap Ed" gave Rosalind professional advice and input that was totally unauthorized, and she would change her onstage patter in the middle of the act. It would totally throw off my performance and put me on the defensive. Our shows were timed and scripted very tightly, and they were specially designed for us by Maurice King and Johnny Allen. Now I never knew from one show to the next what was going to come out of Rosalind's mouth. Worse yet, she began to sing different harmony notes than the ones we rehearsed. I could sense that our final showdown was about to come.

While all of this was transpiring, another unfortunate event took place: I met a man named Walt on the road, and he introduced him-self as a manager of James Brown's. He seemed to be on the level, and I considered him to be an interesting business associate.

While in Atlanta I ran into him again, but I was fooled by outer appearances and manners. I believed him to be a friend and a gentle-man. He falsely put me at ease by announcing that we were both from the Big "D"–Detroit–so I felt safe.

Walt spoke to me about a business deal that would bring me the kind of money I had never seen before. Now that I knew the reality of my "riches" at Motown, this appealed to me greatly. When he asked if we could continue our discussion in my hotel room, I thought nothing of it. Besides, I was an adult, not an all-trusting child.

However, the minute the doors were closed, he tried to get inti-mate with me. I didn't feel romantic, and I could never pretend. This angered him in a very unreasonable fashion. He got this demonic look in his eyes and started hitting me. He turned into a raging maniac, knocking me up against walls, over and under beds.

As though chanting, I kept saying over and over in my mind as I always did, "This too shall pass . . . this too shall pass." He soon left after tiring of hitting someone who would not hit back or react to the pain. I had taken the punches that should have been thrown in a boxing ring, but I think it was the only way under the circumstances.

For the next night's show, I hid my blackened eye with makeup and brushed out curls of hair to cover my bruises. It only hurt when I hit the high notes! I was even able to take the teasing from the band, with whispers and snide insinuations, for they had heard the com-motion and not come to my rescue. The walls were thin at that motel, and if Lois had heard me, together we could have dealt with Walt.

The next nightmare came one night after the second show, at a nightclub in Chicago. I was worn out, sleepy, and about to fall asleep on the counter of the dressing table, which was the most comfortable seat in that changing room. As I sat there with my head resting on my arms, I was asked by "Cheap Ed" if I wanted something to keep me awake. I trusted him, although he and Rosalind had become unfriendly of late. He had recently deserted his own singing group, and had latched onto mine.

Our 3:00 A.M. show was scheduled to start in fifteen minutes, and

I had just weaned myself away from the prescription "downers." He said to me, "You won't feel a thing, and tomorrow you'll be just fine."

I knew that our pay depended on this middle-of-the-night show, and it was nearly showtime. He convinced me that this was a harmless diet pill and totally cool. I put the small, orange-colored pill in my mouth and swallowed it without water. Well, I became energetic, all right. All I wanted to do was stay awake, and instead that little pill became the last straw in my system. The simple word "no" would have saved me a fortune in lost time and wages. Instead it threw off my nervous system so badly that it took a ten-day hospital stay complete with convulsions, sleepless nights, and embarrassment to get over that one tragic mistake.

Again I found myself flat on my back in the hospital, coming down from another unplanned "trip." Lying there I thought to myself, "Why is this happening to me? All I want to do was to perform, deliver good shows, spread some cheer, and keep up the pace." What I got instead was another living nightmare I couldn't seem to wake up from.

CHAPTER 9

In and Out of
My Life

"MISTY" MARTHA REEVES

You've got to fight
To have some peace
Fight the urge to casually
Eat or drink
When what you need
Is to sit and think

You've got to fight
The urge to doubt and swear
Learn to sit still and watch
It will be all right
With no crosses to bear

You've got to fight
While you're waiting
Until time brings a change
And try to be patient
Between loses and gain

You have to fight
Contradictions
And friendly advice
Try hanging out with people
Who know how to treat you right

Hold firm to
Your own convictions
Work hard and do it right
Think yourself past the dark clouds
Keep your outlook bright.

I had to put my life together. The first step was bidding Rosalind farewell. Lois got on well with her, but I was tired of battling with her onstage. I found it an unpleasant task asking Rosalind to find something else to do with her life, but I felt I had to go through with it.

Here I was Vandella–shopping again. Who should I run into but another member of the Velvelettes who was between groups! Sandra ("Sandy") Tilley not only sang with the Velvelettes for a spell as a replacement, but she had just finished a stint with the Orlons ("South Street"). She was filling in for one of the regular members, and now that the girl had returned, she was looking for work.

Sandy always made me smile the way she used her eyes when she talked. Although she had some throat affliction caused by a growth underneath her chin, I overlooked her slightly hoarse voice because of her natural beauty and grace. Both of her parents had been dancers and were tragically killed in a car crash when she was an infant, leaving her to be raised by her grandmother. Sandy had only been a Velvelette for a short time, and I felt an immediate connection with her. We seemed compatible, so I asked her to be in the group.

The rehearsals were a breeze. Sandy caught on very quickly, and I consider her and Lois to be the best coordinated pair of girls ever to be Vandellas. They moved with a beautiful fluidity on stage, and she became a welcome addition to the act.

Our 1969 album *Sugar n' Spice* was compiled from various cuts of Martha & the Vandellas. There are recordings of ours from the Holland–Dozier–Holland days ("I Can't Get Along Without You" and "I Hope You Have Better Luck Than I Do"), and my first work with Ashford and Simpson ("It Ain't Like That" and "I'm a Winner"). Although I was photographed on the cover with Lois and Sandy, the album's one single release, "Taking My Love (and Leaving Me)," was recorded with Betty and Rosalind.

The first recording that Sandy did as a Vandella was the Beatles' song "Something," which was on our 1970 *Natural Resources* album. That album contained some very good material. There was even a solo jazz number that I did on it. I had the pleasure of having Earl Van Dyke accompanying me on the piano on Jimmy Webb's song "Didn't We." It was my own personal arrangement of the song, one of my best attempts at singing ballads. In addition to the Beatles' song, we also dipped into the songbooks of several other contemporary non–Motown singers and writers: Jackie DeShannon ("Put a Little Love in Your Heart"), Harry Nilsson ("Everybody's Talking"), and the Rascals ("People Got to Be Free"). I even snuck in an old Aretha Franklin song, Clyde Otis's "Take a Look," a really great tune about world harmony and self–worth. I was glad to be able to put my own interpretation of "Take a Look" on this album.

The most controversial cut on the album was our single "I Should Be Proud," backed by the Andantes. It was a song with a strong anti–Vietnam War message, a narrative story song about a soldier coming home in a pine box while the girl singing the song questions the sense of it all. This was the era of war protest songs, and I was the first Motown artist to have a song like this (Edwin Starr's "War" came months later). Unfortunately, the single was killed right after its release because several radio stations were afraid to play it.

Although this album contained a lot more serious contemporary material on it than our previous ones did, *Natural Resources* received very little promotional attention. It seemed that Motown was too busy concentrating on this new group of children from Indiana that the company had just signed to a recording contract: the Jackson Five.

Unhappy with the nonsupport that I was receiving for Martha Reeves & the Vandellas, I recorded two solo songs during this time period, "I Won't Be the Fool I've Been Again" and "Baby (Don't You Leave Me)." They remained unreleased for twenty–two years.

During this time, I had begun to date a smooth and handsome man named Gerald. This turned into a disaster as well. As dysfunctional as our affair was, I still considered it to be my first really meaningful relationship. He was an athlete, a successful businessman, and a charmer in his own league. He was also involved with another woman for the duration of our affair.

Gerald and I had a big fight after I returned from a six-week tour and found him missing. I tried relentlessly to contact him, but I guess his woman wouldn't let him "service me," which was about the only way to describe our relationship, if it could be called that.

When I made up my mind to quit him, I went out with Sandy for a night on the town and had a fling with someone that I didn't know he knew. When this other man let word get back to Gerald, he showed up finally—and enraged. He had my brother Victor let him into my house. Victor had moved in as well, and initially he thought it was all right for Gerald to join us, even after I had asked—ordered—him explicitly that morning: "Don't let him in!"

Victor thought it was funny, a real joke, seeing Gerald so upset. I was in bed, tired from getting in about 6:30 A.M. Around noon, he entered my unlockable bedroom door unannounced. I had done my dirty deed in retaliation for being neglected. I had anticipated seeing him so much, and as far as I was concerned, I was justified in my actions. I wasn't married to anyone, either.

Gerald disturbed my privacy boldly: "Get up, put on something, and come into the living room. I've got something for you," he said quietly and so calmly that I felt I had to deal with him whether I wanted to or not. He had me at a disadvantage, for I was undressed and off-guard, never expecting to see him again. I proceeded to get to my feet, reaching for my robe that lay next to the bed on the dressing table bench. Before I could stand upright, he hit me with a right, knocking my head into the baseboard of the closet door. When I cried out in pain, he pulled a gun from the pocket of his leather jacket and growled to me: "Shut up, or I'll pistol whip you!" Just then, my brother and sister burst into the room to find me with nothing on but the blood that was now gushing from a cut on my forehead.

Lois yelled, "Leave my sister alone, or I'll call the police!" Gerald put his gun hurriedly in his pocket and left without a word as Lois draped my gown about me and tried to stop the bleeding. She then tried to determine if it was necessary to go to the hospital. I feared a scandal and decided not to go public with this incident, I felt so ashamed and cheapened.

This humiliation should have been enough of him. I should have been convinced that I could forget about him and go on with my life. I had always told myself that I could understand plain English, and I wasn't going to be beaten anymore. My childhood was over, and fighting belonged in a ring. But I was so in love with him, and he was so much help to me. He knew the game and taught me profound things. I loved him so much until it was all over and I tried to go crazy. I learned to rest in his love, and depended on him to keep me happy instead of relying on my own self-esteem.

I was so love sick, and so regretful of a lot of wrong things that I had done, that I took a handful of quaaludes. I just wanted the world to stop and let me off! When I asked him to spend some time and talk with me, help me straighten out my whirling thoughts, he told me, "Slim is having a surprise party, and I want to be there." That should have been a clue. I stood in the doorway, screaming to him, "Don't go, stay with me," acting just like a spoiled child who always got her way.

While everything was crumbling around me, I needed someone around me to offer me some stability. I didn't realize it at the time, but what I needed could not be supplied by another person.

Gerald's stupid manly pride had been damaged. When his male friends laughed at him for not controlling me, "the other woman," he felt justified in slapping me around. Confused, bruised, but still lovesick after about a week of not eating, not sleeping, and having to face the road again, I allowed him to come over and make up. My bruise had nearly healed and could now be hidden under tresses. We made sweet love, trying to forgive and forget. I conceived—and I knew exactly when it happened: We had fought, made up, and made a baby. I had longed for a child of my own. At twenty-eight years of age, I heard my biological clock ticking. When I was going with David, I had considered getting pregnant as a way to entrap and hold him. Since this scheme had failed, I decided that I wanted a child by this handsome man. We were never together again, and the cheap trick of attempted suicide only drove him further away.

Sandy had moved into an apartment building in downtown

Detroit, and when I got pregnant after dating Gerald three years, I felt a drop in finances and moved into the same building upon her recommendation. With Lois also leaving my fold, she too moved into an apartment in this same building. All three of us–Martha *and* both Vandellas–held down the eleventh, fifteenth, and seventeenth floors regally! They should have renamed it "Vandellas Arms"!

I spent the last two months of my pregnancy closing out my house on LaSalle and recovering from the theft of my 1969 Fleetwood Brougham, which had been stolen from the airport. I nearly caught pneumonia standing in the rain in the parking lot at Detroit Metropolitan Airport that day, not realizing that my car was gone.

Gerald left me as soon as I told him "I'm pregnant."

He asked blatantly, "By whom?"

I felt my blood rush to my head as I felt the words escape me: "Not by you. I just thought I would tell you so that you can keep the f--- away from me," and with those words, he did.

What was I to do? I had said enough for the father of my child to leave me with no one to see me through. I wanted a baby, and I made the decision to become a single mother. I gave birth to Eric Jermel Graham on November 10, 1970. When Eric was born, he didn't even have to be slapped. He came out crying, ready and full of life. Hallelujah!

I'll admit that I know exactly who I was singing to when I recorded "My Baby Loves Me" and "In and Out of My Life." The latter song was recorded two weeks after the birth of my son, and I sang it with Gerald in mind. I can honestly say that I carried, birthed, supported, and raised my son with the help of my understanding parents, sisters, brothers, and caring friends. Gerald provided nothing, although his parents, brothers, and sisters were generous and loving to my son.

When a tour of England suddenly came together for me, it was a family decision to give my mother legal guardianship of my baby. This way, I could continue my career and still rest assured that my baby was properly cared for. It happened two weeks after Eric's birth, and the day after the "In and Out of My Life" recording session.

Until Eric was born, I felt like I was nobody. He was the miracle that God gave me and a reason to live a purposeful life. He is the greatest gift to me in this whole wide world. I wanted him all of my life. The way I looked at this whole situation was that God used Eric's father to give me my heart's desire. Sure it was going to be rough being a single working mother, but God blessed and kept us, and Eric is not an unwanted pregnancy, and certainly not a "mistake." Even when he was an infant, I could speak my heart to my child and feel he understood what I said.

It was in 1971 that Motown suddenly moved out of Detroit–and I was the last to know. I called Motown from time to time, and after a few months of no response, I finally got a secretary on the phone. I asked to speak to Berry Gordy because we'd been so close in the first days of the company. As Motown grew, we didn't talk as often as I would have liked, but I needed to talk to him now. Finally a receptionist who took my call said, "Don't you know the company has moved to Los Angeles?!"

No, I didn't know. They didn't even have the courtesy to tell me. It was a big disappointment to me when Motown moved to the West Coast, but I knew why. Motown had grown so large that it was too big for Detroit. The company couldn't service all of us because we'd all grown to such proportions. Berry zeroed in on the one act that was likely to be able to personify his dreams–and that was Diane's solo career. Unfortunately, we lost Florence Ballard in the process. Her try at a solo career stalled after two solo singles. It was disheartening to see how Motown had turned its back on her. Mary Wilson proved herself to be a strong entertainer, continuing with the 1970s Supremes and beyond. Somehow I felt lost in the shuffle.

When I first started at Motown, there was a game plan, a strategy, and goals for my career. Now that I had recorded million-selling records, had headlined prestigious nightclubs like the Copa, and became an international star, Motown treated me like a poor stepchild. Free-floating without a direction or a safety net, I felt lost in the shuffle.

The move to L.A. signaled many changes for Motown. The Temptations still continued with the company as hit makers, but the Marvelettes disbanded. Gladys Knight & the Pips were soon to leave the label, as well as the Four Tops. Berry wanted to be near the movie world because he wanted to make Diane into a film star. Other than Marvin, Stevie, and Smokey, who all wrote and produced their own material, the rest had to fend for ourselves.

It was October of 1971, and I found myself on my way to Los Angeles. There was some discussion about a new musical direction for me. The New York Street Band was something Motown's vice president, Ewart Abner, had planned for me so I could continue my career. I was on my way to California to see what they were all about.

We boarded the plane, Pampers and all, and Eric found it fun to go from flight attendant to flight attendant and be carried front to back down the aisles, because he refused to sit still. Some children cry the whole trip, but my child didn't want to sit strapped in, and was passed around from one stewardess to another.

Willie, the son of a friend of my father's, begged, pleaded, and even cried to go to California. He wanted to travel with me with a one-way ticket, and promised to help as bodyguard and assist with the care of my eleven-month-old son. I finally agreed. Willie had a wife and child, and his family lived the next cross-street over, so I felt that he was a friend.

It was crowded on a 727, and the people sitting in front of us would turn around every so often to play with my sweet baby. Soon the five-hour ride rocked him softly to sleep. The meal came just in time, and the white wine, bitter as it was, relaxed me even more as Eric slept peacefully.

We landed, and the three of us were taken to the Player's Motel. Willie was off and running the moment we arrived. So much for me having a dependable bodyguard and baby-sitter.

The day we arrived, I rested–after a brief introduction to this six-man band who called themselves the New York Street Band. They were an interracial group of the finest of the land. Every player was an accomplished soloist, and although the volume damaged eardrums, they played intriguing music. I'd love to hear the tapes that were made during those rehearsals. I was sure the records would introduce a new sound of jazz that would encourage others to study and give me the training I wanted in the art of straight-from-the-heart song.

The rehearsal studio was rigged with the biggest of sound systems. Heard separately, the melodies and arrangements were the strangest, but when the band played together, they sounded beautiful. We embraced each other's artistry, and I withstood the sheer volume of the music. Bill, the guitarist, was the major creative force, and he seemed like the leader. He had a real pure musical style, but his lyrics were pretty strange. There was one song about nuns and abortions and a gardener discovering bones in the garden. *Strange* songs. What did any of this have to do with my career, or what I should be singing? But the music business was evolving, so I was willing to try anything new.

I thought Eric was old enough now for me to get busy with my career again—a career I was used to. I didn't want to stop singing, creating, traveling, and getting my daily healing. There were now voices in my head that kept asking me, "Why do you keep on singing?" I should have been smart enough to tell these voices, "The next sparrow you hear, ask it why God blessed it with song and commissioned that homeless creature to sing in the rain, sunshine, whatever comes its way."

I began to retreat into my poetry. Although I never recorded my own compositions at Motown (with the exception of the "B" side of my first single), I continually wrote poems and songs about what was on my mind:

WHY?

Why Lord did you give me
This beautiful voice and song
That causes me to feel good all over
And sing all day long?
Why Lord did you find me worthy
Of such a big responsibility
Put a desire in me
To please you from the soul?
You must have known it would heal my wounds
Cure my illness the way music does
I get so much satisfaction when I sing of your love
Why Lord, oh I know Lord
It's because you first loved me.

The redbird sometimes turns me all the way around to hear the variations of its song. But it wasn't long before some of the music I

From the cover of our *Ridin' High* album. I was wearing a top hat with a chiffon scarf, which was blown by a huge fan for effect. *(Joseph Shillair Collection)*

(*Top*) Rosalind, Betty, and Martha at the Twenty Grand in Detroit. David Walker was the conductor, and Thomas "Beans" Bowles is on the baritone sax.
(*Joseph Shillair Collection*)

(*Bottom*) Martha Reeves and the Vandellas, the third version of the group, with Rosalind, Martha, and my sister Lois in 1968. We were decked out in pink gowns with sequins, and beads and bows on the back.
(*Photo by James J. Kriegsmann/Joseph Shillair Collection*)

(*Above*) In our vinyl and boots "Mod" look. (*Martha Reeves Collection*)
(*Below*) Martha, Rosalind, and Lois in our white off-the-shoulder gowns from Saks Fifth Avenue. During this era we debuted at the Copacabana, playing to ecstatic audiences. (*Photo by James J. Kriegsmann/Michael Ochs Archives*)

Backstage between shows: Sandy, attorney F. Lee Bailey, Martha, and Lois. This was taken at the Copacabana in 1968. *(Martha Reeves Collection)*

Lois, Martha, and Sandy sitting in the picnic area at the Hollywood Bowl in Los Angeles. *(Joseph Shillair Collection)*

This is the original art for the Martha & the Vandellas album *Sugar n' Spice*. I love this album cover.
(*Joseph Shillair Collection*)

I've always felt that Sandy, Lois, and I made the most elegant trio of Martha & the Vandellas. I felt good in these gowns by Bernard Johnson: mauve dresses with chiffon and ostrich feathers. (*Photo by James J. Kriegsmann/Joseph Shillair Collection*)

was hearing from these musicians disturbed me. I should have realized that something wasn't right with this situation. The music of the
New York Street Band had satanic lyrics, but those were some fine
musicians who guessed that if they got rid of me, they would get
their own spot on Motown. We rehearsed every day for a week.

Since Willie was nowhere to be found, I couldn't really concentrate on the music and watch the baby, my precious Eric. I was so
afraid of the big Siberian husky with the gray eyes who was at the
studio. I was scared that he was going to eat my baby if Eric toddled
near him.

One evening while there I was invited to a Marvin Gaye recording session. Marvin had just catapulted his career successfully into
the 1970s with his socially conscious *What's Going On* album. He was
now at work on his follow-up album, *Let's Get It On.* I asked someone
to hold my son while I sang "I aye, aye, aye" in harmony with Ed
Townsend, coproducer on Marvin's song, "Let's Get It On." It was
good visiting with Marvin, and it reminded me of the old days in
Detroit when I sang for him on his first hits. This reinforced my interest in advancing my career out of the 1960s sound as well.

That evening Willie had finally returned to the Player's Motel–for
food and compensation. He agreed to watch Eric–now asleep–while I
went to get some food for us.

It was Hollywood in the early 1970s and cocaine was now the
prestige drug of the "in" crowd. Sure, I did coke occasionally–it was
very big in the music scene. But I was about to get something more
than I bargained for.

I was coming from a restaurant with take-out meals for Eric,
Willie, and myself. As I walked by the door of the corner ground floor
room of the Player's Motel, Z–Man, the band's bass player, beckoned
and asked me, "Do you want to get high?"

When I thought of getting high, I thought of something pleasur-
able, which is usually how you feel about the coke you're hooked on.
But after these illegitimate druggists doctor it up, you can get your
mind scrambled, and if you're not taken to the doctor soon after it
happens, you stay that way. You forget about breathing, and while
you can hear all that's around you, you've lost all control. That's what
happened to me.

As soon as I snorted this coke, I knew something was wrong. It was my fault, because I shouldn't have trusted the good-looking, kind-faced bass player on the mission of messing me up.

All of a sudden I was wild. I couldn't calm down, my legs wouldn't move, and I couldn't raise my arms. I could see, but I couldn't turn my head if I wanted to. I don't remember it all because I must have had convulsions. I could feel my leg tapping and my body drawing up, but I had to wait until it stopped to see in one direction. I should have been warned! No illegitimate druggist should be able to obtain and administer this drug to anyone—especially me. Perhaps I was not expected to ever recover. Maybe that was the plan all along.

Through the fog that my mind was in, I could see myself being taken to a mental hospital by two business-suited white men who gathered me up and took me away. Amid the haze, I watched helplessly as my eleven-month-old son stood at the top of some stairs, crying for me to come get him.

The next thing I knew, I was in a hospital bed. Even while it was happening, it seemed like it was part of a surreal dream—and that this was all happening to someone else. I stared up at the ceiling, and thought to myself that it was as if I had been tempted and had fallen into a trap.

Thank God it wasn't as deep as a gutter, but it felt like one. While in the hospital, I saw some dark places, shared rooms with dark creatures, had truth serum, shock therapy, and was strapped in stirrups. For ten days I felt like I was in a cage. One morning while everything was quiet, I awoke at about 5:30 A.M. My dosage of medication should have rendered me out of it for hours, yet I was wide awake.

There were beads of dust on the ventilation screen overhead. I have always suffered from hay fever, so all of this dust in the air began to irritate me. As I lay down, my sinuses started running. Once asleep, I awakened choking and gagging. I didn't want to wake up my roommate, so I went to the desk where the attendant was fast asleep. I must have startled her, because she shouted to someone and I was grabbed by a man. He tried to put his hand over my mouth, and I bit him. This must have been his wife who worked the desk, because she wouldn't let me explain that I meant no harm, that I simply needed a throat lozenge or something.

After she called out for him to come, she yelled to me, "You'd better get back in there!" I went back into the room as I was told, after begging for some relief so that I could sleep. He was in the room, and on me before I could turn around. She called to him to put me in a padded cell. I only resisted because all I needed and required was some water, or something for my throat.

I guessed that I was probably coming down from something, and there was no one to help me understand where I was or how I got there. Besides, who would take the word of someone considered unbalanced? That's why I was there. Locked in a padded cell, I learned fear firsthand. I'd seen such cells in movies, and never in my childlike mind had I ever visualized myself actually bouncing from wall to wall, looking for the door that would let me out and put an end to this humorless joke.

This couldn't be real. Here was another time that I told myself, "Momma don't even know where I am." I had overheard talking in the next room after I first got there. They were saying that they were going to take my baby home.

They had spoken to my momma, and she had sent the money that Daddy gave her for my son's return home. Momma had told me not to bring Eric with me, but I missed him so much when we were apart. I thought I could trust this male nanny, but realized too late that I was alone. Meanwhile, Willie's white wife had shown up at the hospital very upset. She screamed at the top of her voice, "Where is she? I want to give her baby to her. She ran away with my husband!" Willie stood there with his tail between his legs and didn't say anything but "we'll take Eric home on the next flight."

I was helpless in my struggle to sort this all out. All I wanted to do was recover. I needed for this to work–to be able to afford a proper home, nurse, and security for my child and me. By my faith I had to do it all by myself, which is how I have been in most troubled times. Well, I had gotten myself into all this trouble without asking God for anything. Instead, I just wanted to get high and change the pain–instead of getting the cure, straightening up and flying right, onward and upward.

I couldn't get out of this tiny room I was trapped in. I didn't see anything but lights reflecting on the tops of the padded wall. I flashed back to playing on the mats in gym class as a little girl. I had never really hated the roughness or the smells of the knotted ropes as we climbed up them and then dropped to the padded, mat–covered floor. The rope burned on the slide down, but you were always happy for the victory. Well, now the rope was gone, and this wasn't fun or teaching me anything. There was no love in here, and there wouldn't be until these illegal drugs wore off.

Suddenly I cried out loud for the first time, then I was finally able to settle down and sleep–in spite of the straitjacket two attendants had put on me. I knew better than to struggle. My energy was already spent after wrestling with both of them. I'm relieved now to think that the blood I saw on me wasn't mine, and I was so glad that they didn't give me the shot she suggested. But God, was this nightmare ever going to be over?

I woke up and surveyed the padded cell around me. I'd been locked in there for two whole days as far as I knew. I had no idea what day it was, and I only watched the clock because it meant more pills. "Perhaps when they come with more medication, they'll let me out of here," I thought to myself. Somehow I longed for visitors. Bed–time was spent on the couch that served two purposes: as a bed at night and the only place to sit during the day. You were told to remain in your room, and on your side.

My roommate was a real pretty girl named Toni who boasted that her mother had had her top eyelashes replaced and that's why they were so long. It seemed that Toni lived alone and apparently couldn't cope with life and love. She had long black hair with bangs cut straight across, and she wore red lipstick all day long. She said she was a model and a temporary secretary. We talked about everything but what put us there. She was diagnosed as a manic–depressive. My condition was termed a nervous breakdown.

I was broken down, all right–by the bass player Z–Man and his "gift." It only took a second to get me put back on the shelf. While at the facility, I lost precious time, making ashtrays, answering ques–tions, and being revived from a living dark place. This was not a serious enough experience to teach me a lasting lesson about recre–ational drugs. I just thought, "It was a bad trip. All drugs don't make you go off." These are things I told myself when I took my next Fan–tastic Voyage. Some lessons in life aren't easily learned.

Elaine Jasmin came to visit me in the hospital. She's the author of a fable about the music business called *Number One with a Bullet*. It is rumored to be about Motown. Though the book had a limited print–

ing, she caused a lot of controversy and bad feelings with it. Perhaps she saw a side of the characters I found difficult to understand, that I never witnessed. She tried to expose some darkness, but the light was brighter than the facts.

She came especially to let me know some suspicions. "I heard what happened to you, and all of this was *not* an accident," she said. "Watch yourself. Hurry up, get well, get out of here. It's only temporary." I kept asking her how she knew I was there. I hadn't spoken to anyone at Motown–no phone calls, I didn't want anyone to know. She remained secretive.

I didn't have many visitors even though I had many friends and acquaintances. Motown called only once to see how I was. I later found that they had been helpful in getting my mother in touch with the people who brought my baby to her. Although I still had a long · way to go to full recovery, after ten days I was ready to check out of the hospital. When it was time to leave, I was the last one informed, so I had to gather my belongings quickly. All I had was what I wore in there, and I washed those items every single night. That afternoon a nurse came in and asked me to sign a form regarding an "operation consent." When I asked her what operation she was talking about, she refused to explain it to me, finally insisting, "If you don't sign this paper, we're not going to let you out. I'll just have to give you a blood test if you don't write you name here." So I signed the paper, and I was told that my brother, Thomas, was waiting to take me home. He had driven up from San Diego.

The pieces of a jigsaw puzzle sometimes have to be turned around and around before they fit. I hadn't learned yet that you can hang out with people who don't like you or have something against you, and that they will mess you up in the game with a smile.

"YOU MESSED ME UP"

Yes, messed up in the game and play
Because the man I love has gotten away
There was never a need or crave
He left me in a crazy rage
With child in arms, empty bed
And drug pushers messing up my head
You messed me up.

Thomas had driven all day. He came to get me and we took our time making sure he had the authority to get me out of there. We went straight to Berry Gordy, and I was left alone with him in his Sunset Boulevard office.

Behind closed doors he told me, "Go away, and get well." He cut the hospital band off my wrist and dismissed me, saying, "Go on, go take care of yourself."

I kept asking him questions about my career, and "Berry, when can I call you again?"

He never answered my question. Instead he told me something about "self-contained groups" like his latest discovery, the Commodores, and a lot of new acts. He then promised to call me real soon—you know, "Don't call us, we'll call you." Little did I know I had officially left Motown Records. Unlike the old days, the company was no longer there for me. I never saw another royalty check from Motown after that day. The man who was once my hero had turned his back on me.

Thomas secured my checkbook, the one that Motown had left with me—for the first time. It was found among my possessions at the Player's Motel. The bank in San Diego informed me that the account was empty. I remained at Thomas's home with his wife, Florence, and children, Earl, Tommy, Keith, Wendy, and baby William, until I could see clearly. I got back to Detroit—somehow. Maybe in time, I'll remember that, too.

Back to reality: I had a son and responsibilities. By now, whatever I was given by Z-Man had totally worn off. I had to make a living, so I decided to quit trying to swim upstream against impossible odds. That was it. I decided to quit show business right then and there. I figured that my singing career had hit the rocks, and I decided that I would look for a job and buy myself a modest car. In the past it had been grand driving my '68 and '69 Electra 225s. The Buick was my car because it had very few problems, and I loved a smooth ride in a long, smart-looking new car. This time I settled for an Opel Cadet, a German-made car that stopped every time I got ready to accelerate on the freeway, or was faced with going up an incline. Even at speeds of fifty-five to sixty miles per hour, it had problems. I found myself downscaling for the new financial reality of the seventies.

In March of 1972, the final Martha Reeves & the Vandellas

album, *Black Magic,* was released. Ironically, it is considered one of the finest albums of our recording career. At least my group was going out in style. To top it all off, we hit the Top 40 with our three last singles that year: "Bless You" (Number 29 R&B, Number 33 pop, Number 33 U.K. pop), "In and Out of My Life" (Number 22 R&B), and "Tear It on Down" (Number 37 R&B).

When I had been given demos for the album, most of the tape cases had Diane Ross's name on them. She evidently didn't like the songs, but I did. However, the song "Tear It on Down" was all mine, written for me by Nickolas Ashford and Valerie Simpson, and it has always been one of my favorites.

At the photo session for the *Black Magic* album cover, the three of us were angry at being made to sit and wait for hours. When the photographer was finally ready, he played a tape recording of crickets chirping to set the mood he wanted in the studio, and we were instructed not to smile. The somber photo of us was lit in blue lights, and our serious expressions speak for themselves.

I tried to get on with my life in Detroit. I felt all alone since Motown had moved to Hollywood to make movies. I didn't want to leave my baby and I turned down too many jobs, leaving Sandy and Lois in a bind. They both had rent, bills, and taxes pending. They eventually had to make a move, and with my blessing we agreed to break up. But first we performed our final concert on December 21, 1972, in downtown Detroit's Cobo Hall.

On that same gig, David Ruffin made a special cameo appearance. It was an upsetting evening, knowing that this marked the end of an era for me. I felt that we were being rejected because of a decline in attention from Motown and a lack of steady work.

Martha & the Vandellas officially said good-bye, and we were all in tears. Sandy moved out of the city and eventually moved to Texas, and in time I lost touch with her. She was reported to have married some rich man. I prayed for her happiness. Lois joined a management team formed by Otis Williams and Melvin Franklin of the Temptations, and they put her with two other girls in a group called Quiet Elegance, who sang locally in Detroit. She also performed with an eight-piece group called Swiss Cottage. They had a real good sound and they put on an entertaining stage show.

I was proud, and stayed in the background of the business—until one day when Eddie Kendricks showed up unexpectedly and cursed me out that one and only time. I was living in my apartment in Detroit, and I was sitting in my front room, a combination of dining area, counter, and kitchenette. Eddie rang the downstairs bell. As I pushed the buzzer to let him in, I was surprised indeed. Eric was asleep at the time, so I opened the door to watch Eddie step from the elevator. He walked toward me with urgency, and started to yell a flurry of questions at me from the very doorway: "What the hell do you think you're doing? Why aren't you working on your career?"

I was astonished, and I tried to get him into the apartment. I quickly closed the door so that the neighbors couldn't hear what he was saying. "You can't quit show business!" he shouted at me. The names he mentioned as having informed him were people I've never taken as being kind or nice, which made his words sting even more.

He called me nearly every name in the book—the most painful one being "quitter." I thought I had long since stopped doing anything that would cause me to be called such things.

I was shocked by his outburst, but I took Eddie seriously and took his rough tactics as an offering of love and concern. He didn't stay long, and after going off on me, he was his mild, sweet self again. By the time he left, he was satisfied that his message had been successfully delivered.

That afternoon he talked me into picking myself up, brushing myself off, and getting on with my singing career—an occupation derived from my God-given talents. Starting the very next day, I began to pray for a continuance of my career. I have to thank God for Eddie every time I think about this period in my life when I almost called it quits. Because of Eddie, my faith in my talent was restored. I vowed that I would find a way to piece my once-glorious career back together. I had to—for me and for my son. I'd find a way. I was determined that nothing was going to stop me this time!

CHAPTER 10

Wild Night

LET ME BE YOUR ONE–STOP LOVER

Here is some happiness
And I'll do my best
To satisfy your every need

If my eyes light up
When I look at you
You can bet I will be true

Let me be your one-stop lover
You don't have to go nowhere else
Let me be your one-stop lover

Here's some friendship
From my heart
Take me over, let it start

Forget your troubles
Just relax
An even chance is all I ask

Let me be your one-stop lover
It's an invitation to my heart
Let me be your one-stop lover

As you fill me up with sunshine
You can get all you need right here
I will soothe you, never fool you
There's no reason to doubt or fear

Let me be your one-stop lover
You can do it all for me
Let me be your one-stop lover.

I didn't realize how strong the entertainment business was in my heart until I thought about leaving it. Once you've been on top, you can't just turn your back and walk away from it. I thought that I could just go off and do something else with my life–especially after having a child. But I found out that I'm too much of a gypsy and that show business is so deep in my blood that it's a part of my life I just had to continue to live.

Everything had changed. After years of being lead singer of a girl group, I was once again a solo act. After a decade with the Vandellas, it felt good to be out on my own, but it was a little frightening as well. In a way it was like starting all over again. I started out slowly getting my stage legs back. I took my time–accepting low visibility, low-paying gigs, trying this band and that band, deciding what direction I was going to take musically. I also checked out several different personal managers. After all of those years of Motown calling all the shots, it was intimidating to have so many decisions on my own shoulders.

Lois began traveling with Al Green after her group Quiet Elegance landed a contract with his label, Hi Records in Memphis. Willie Mitchell, who was Al's producer, also produced Quiet Elegance's album. Lois was there to help Al through his infamous "grits ordeal." One of Al's girlfriends threw a boiling pot of grits onto his back while he showered, the dramatic end of a "heated" argument. It was widely reported in the press.

Lois and Al became close friends, and I was glad that she could help nurse him back on his feet. Quiet Elegance went on to land a job backing Engelbert Humperdinck, playing Atlantic City, Las Vegas, Reno, Palm Springs–all of the places I longed to play. In her travels, Lois met Ron Strasner, manager of former Motown act Rare Earth ("Get Ready").

Lois introduced me to Ron, and when we discussed some projected goals for me, we seemed to be on the same wave length.

Ron Strasner came by at a time when it was dry and I was about to get into my business suit and prepare myself for the inevitable–the dreaded unemployment queue. It wasn't long after my introductory meeting with him that I was up and at it again. Ron's first matter of business was formalizing the paperwork to sever my ties with Motown Records. Once that was taken care of, he set about keeping his promise to get me a record deal with MCA Records. As soon as the contracts were signed, I finally felt like I was back on the right track.

Meanwhile, in my personal life, I met a man and hastily got married again. This time I was even more convinced that this was the real thing. It was so magical that I thought it was a blessing. In a way, we filled in some time in each other's life and kept each other warm. He was always hot, almost feverish, and I'm the type of person who always felt cold and chilled. I have heard that opposites attract, and it seemed true in this relationship.

I was backstage at a theater in Toronto, in an upstairs office. It was one of those offices where everybody comes and goes at will. I was sitting there with a needle and thread, making some necessary last-minute dress repairs. Suddenly the door swung open, and a head popped in and said, "Hi, Martha. I'm Willie Dee, let me help you."

In walked this tall, handsome man, and without missing a beat he took the sewing needle I was using out of my hands and started to sew my up dress. And he did it well. In my mind I said, "Wow, a man who can sew! Now I'm into the man. I'm ready for a new affair! I don't belong to anyone!"

I enjoyed his companionship from that very first moment, and he stayed. He told me that he was a DJ and that his radio show started at 2:00 A.M. He asked me to join him on his program that evening. He told me that he wanted to make his show a tribute to me and my music. We would have listeners call in to ask me questions, and make song requests.

Up until this point on this gig, I had been overwhelmed. I was working with an all-Canadian clientele, and everyone was a stranger to me. There hadn't been enough money proposed to bring other players there on that trip, since it had such a low budget. I suddenly felt that I had someone to talk to. Willie seemed to be knowledgeable about nearly everything, and he was warm and very affectionate. He was kind of all over me, and I needed that at the time.

Several times I drove from Detroit to Toronto just to be with him. We suddenly began making snap decisions, and we got married and together set up housekeeping in California. It turned out that much to my surprise, Willie had some "unfinished business" in Canada that required him to return to that country permanently. My mad affair with Willie Dee lasted only fifteen months: from meeting to marriage to annulment!

Although my marriage was fleeting, my career and personal growth were both booming. Newly settled in my new life in Los Angeles, one of the things that Ron encouraged me to do was to enroll in classes at Lee Strasberg's Theater Institute for acting theory so I could bide my time during studio breaks. I was on a self-improvement kick and I began to stretch myself into several personal development areas. I had my eye on possibly acting, and I utilized the classes to remove some of the southern drawl from my speech. I really enjoyed the Theater Institute–and I was fascinated to find that acting classes don't teach you how to act, but how to be yourself, how to relax, and how to get your emotions settled by using total recall to express feelings of experiences you've lived through and dealt with. I thoroughly enjoyed them.

My first project on MCA Records was one of my best accomplishments, thanks to director Gilbert Moses and composer J. J. Johnson. I was the star vocalist on the soundtrack album for the 1973 film *Willie Dynamite*. In the early seventies after the success of *Superfly* and its Number 1 hit soundtrack album by Curtis Mayfield, suddenly "black pimp films" were all the rage. *Willie Dynamite* was directed by Gilbert Moses III, who also composed the score. It was one of those films where *everyone* wore flashy clothes and platform shoes. Its one touch of class came by featuring Diana Sands (*A Raisin in the Sun*) in the cast. This would be her last film.

On the soundtrack I was accompanied by a group of background singers billed as the Sweet Things, who consisted of noted background singer Clydie King and her friends Jeanie and Fran. I cut three songs: "Willie D," "King Midas," and "Keep on Movin' On." It was fine for testing my wings at recording apart from Motown Records, but I had my sights on much bigger things.

As early as 1969 Richard Perry expressed the idea of recording with me. He had just started producing, and he told me that he loved my voice on "Quicksand," "Dancing in the Street" and "(Love Is Like a) Heat Wave." But at the time, Motown only used staff writers and producers. Ron introduced us after telling me of his desire to record me, and I loved the idea.

By 1973 Richard had launched himself on a remarkable career and had already produced albums for several of the top people in the rock, pop, and jazz worlds, including Ella Fitzgerald (*Ella*), Barbra Streisand (*Stoney End* and *Barbra Joan Streisand*), and Carly Simon (*No Secrets*). I was fascinated by him and loved working with the hottest producer around.

It was a busy time for Richard. Harry Nilsson had an album in the works. Carly Simon was having a baby and was waiting on the completion of her album *Hotcakes* before she went into the hospital. He was working with George Harrison on some things, and he was already producing Ringo Starr's platinum album, *Ringo*. In fact, I did background vocals with Merry Clayton on Ringo's song "Oh My My" from that album.

Richard and I sat for weeks listening to stack after stack of demos that he pulled from boxes he had collected. We started recording, but Richard had to go back to England and my album had to be fit in between his other commitments. I really put my best efforts into it, and we had some of the finest people in the business involved. Billy Preston contributed a song he wrote called "You've Got Me for Company," and played the organ on my version of Carole King's "Dixie Highway." Hoyt Axton and Dennis Coffey played guitar on "Sweet Misery," and on "Power of Love" James Taylor arranged and conducted the horns while Joe Sample played piano. I was also thrilled to have my Motown buddy James Jamerson on bass on my version of Van Morrison's "Wild Night." I even got to record one of my own compositions, "Facsimile." This was one classy production from beginning to end.

I have nothing but glowing things to say about Richard Perry as a producer. I think he's a genius, and I'd jump at the chance to work with him again. I was thrilled to hear him talk about how he revered me. *Rolling Stone* magazine quoted him as saying " 'Nowhere to Run' and 'Dancing in the Street' are two of the greatest records ever made, but I was amazed at how much more she was capable of doing with her voice, how much depth there was, and how far and in different directions she could move and still be very comfortable." With energy and good thoughts like those behind me, how could I do anything but excel in the studio? This album entirely restored my self-confidence.

It was a luxurious process recording this album, because all I had to concentrate on was taking care of myself and my voice. After I recorded my vocals, then the strings and horns were added. Most of the time I had recorded to rhythm tracks, with no horns to inspire me. On this album, it was I who inspired them, because they would play their parts to accentuate what I had recorded, and not the other way around. This was such a nice contrast to the way things had been done at Motown, when most of the tracks were prerecorded and used by one and all.

Another song that I cowrote, "Stand By Me," was used as the "B" side of my first two MCA singles, and I also recorded a great song called "(I've Got to Use My) Imagination." When Gladys Knight & the Pips were recording their first post–Motown album, they chose that song as well. Neither of us knew that the other was recording that song. I guess we both knew a good song when we heard one!

What a joy it was picking my own material to record, especially after ten years of being given specific songs to record at Motown. If you couldn't adapt easily to the tune, the song was passed on to another artist waiting in the wings. Choosing songs with Richard, I liked "(I've Got to Use My) Imagination" immediately. I didn't care who wrote it, I could identify with the lyrics and the way Richard cut it—mystifying and dreamy, set a nice tone. I sang all of the background vocals myself to keep the mood in that groove. I would not be surprised if Gladys had never heard my version before she recorded hers, because we are both expressive and have the knack of creating our own styles and making a song our own. She made hers happy and upbeat, while I made mine more serious and moody.

At Motown we had all been coerced into recording each other's material. How ironic that Gladys and I both leave Motown for more artistic freedom and personal expression, and we record the same song on our first albums. And I've always loved both versions of the song.

The good news was that my MCA debut album *Martha Reeves*, released in the spring of 1974, was an incredible critical smash. The *New York Times* claimed, "Miss Reeves can rock 'n' roll just as well as she can sing soul. . . . Perry has created an album that truly showcases Martha Reeves's unique talent." At long last, after all of the nonsense that I had been through over the last five years, I had a triumphant album of which I was truly proud.

I still love this album, and I feel that it is one of the best of my career. Because of it, and my appearance on Ringo's album, I suddenly found myself highly revered in the rock world. It was like I was suddenly taken seriously in the music business, unlike all those years of feeling like I was a number two priority at Motown. Both *Rolling Stone* and the *New York Times* did extensive articles about me and this new album. Suddenly I became hot on the rock nightclub circuit, including New York City's Bottom Line and L.A.'s the Troubadour. In a very big way, the album did what it was supposed to do: It launched me as a single performer and gave me a fresh direction.

The bad news was that while I recorded it, I had lived for a year and a half on advances from MCA, and Richard went way over budget. Costing $250,000 to produce, when it was released the *Martha Reeves* album was declared the most expensive album *ever* produced!

Although an acknowledged masterpiece, it's debatable whether or not the sales recouped the initial expense. To compensate, they dragged their feet on the promotional budget that it needed to succeed saleswise. Three singles were released from it: "The Power of Love," "Wild Night," and "My Man (You've Changed My Tune)"—each receiving little or no airplay. "The Power of Love" became a minor hit (Number 76 pop), and then MCA was all finished with me.

After that I severed my ties with Ron Strasner as well, because I was left with all of my money tied up at MCA. This was another of my expensive lessons in life: Ron had signed me to MCA Records through a "production deal." This kind of a transaction places someone in-between you and your money. If they decide to give you money, then it's out of the goodness of your choice of trustees if it gets to you at all. If they advance you money, they might place their own rate of interest on it, and if you never pay them off, they end up collecting for you and exercising "power of attorney."

My Richard Perry album at MCA should have been a roaring success. Instead, it left me without a label, and I wanted nothing to do with Ron Strasner after that. Island Records was immediately interested in signing me, but I found out that Ron was to own a cut of the deal, so I declined. Instead I signed with Clive Davis at Arista Records. At the time they were having a lot of good fortune with Melissa Manchester and Barry Manilow, and Clive seemed genuinely interested in steering me into a hit album. I signed with Arista in January of 1975 and began working with four different producers. Unfortunately, the resulting album, *The Rest of My Life*, didn't have much of a central focus. Since all of the producers were working independently, it didn't quite work as a unified album. I was the first to record a beautiful song called "This Time I'll Be Sweeter," which is a masterpiece written by Gwen Guthrie and Pat Grant. I also recorded the O'Jays' song "Now That We Found Love," which has since been a hit for Third World and Heavy D & the Boyz. I had four songs released as singles off of this album: "Love Blind," "Higher and Higher," "The Rest of My Life," and "You've Lost That Lovin' Feelin'." "Love Blind" is a song that I wrote myself, which tells how I felt about my lost time playing married. I debuted my version of Jackie Wilson's "Higher and Higher" on "Saturday Night Live" in December of 1975.

Having broken my ties with Ron Strasner, I enlisted a pair of managers from a Toronto company called Dixon/Propas. They were helpful with my 1975 British solo tour, but our relationship didn't last long. I sensed that this wasn't going to work out, and I referred to my new managers as "the odd couple" when I wrote about them in my diary.

In December of 1975 I was booked at a hot little cabaret nightclub in Greenwich Village called Reno Sweeney's. My brother Vic was on drums, and two Canadian sisters were my background singers. When *Record World* magazine reviewed my act, they called me "a phenomenon!" It was freezing cold in New York City, and my hotel room at the Chesterfield overlooked Central Park, where I could see the skaters in Wollman Rink.

It was a Friday night, the evening before my "Saturday Night Live" performance. After the show that night at Reno Sweeney's, I met a slender young man who introduced himself as Paul Eaves. He was a Martha & the Vandellas fan from Washington, D.C., and he worked as a flight attendant for American Airlines. He seemed like a fun, caring person, and he was nice to talk to. We both agreed that we wanted to continue the evening, so we went back to my hotel so I could change clothes. When I we got back to the hotel, I freshened up. When we got to the disco, we danced into the wee hours.

Saturday morning I woke up on the floor of my hotel room, hung over from the night before. As the room came into focus, I saw Paul sitting patiently on the couch, waiting for me to awaken and face the new day that I wasn't ready for. I don't remember what combination of quaaludes, tranquilizers, and other prescribed medications or street drugs I had taken. I don't even remember getting back to the hotel the previous night. Thank God Paul was with me and had the compassion to sit with me while I desperately tried to get myself together.

This flight attendant was obviously my latest guardian angel sent to me at a time of need. This was another one of those cases where you meet someone and you know instantly that you have just met a lifelong friend. Like the firemen who saved Thomas and me when we were lost as children, like Mary who fed me in Boston when I was a stranded teenager, Paul was sent here to bring some light into the darkness that I was slipping into.

Hadn't I learned my lesson with drugs yet? I had recently witnessed what drugs had done to James Jamerson. For my 1974 performance on "Don Kirshner's Rock Concert," I had hired him to play "Wild Night" and three other songs during the taping. For whatever reason, James drank beer and took tranquilizers before the show. He was so out of it we had to set up a stool on stage to prop him up, because he couldn't stand on his own. I finally had to eliminate one of my songs because he was too drugged to continue. He died several months after that. You'd think that I would have gotten a clue by now.

Paul had to work on a flight that afternoon, but he vowed to come and meet me at NBC-TV during the "Saturday Night Live" taping. I straightened myself out and got ready to go to NBC in Rockefeller Plaza. I had prescription pills to wake up with or go to sleep with, and anything else that well-wishers or so-called friends brought by.

Paul met me as scheduled, and stayed with me until I left town a few days later. He observed my daily routine and saw the dependency on pills that I had again developed. I was now living Return to the Valley of the Dolls. I had let learned chemists with degrees give me tranquilizers—five milligrams of Valium, then ten milligrams, fifteen milligrams, then Librium after the next few visits, followed by quaaludes and finally Thorazine. To function during the day, I would need "ups."

Before we parted, Paul sat me down and had a talk with me about my drug consumption. He wasn't telling me anything that my own common sense didn't know, he was just making me take a good hard look in the mirror to see what I was doing to myself. I felt that this was also a message from the Holy Spirit—and my first real step to normality. I was very aware of the fact that another guardian angel had entered my life at the moment I needed him, and I made up my mind to heed his advice.

In 1976 I made my screen debut in a movie called *Fairy Tales*. With a brief walk-on role, it was a good place to start. My part in the production featured me doing a musical number after emerging from a big black cauldron, the kind that Halloween witches might have bubbling on a fire. I sang a beautiful song entitled "You'll Feel the Magic in Me." I heard a thunderous round of applause at the screening at the Preview House on Sunset Boulevard. But I was embarrassed by the rest of the film, because I didn't know it was X-rated, and I had brought along several friends of mine from church!

Speaking of fairy tales and childhood dreams, ever since I was eight years old, I had dreamed about Egypt, pyramids, and life along the legendary Nile River. Well, in 1976 I finally got to go there and see it all for myself. It was like going back in the history books, as very few things are modernized there. So much of Egypt looked just like it must have been in 2500 B.C.

The journey started with two weeks in England. I had rehearsed with two background singers named Janice and Jaison, and at the last minute Janice took ill. I needed to replace her at a moment's notice. I quickly phoned my friend Jean Trimble in Los Angeles. As I cried on her shoulder, she cheerfully said that she'd go. I was so relieved and thankful that she knew the music, had traveled extensively, had a passport, and was available.

Ultimately, though, my trip abroad was a series of one disaster after the next, but an adventure nonetheless. My latest manager, Tommy, met me at Heathrow Airport simply to tell me that he wouldn't be accompanying me to the Middle East as planned. He then introduced me to Tom, his last-minute replacement, and promptly left. Here I was, set to leave with a ten-piece band of Englishmen and a new road manager thrust upon me. "How on earth did I get talked into this one?" I asked myself as I boarded the plane. It should have been an omen.

What an international cast of characters this was. The promoters consisted of Bob from England, Sheikh Muhammad from Kuwait, Clive from Germany, and now road manager Tom, a bald white man from Atlanta. Tom's weakness was white blond girls–the exact description of two of my entourage. To top it off, I was traveling with these dancers who appeared in my act, and I found out in midtrip that one of them was Jewish and forbidden to travel to several of the countries we were heading toward. I should have gotten off the plane and ended this impossible tour, but I was determined to see the pyramids.

The airplane ride from London to Cairo was extremely long. The tour was then to go to Kuwait, Abu Dhabi, Dubai, Teheran, and Bahrain. We landed in Cairo and were taken directly to the Sheraton. Upon arrival we immediately felt the arid Sahara heat and started shedding our clothes, but we ladies were then warned not to show our faces, armpits, or kneecaps, for this was considered offensive in this Muslim country and we could be treated like sinful women. They still *stoned* people here for punishment!

The Sheraton Hotel seemed to be the newest building in all of Cairo. Everything else there was old and ancient-looking, crudely built, and showing signs of aging. I was fascinated by the minaret towers for prayer that peaked above the buildings. The Mohammed Mountain towered above the city, as there were no buildings taller than six stories. There were open marketplaces, and brahman bulls could be seen running amok in them. The marketplaces were either open stalls with shades that were pulled down upon closing time, or makeshift sales places that were removed after a merchant's day of bartering.

We checked into our individual rooms and found it nearly to American standards, only it lacked completion. The faucets dripped, the ceilings had obvious open spaces where insects made homes, and air came in freely–hot during the day and warm at night. I got to know that room real well, for upon arrival, I used water from the tap in the bathroom to take some vitamins I needed to supplement my diet while eating new and strange dishes. Thanks to the water, I fell deathly ill.

This disgusting desert disease was a whole new experience for me. I was so sick at both ends of the spectrum that I would have to sit on the commode and lean my head over the bathtub at the same time. I have never felt that bad in my entire life. I called the house doctor, and he prescribed some pills for the virus, and warned me to *never* drink tap water in this country ever again. I learned my lesson the tragic way.

Stuck in my room for several days, I observed this very different country from the window, on the radio, and on television. I had brought an AM/FM radio with me that I would fill the time with, for there was only a five-hour television broadcast period per twenty-four hours. But I would always stop what I was doing to acknowledge the five times a day that the world would stop. The radio broadcast would suddenly end, stores would close, restaurants didn't serve, and traffic came to a halt for everyone to kneel down and pray. I always prayed right along, knowing God was worthy to be praised.

Egypt was a whole new world to me. The midday temperature felt like 140–160°F at that time of year. I was obviously in a very rich country, where oil wells towered high with eternal flames burning on top. There were also souks, little shopping stalls with more gold than I have ever dreamed of. The women in their Batman-type shrouds would walk behind the men, and the men–who were clearly first-class citizens here–held hands with other men, talked freely together, and kissed each other openly on many occasions.

After our arrival we had to wait ten days before our first show. There had been a helicopter crash, and a well-known sheikh had died in the accident. Teheran was suddenly taken off the list of places to perform. All of the Arab nations canceled every event to mourn the customary time period. For me it worked out perfectly to allow time for recuperation.

In my virus-induced delirium, I imagined I had been poisoned deliberately, being so distressed with Tommy's quick exit at the airport. I needed a manager in that country to make sure I fared as well as possible and got properly paid–for everyone's sake. This was quite a lot of responsibility for me to have, being the head and lead of it all. It also meant that I would be the one everyone would blame if things went wrong.

I felt like I had been deserted in this foreign land. The hotel room began to feel like a jail cell to me. Jean and Jaison were out discovering Cairo, not even checking to see how I was doing or if I was going to live or die.

It was dark in the room that evening as the door was opened with a passkey. An attendant had been sent to retreive a tray that I'd ordered at lunchtime. The second shift of housekeepers had taken over the duties of serving. This non–English-speaking young man, who looked about twenty years my junior, came in to get the tray and noticed that I had not touched the food. He put the tray outside the room, came back in, and fanned the flies out that had collected and were buzzing overhead. He looked around the room, and I asked him, "What do you want?"

He answered something in Arabic. I didn't understand a word, but somehow I knew he was an angel on a mission. He came very close to where I was. I knew I was looking as sick as I felt, and he placed his hand on my forehead. I was too weak to turn away and felt safe, for he was gentle, quiet-spoken, and very handsome. He went to the telephone about to place a call when he noticed my new medicine bottles there on the stand. He walked directly out of the room and shut the door behind him.

I drifted off because of the medication, only to hear the door open in the half-lit room. There he was again. He pushed a serving cart into the room. On the tray was a big metal bowl filled with some kind of broth and a serving of unleavened bread. The bread was similar to toast only thinner, and as he took the ladle and filled the bowl with broth, he beckoned to me to have some. I was too weak to sit up, so he made a gesture for me to lie still and came with the bowl, still warm, and fed me small spoonfuls of it until I couldn't swallow anymore.

He uttered something else as he wheeled the tray out. After I had taken all of my medicine, he turned my light out as he left. I went to sleep feeling better, with my head full of prayers. I thanked God for this kind spirit He had sent to rescue me. I had no more fear of being poisoned or hurt, and completely forgot all the negative thoughts, only praising and thanking God for this young man. This stranger had shown me kindness and intensive care that was very badly needed and very much appreciated.

He came to check on me the next day at 6:30 P.M. as soon as his shift started. Thankfully, my diarrhea had subsided. I had actually gotten out of bed, washed, changed out of my sick-smelling bed-clothes, and I tidied up my hair that was sticking up from being bedridden.

The other girls seemed to be busy for two whole days. I had assured them on the phone not to be concerned, because Niole, my guardian angel, was taking very good care of me. They chuckled with tongue-in-cheek remarks, but this was a heaven-sent kismet, and I don't think he was attracted to me in that way. The God in him saw someone about to die, and he helped me recover. The second day, we exchanged names with pen and paper. He pronounced mine, and I attempted to reciprocate. He made it a point to come to my room every night about the same time with a tureen of soup and bread, and never let me give him money.

This crisis was the moment that began a long road to regaining my faith in God. In 1976 I was struggling with different spirits, having tried all kinds of mind- and spirit-altering substances. I had reached the bottom, and now had to stand up and get on the right track.

Finally, after my physical recuperation, we played our first Cairo date. This was Jean's first time ever onstage, and thanks to Jaison, who drilled her relentlessly, we pulled it off.

What happened next I can talk about with humor now, but it wasn't funny at the time. While we were in Cairo, a local newspaper reported that Idi Amin had ordered his officers to take a razor blade to any African woman they saw in the street with braided hair. The three of us singers all wore our hair in braids during the day and put our wigs on at night because the heat was unbearable.

One night before the show, Jean had her wig sitting over her eye-brows and had a fit in the dressing room that night, claiming that she didn't want to wear it. I insisted that she put it on in spite of her feelings. The show was great, but she pouted through the whole thing. The musicians shined as if we had been together for years as opposed to a total of three weeks.

Later in the dressing room, which was also a ladies' room open to the public, Miss Jean snatched her wig off in front of about eight local patrons and went into a spiel: "This ain't my hair—*this* is what my hair looks like," and she began pulling at her braids. Then she said, "I don't have to do this! I don't like show business, and I ain't gonna put this thing back on my head," and promptly threw it on the floor, stomping it.

It took all my strength not to laugh at her, for she was comical, even though her irreverent actions could get us all arrested—or worse. I calmly explained to her, "I brought you here, there was a lot of danger around us, we can't afford to anger the people we're working for, so calm down and remember why we're here. We'll all be stoned in the streets if you don't pull it together!" I had no more trouble out of Jean the rest of the tour.

Usually, during the finale, it's natural to ask for audience response, and that's where I goofed. Through my onstage friendliness, I found that I had made friends with a Middle Eastern man in the audience. There he was, sitting in the front row with a blond lady, looking like my Uncle Sylvester with a deep, cherry-red tan. When I extended my hand to get approval, he held it and wouldn't let go. After my hasty departure, he followed the three of us to the dressing room. He was a well-known actor who spoke enough English to make it to my room after the show.

The minute we were behind closed doors, he got fresh and wrestled with me in an attempted rape. I was just regaining my strength, but I wasn't about to be assaulted by this sneaky, arrogant stranger. In my struggle to defend myself, we both tumbled down on the floor.

Amid our downward scuffle, he grabbed me by the hair, and to my horror he pulled one of my braids right out of my scalp! The sight of this patch of hair underneath his knee, and the blood dripping from my head where the braid had once been, startled him enough to turn me loose. I ran to the bathroom, locked myself in, and he let himself out. Boy, did that hurt—but not as much as it would have had my pride and person been violated.

We had the next day off, and I had a chance to relax and lick my wounds. We made plans to go to a camel farm and later to the pyramids. We rode a long way into the desert in an open Jeep, one of three that caravaned on this tour. The camels were beautiful when viewed in such numbers, and the bedouin herders were cordial and volunteered information. They let us have a close-hand view of these disgusting animals that would spit on you if you got too near. The bedouins lived in a tent and ate out of tin cans, amid the sand that blew in the wind at all times. I can remember thoughts of the ocean and the relief of the water that was nowhere near at the moment. We rode on and finally arrived at the tombs that lie at the foot of the pyramids. There were twenty or more men dressed in wrapped cloths and riding on camelback, who raced by as we were shown the tombs, the Sphinx, and the surrounding valley.

When an announcement was made to inform us that we had to leave to prepare for showtime, I reluctantly boarded the open Jeep and complained as our driver prepared to pull onto the highway and head back to the city. I kept loudly insisting that I wanted to go inside the pyramids. A local man who had overheard me approached us. He immediately took a look at Jean, Jaison, and I and addressed us as "Nefertiti, the Queen of Sheba, and Cleopatra." Those became our nicknames for the rest of the trip.

I thought it magical and mystifying how much this man resembled Sammy Davis Jr. He was the first person we saw after turning the Jeep around and stopping just short of the entrance to the pyramids. After he walked directly to us and gave us our new names, we followed him like sheep. My wish to enter the pyramids was granted. I was entirely fascinated by this exploration. The climb up the narrow, dark passages took us into the world of ancient history. It was dangerous and exciting, and rocks fell as we climbed. I shall never forget this experience.

We went from Cairo to Kuwait, where the Women's Society called us to their meeting on our night off, prior to our first show. We met our first and only "sheikhress." Since it's a known fact that the person with the most wealth rules in this country, she must have been extremely rich. We were thoroughly entertained by a band of South African women beating drums held under their arms and strumming them with mallets. When we were introduced to them, one of them was translated as saying to me, "Come home with me, you need to eat. I will fatten you up." I was flattered.

Amid all of our adventures on this fascinating and dangerous tour, tragedy struck. The money from our past week's engagement was stolen. We had a regular payday scheduled, but because of the sudden death of the sheikh and other excuses, we hadn't been paid in three weeks and everybody started disliking me–as though this was all my fault! Sheikh Muhammad had a heart attack, which angered all of the Arabs involved, and here we were–stuck with Tom, who was now panicked because we had four more weeks scheduled and he was stuck there. We agreed to continue and make up the losses with future dates, but things just got worse with each attempt to overcome.

Our shows were good, but it's uncomfortable working with people who haven't been compensated. I had fulfilled my end of the bargain to no avail–and now, no available cash! Stuck in this unfamiliar country, we had no choice but to do our shows and get out of there as soon as possible. We lived each moment in uncertainty, but at least we arrived at the day when we could leave the United Arab Emirates. I said good–bye to our ten-piece band and headed for London. They smiled but were very disgruntled. They all had terrible hangovers, because once they heard we were not going to get paid, they went to the bar of the hotel and charged themselves a good number of drinks.

When we arrived at Heathrow Airport, it was freezing cold, and we had checked our coats in baggage because of the stifling heat we left in the Middle East. To top it all off, when we arrived in London, there was a bomb threat, and we were stuck there. Ah, the glamour of show business!

Jean and I returned to Los Angeles eventually. There have been several other shows that she assisted me with as a Vandella, road manager, and best friend. We have gone through so many adventures together. Not long after our Middle Eastern tour, I was booked for a one–nighter at the Coconut Grove in L.A. Jean introduced me to a pair of junior dress designers, who professed to have such clients as Freda Payne, Deniece Williams, and Patti LaBelle.

They said that they would love to design a new gown for me, and I agreed to let them come up with a new outfit for me for the Coconut Grove. They promised my costumes in time for this show, but didn't deliver them until minutes before curtain time. Unfortunately, I had a mirror that you could only see when you were standing–and even then, you could just see your shoulders and head. Therefore, I couldn't really see what I looked like in it. Looking down at my body in the dress, I felt beautiful. It had metallic designs riddled through and through it, and it was comprised of layers and layers of sheer fabric. Besides, everyone oohed and aahed when they saw me in it.

However beautiful it looked backstage, these dress–designing novices had neglected to calculate what several thousand watts of spotlight were going to do to it. I performed my show, singing wonderfully and feeling so beautiful in this colorful dress that the audience couldn't seem to stop staring at. Well, when I finally got backstage, I heard the shocking news. When I stood in the spotlight, the material of the dress had turned absolutely transparent, and I had stood there with a smile on my face, looking totally naked from the waist up! How embarrassing! I was reminded of the sundress of cousin Veola's that I had worn in elementary school. I live in fear that photographs of this evening will one day surface! I'm prepared to explain that the nude appearance was unintentional.

Another adventure that I went through with Jean came while I was scouting for engagements around Los Angeles. I had met a man named Mojo. He claimed that he owned three clubs called Name of the Game I, II, and III, and I agreed to perform at one of them. I rehearsed the girls and went to rehearse with a band that would never–and could never–play my music correctly in a million years. It was obvious I was in the wrong place, but I went through with my part of the bargain and faced the night and the first show.

It was so bad that I stopped after three songs out of ten, went to my dressing room, and proceeded to pack my gowns and leave. Jean, being one of my backup singers and also the road manager, had parked her car just outside the back door in the alley. This Mojo person became irate. He hadn't met the first half of his financial obligations, and he wasn't about to pay me any money. He then threatened to shoot us both if we left. Upon hearing this, Jean said softly to me, "We're getting out of here! Don't stop walking." We were in her car so quickly it seemed our feet never touched the ground. She had the car started in a second and was burning rubber up the alley driving in zigzags in case he did start shooting. We drove at high speeds until we felt secure and safely out of reach of that madman, then we both broke up into uncontrollable laughter.

It was in 1977 that I turned in my charter membership to the Valley of the Dolls club. I had used pills to shield myself from pain, loneliness, and frustration, and I was feeling hollow inside after weaning myself from their use. It was with Jean Trimble that I began attending prayer meetings with former Motown producer Frank Wilson. He is best known for his 1970s Supremes productions ("Up the Ladder to the Roof"). He had since moved to California, became a minister, and appeared in my path at a very good time in my life. Frank's wife, Bunny, took me on as her personal prayer partner, inviting me to a series of prayer meetings. We attended prayer retreats along with Rita Ross, Jayne Kennedy, Leon Kennedy, Esther Phillips, Stevie Wonder, Smokey Robinson, Claudette Robinson, and Ivory Davis, to name a few. Jean and I were both baptized the first Sunday in July 1977.

I was a changed person after that. It was at a seminar revival at Lake Arrowhead, California, that I became "born again." It was a thrill enough to be cleansed of demons and receive an exorcism that July. I received the Holy Spirit, and I felt my greatest "heat wave." A burning fire shot up in my bones. I couldn't sit down and I couldn't stand still. I couldn't stop praising my God, though I tried to remain calm. I realized that after the wonders and signs that I witnessed firsthand, nothing else in life will ever make me stop, stare, and drop my jaw. There is no longer anything in life that could surprise me, and I now expect to see the unusual and know that the war of the spirits is raging.

As I paced around the auditorium, raising my voice and hands to offer praise and thanks to God, I was comforted in my tears by a girl named Patricia.

"Call the authorities, I've lost my mind," I said as she paced at my side.

She just kept telling me, "Praise Him, our God is worthy of being praised."

As Reverend Hill at Mt. Zion Missionary Baptist Church says, "If someone wants to pray, not only can one feel free to do it, but there are angels sitting near who will help you worship God."

I said to Patricia, "I can't stop thanking Jesus, and I can't sit down, and I can't stop these tears that keep streaming from my eyes. I know I've gone crazy!"

Pat didn't seem alarmed or changed by what I couldn't help but say. "Let it out, you are cleansing your heart, soul, and mind. Let yourself go, feel free to worship God. Hallelujah!" she exclaimed.

To me, "hallelujah" is like the magician's "hocus-pocus." When I repeated "hallelujah" after hearing Patricia say it, my soul shook. Then I was called on to sing. As I took the stage, I was tingling from my head to my toes. I had never felt like this before. I was told by the Holy Spirit to sing "You'll Never Walk Alone." I gave the accompanist the title, and began to sing like never before. I felt quakes of emotion during that experience. God provided me with an additional octave to my singing range, for I kept inverting and singing higher- and higher-pitched tones.

I was released from Satan's grip, and from that day forward everything had changed. I was finally able to put the drugs and nonsense behind me. Even stronger now was my outlook toward my life–both my future and my past. At last I was able to make plans for my life without all of the emotional baggage I had been carrying around with me. I was truly ready to begin my onward and upward journey.

CHAPTER 11

Free Again

COME HOME, MY SWEET

The music's stacked on the record player
I've been cooking all day long
I've fluffed the pillows way up high
I don't like to be alone
The food is waiting
Newspaper waiting
And so am I
Come home, my sweet
    Come home

One week has seemed like a long, long time
When you left I lost my way
I've counted hours by the seconds
My love grows stronger every day
The cat is waiting
Dog is waiting
And so am I
Come home, my sweet
    Come home

Now I'm sure that we were meant to be together
It's clear we're headed for happiness
When you leave me again, I can face it
Because your coming home is what I like the best
My heart is racing
Anticipating
I'm pacing, ready for you
Come home, my sweet
    Come home

$\mathcal{Living}$ on the West Coast presented all sorts of new experiences for me. There were many new friends and several new voices to blend with–including Scherrie and Freda Payne, Cher, Merry Clayton, Dee Dee Warwick (Dionne's sister), Linda Hopkins, Clydie King, and Doris Troy. I found myself associating with some very talented and brilliant women, and it inspired me to hurry up and get myself together as quickly as I could. It was the mid–seventies, and Brenda Russell, Patti LaBelle, Chaka Khan, and Natalie Cole were all working and making some great music. I thought to myself, "Please let me find some of the gold in these hills–Beverly Hills that is!"

I was also surprised to run into as many former Motown alumni as I did. Right after my "rebirth," former Motown producer Hank Crosby showed up at Bible study at Frank Wilson's house right after the opening prayer. I didn't see him at any of the other gatherings, only this one time. He had been the producer of my hits "I Promise to Wait My Love" and "I Should Be Proud." It was really great to see him.

He informed me that he was now working for the Berkeley–based label Fantasy Records. He gave me his phone number, and I promised to get in touch. I was between record deals, and it was as though Hank just showed up at the right minute. The next day I called just as he requested, and I instantly had a new record deal.

I had been writing new songs with my current music director, Mickey Durio. We penned several tracks together. We would first record our efforts in his bedroom with a four-track tape recorder, and later–as we made money–we recorded in his studio. It was a pleasure to collaborate with him. Mickey and I had met through a mutual friend, and we immediately hit it off as creative partners.

Among the songs that Mickey and I wrote, four of them appear on my debut Fantasy album: "I Feel a Magic," "Dedicated to Be Your Woman," "Special to Me," and "You're Like Sunshine." The song "Love Don't Come No Stronger," backed with "You're Like Sunshine," became my first single on Fantasy. There was also a twelve-inch disco remix single version of both of those songs because disco was the big rage in the 1970s.

I also recorded my version of the Barbra Streisand hit "Free Again." My recording of it opened the album, and I sang it like a heartfelt anthem, for it was I who felt free again since my rebirth.

I was working on my *We Meet Again* album when I got a call informing me that NBC was producing a television special starring operatic soprano Beverly Sills, and she personally wanted me to appear on her show along with Lily Tomlin. This was wonderful, except for one major dilemma: I didn't have anything appropriate to wear! I had a dress that I liked, but it was the wrong color for television. It really needed to be dyed. Very quickly I ran out to the store and got several boxes of Rit dye. Dyeing my dress in my bathtub, I spent the evening transforming this dingy white polyester dress into a beautifully rich and vibrant shade of yellow. It looked just fine on camera. Quick thinking had given me the age-old answer: "Make do with what you have, and be thankful."

The next day at the television studio, I found that it was a thrill just being in Miss Sills's presence. She was so regular and down-to-earth. We held several warm friendly conversations between takes, and she inspired me. On the show I had the opportunity to sing a song with her that was written by her close friend, Michel Legrand. Beverly and I sang a duet version of Legrand's romantic composition, "What Are You Doing the Rest of Your Life." She had heard my attempt of this song on my first Fantasy album, and she showed me another side of the song with her treatment of it. Thanks to Beverly Sills, I learned a thing or two about pacing and grace, and I'll always cherish the time I spent with her.

When *We Meet Again* was released, I received some great reviews and a lot of press coverage, but it didn't sell all that well. The success

I did have was on the disco charts with the twelve-inch single. There was little or no airplay. I was getting used to this by now; this was my third solo album.

With the exception of "What Are You Doing the Rest of Your Life" and "Special to Me," my recorded product on the Fantasy label had been altered after I had added my vocals. It was speeded up, motorized with disco-sounding effects, and passed off as disco. I wasn't very happy about this, but disco was what was selling, so reluctantly I was thrown into the middle of the disco scene.

My life and career seemed totally threatened in 1977, 1978, and 1979, when the whole disco craze really hit. It was like my life was on hold, because a lot of the clubs removed the stages, expanded the dance floors, and started playing records that thumped and jumped. No one seemed to mind who was singing or what they were saying, as long as the beat kept playing nonstop. I went to dozens of darkened places with enough flashing lights to drive the average person mad. I felt lost in the pulse of sheer panic.

Stranded on Disco Island, I penned this song:

"DISCO-ITIS"

My body's shaking with the heartbeat
    Rhythm's got me rocking in my shoes
My eyes are rolling back in my head
    While I dance off these boogie-woogie blues

I've got disco-itis
    Music is thumping and bumping
Feel like they might expedite us
    The way we're shaking and bumping

My partner is a junior acrobat
    Who can kick high over my head
Ooo, this is the part where your hips gyrate
    And you pretend we're both in bed

I've got a case of groove-atism
    That I must stop with the next disc played
But the floor keeps on vibrating
    To go home is what I crave

Disco music in the 1970s was just a call to go wild and party and dance with no thought of conscience or regard for tomorrow. While I was glad to see the coming of a new art form and some of the glorious artists who came with it, the Motown Sound was what I longed for.

The ironic thing was that even Motown was getting into the disco act as well. Smokey Robinson, the Temptations, and the Supremes were recording disco. Cher jumped into the swing of it with "Take Me Home," Rod Stewart recorded "Do Ya Think I'm Sexy?" and Barbra Streisand and Donna Summer teamed up for "Enough Is Enough."

Well, what was I going to do? In 1980 I released my disco album, *Gotta Keep Moving.* Disco rollerskating was suddenly the hot new thing, and this album kicked off with "Skating in the Streets," a disco version of my Vandellas hit. It wasn't the height of my artistic career, but it did make several Top Ten disco playlists at the time. On the album's cover I was depicted in tight spandex with a glittering tube top.

One of the highlights of the *Gotta Keep Moving* was that I had Lamont Dozier produce two of the cuts: "Really Like Your Rap" and "Gotta Keep Moving." He wrote both of those songs, and it was great working with him again. The song "Really Like Your Rap" was a cute hip–hop kind of song and became the second single released off this album. I was slightly ahead of the trend as rap music was making its entrance.

As though that weren't enough disco material from me, Motown released a series of albums by their classic artists, taking five or six of their greatest hits and edited them into a disco medley. The remixed tracks became a "mega–mix" twelve–inch disco release. With that came the Motown album *Martha Reeves & the Vandellas: Superstar Series Vol. 11.* It included an eight–minute medley of "Nowhere to Run," "Dancing in the Street," "(Love Is Like a) Heat Wave," "I'm Ready for Love," and "Jimmy Mack."

One night in 1980 I was in Hollywood at the Troubadour on Santa Monica Boulevard to see the Average White Band. I was introduced in the audience, as were several of my singing star peers. The next thing I knew I found myself up on stage singing "I Heard It Through the Grapevine" with Cher and Elton John. We sounded so good together that we just sang on and on until we were just singing to the drummer's beat. I had a ball that night.

In 1981 I received some sad news: Sandy Tilley had died of a brain aneurysm. Sandy had opened her own boutique and was doing fine. She had undergone a serious operation to stop the bleeding from the aneurysm caused by a tumor she was born with. The doctors were at a loss, and she had not made it off the operating table. Sandy had a lot of good friends when she died, but there were only a few people at her funeral services. Her mother and father had died and she had no children. She was survived by her husband and a grandmother. Lois and I went to the funeral, and Duke Fakir of the Four Tops sent his wife to represent him, as he was out of town. Sandy Tilley was one of my favorite Vandellas, and she is dearly missed.

Los Angeles meant a lot of things to me, but never seemed like home. It was more like a place to regroup. I was all the better for some of the experiences, especially my rebirth. I was working sporadically, taking local one-nighters in places like the Backlot at Studio One, Tabasco, and Greg's Blue Dot. I also went to San Diego to play the Catamaran, and I headlined the El Mocambo in San Francisco for a great two-week run.

While living in Los Angeles, I met several men in show business whom I enjoyed talking with. It was exciting to get to know Little Richard, Richard Pryor, Clifton Davis, Mel Carter, Jim Brown, Gary U.S. Bonds, James Darren, Robert Mitchum, Gilbert Roland, H. B. Barnum, Lou Rawls, Benjamin Wright, Louis Price, Solomon Burke, the Nicholas Brothers, Lester Wilson, and Michael Peters. They've all said kind things to me and have given me the inspiration I needed to keep a smile on my face and hope in my heart. For a while I was dating a very nice man named Lonnie, but a permanent relationship wasn't in the cards. Lonnie made a big difference in my life, then he married someone else. We are and will always remain good friends, no matter who he is with.

I struggled with L.A. for nearly a dozen years and saw the demise of Janis Joplin and John Belushi, and the murder of Sal Mineo. The greatest thing to happen to me there was when I was rescued from a life of recklessless. I was lost, found, and suddenly in 1982 I was given a new direction in life.

I was out in the patio of my Los Angeles garden apartment one afternoon working on my plants, hands in dirt up to my elbow, when

I heard this profound voice, louder than anything, calling my name and saying: "Martha, go home."

I said, "What?" and my voice seemed far away and someplace else.

My friend Paul Eaves was sitting on the couch, having just stopped by to spend some time with me, and he asked, "What did you say?"

I quickly said, "Did you hear that, Paul? Did you hear that great profound voice call my name?"

He said politely, "Well, OK, if you say you heard a voice, I'll take your word for it." He could see that I was serious.

"I heard this voice as loud as the defense drill blows its siren. You didn't hear it?" I asked.

He didn't quite know what to say, but said something to the effect that he was happy for me because I was suddenly so overjoyed, and he wasn't going to question it.

When I heard this voice, it seemed that my ears were plugged up. Now my hearing was gradually returning back to normal. Just then the bell rang from downstairs, and it was Perry Fuller, my masseur friend.

I had recently been on a tour of England, and Mr. Fuller apartment-sat for me while I was away. When he was staying there, he would use my apartment to give professional massages. He decided to share his profits with me, and he had stopped by to pay me the percentage he felt was fair to give me for use of my apartment as a place of business.

Seeing how overjoyed I was, he asked quite sincerely, "How are you, Martha?"

"I feel wonderful," I said, explaining, "I just had this voice tell me that I had to go back to Detroit as soon as possible. I really miss my son and my parents, and something tells me I have to get there immediately."

Mr. Fuller handed me the exact amount of money that a plane ticket to Detroit would cost, and I flew there the very next day. When I got there, to my astonishment I found that both of my parents were ill. Instead of visiting them at our home, I would be going from hospital room to hospital room. Mom was released and returned home the next day.

During my visit, they both got better and were soon out of the hospital. While there in the middle of all of this love, I did a lot of soul-searching. I decided that I had been away from Detroit for too long, and I made up my mind to find a way to move back. I asked all of my loved ones for forgiveness as part of my rebirth.

My biggest problem at the time was the fact that I was about to lose the apartment that I was currently living at in West Knoll, California. If I was indeed going to pack my bags and return to the Motor City, I first had to figure out how I was going to pay for this move, being strapped for cash at the time.

Rick James had recently stopped by to tell me that the girl group he produced and managed, the Mary Jane Girls, were getting ready to record my song, "Come and Get These Memories," and he wondered if I would teach them the harmony parts. I knew that I would have some money coming in from that project. This never happened.

By the time I left Detroit after visiting for several weeks, I had resolved to move back as soon as I could. For the time being I had to find a temporary place to stay. My friend John Malveaux found me a little guest house behind his aunt's larger home in Long Beach. I didn't care for the neighborhood, so I simply had bars put on all of the windows. Unfortunately, the bars could easily be pried off with a crowbar, and I was robbed. I lost so many of my precious valuables in that robbery, as well as most of the souvenirs of my career: fur coats, appliances, jewelry, everything nice that I had been given or had earned. My belongings were either missing or strewn all over the tiny house.

To make matters worse, John's aunt was afraid to call the police for fear that it would just draw attention to her house and invite another robbery. Well, three nights in a row the burglars returned to collect everything they had left behind. I summoned the police when I discovered the ransacked mess. The police were polite and told me to come to the station and make out a written report. They would also ask around in the neighborhood to find out if anyone saw or heard anything.

Of all of the items stolen from me, I was the most sick over the fur coats. My leopard, blue fox, two-piece mink wraparound suit, and a long-length beaver that I had loved so much were gone. Divas have always worked hard and been rewarded with fur coats–from Lena

Horne to Lana Turner. I catch cold easily, and in the winter, dashing out of warm clubs into the freezing winter temperatures before my pores can close, I risk becoming very sick. Thousands of times in situations like that, I think that furs have saved my life. I'm sure the cavemen who hadn't obtained adequate fur for the winter stayed in the cave till spring! I'm sympathetic to the cries of animal rights advocates, but I find that most of them hypocritically wear leather shoes or eat pork and beef–so take that! As far as I'm concerned: Divas *need* their furs!

The robbery was the last straw. I started packing, and as I picked up what was left of my belongings, I knew that I could never stay in this space again. I called my cousins Irene and Eunice, to see if I could give them a few items, store some, and leave my car parked somewhere for an undetermined amount of time until I made it home on the Greyhound bus and could come back for everything later. My cousins were a big help, and Eunice was there to see me off at that Greyhound bus station. When I got off the bus in Detroit, I looked at a dirt-covered dog on the side of the road and I thought to myself: "The Greyhound *is* a dog!" The taxi driver who picked me up at the Detroit bus terminal complained that my trunks were heavy, but he helped me anyway. I finally arrived to Townsend Street and to my baby and waiting family. Fortunately, it wasn't cold enough for a fur in Detroit, and I wore a black cloth coat that became my only one for the first part of the winter.

I stayed with Mom and Dad for about a week, and my brother William helped me get into an apartment house. I borrowed bits and pieces of furniture and dishes so that I could move in by the weekend. Although Eric didn't like it, I didn't plan to stay in this one-bedroom apartment for long. It had a kitchen so small that you couldn't open the stove and refrigerator door at the same time. I lasted a year in that apartment trying to save up and get a better place.

Everything seemed to be good for me in Detroit until one night when I was attacked. My apartment at 1740 West Grand Boulevard was down the street from a halfway house for the rehabilitation of drug abusers, and my brother had already been robbed at gunpoint.

I had seen this guy once before, and he had nearly gotten me as I entered the back door from the parking lot when I was unable to find a spot on the front street side. On this particular night I had attended church, gone to Momma's, seen Eric put to bed for the night, and I returned to the building around 9:30 P.M. and lucked up finding a parking place right in front of the building. The door in the back had a lock on it, the outer door in front of the inner front door didn't lock, and that's when I got it.

My attacker was tall, and had a mole on his cheek. Remembering these details later helped me recognize his picture in the police files. He just followed me from the car, and I pretended I was going for a weapon as I got my key and put it in the lock. He looked right in my face and said, "Well?!", and snatched my purse, broke the key off in my hand, and dragged me about 100 feet out of the door and partway down the steps until my purse strap finally broke. He ran off leaving me sprawled in the snow, yelling, "Bring back my identification!"

I did get my purse back and decided to get out of that neighborhood by any means necessary–and as soon as possible. Two friends, Jack and Jim Holland, a pair of singing brothers who owned a limousine service, gave me a letter of recommendation and I moved into a building with better security. That certainly took a load off my mind.

It was in early 1983 that I received a phone call that I couldn't believe I was hearing.

"You say what? You want me to do what?" I said in astonishment. I thought it was a prank or someone playing a mean joke on me. However, it was legitimate–I was actually being invited to a Motown television special. Suzanne de Passe was producing it for NBC–TV as a tribute to Berry Gordy Jr. It had certainly been a long time. In the years since 1972, not only had I not had any communication with Berry Gordy or Motown, I still hadn't received one cent in royalties. Since I left the company, they continued to put my songs on *Greatest Hits* packages, and in 1974 they released a two–record *Martha Reeves & the Vandellas Anthology* in time to capitalize on the publicity that my Richard Perry album was producing–and with the same purple cover packaging.

However, I was at last able to put the whole Motown experience in perspective. Before my rebirth, I used to talk about Berry Gordy as if he had horns and a tail! But I was telling the truth then, and I didn't realize that there was good in him, too. So many good things have happened to me because of Berry and Motown, and after years of bitterness I was finally able to admit that I appreciated him and the role he played in my life.

I decided to take them up on their offer, and be one of the guest stars to perform for the taping of a television special called "Motown 25–Yesterday, Today, Tomorrow." Most of the Motown stars from the 1960s were going to perform on this one–night–only event. The show was to include Marvin Gaye, the Temptations, the Four Tops, Stevie Wonder, Mary Wells, and reunions of Smokey Robinson & the Miracles, Michael Jackson & the Jackson Five, and the Supremes. The lineup seemed like a dream come true.

Again, my biggest problem was: "What am I going to wear?" The television producers solved that problem by providing me with an outfit for the evening. With a few stitches here and there, I was cute in that shiny bronze–colored outfit that still had the price tag on it. I had to keep the tag hidden, since it had to be returned to the store it came from after the show.

It was March 25, 1983, and the Pasadena Civic Center was jumping when I arrived. There were artists onstage rehearsing, set designers making last–minute changes, and acts filing in. This was one of the biggest productions that I had been part of in years. I watched it all unfold with fascination.

I was shown a dressing room and was warmly greeted by the first familiar faces I saw from the Motown family: Mary Wilson and Cindy Birdsong, who had taken Florence Ballard's place in the Supremes. I knew Cindy better from her old group, Patti LaBelle & the Blue-Belles, with whom the Vandellas and I performed dozens of times on the same bill in the 1960s.

Looking for my dressing room, Louis Price stuck his head out of a doorway to say hello. I had known him for years. He had launched a solo career after singing for the Drifters (with Faye Treadwell) and the Temptations.

When I was alone, I collected my charts and waited until I was summoned to take my turn at rehearsing my one song, "(Love Is Like a) Heat Wave." The conductor had already arranged the song in a different key, and I was immediately unhappy with the change in instrumentation. It didn't sound right and made it difficult for me to get into it.

All of this time, Mr. Gordy had been standing watching every-thing going on in the theater from backstage. I was grateful to be inspired by his presence. But instead of feeling connected to all of the activity that was going on around me, I began to feel conspicuously apart from the rest of this production. In addition to all of the Motown stars, Linda Ronstadt was there to sing two duets with Smokey Robinson, British rocker Adam Ant was here to sing a song, and Bill Cosby, Dick Clark, and Richard Pryor were hosting different segments of the show. Seeing all of these people rushing about, I wondered if I could really belong in this gathering of stars.

During the rehearsal I found out that my one song was to be cut to just a verse and a half of chorus. It was like I was only there for nostalgia's sake. Just then Berry Gordy Jr. walked over to the edge of the stage where I was standing, and he said to me, "I know it isn't very long and it isn't the star spot, but give it the old Motown treat-ment."

That at least made me feel better. I didn't let myself get disap-pointed by the limitations of the segment, but I was terribly upset that Mary Wells had also been given only a minute-and-a-half slot. It was Mary Wells who had the first hit on the label, and for those important years from 1962 to 1964, she was the premier female vocal-ist at Motown. I thought that was disgraceful, and done with com-plete disregard for her feelings.

Several people were conspicuously not invited, such as David Ruffin and Eddie Kendricks. They had recently gotten back with the Temptations for their 1982 *Reunion* album on Motown, but there had been a personality conflict within the group and they were missing this evening.

What Motown reunion would be complete without having the girl groups represented? Diane Ross was going to have a solo seg-ment in the show as well as a planned reunion of the Supremes. While I was looking forward to seeing this, I was unhappy that the Marvelettes were unrepresented. They had helped build Motown, too.

My ninety-second segment in which I sang my little snatch of one song came in the beginning of the show, and was over before I knew it. After I was finished I watched from the wings as the taping progressed, and quickly got over the dig they had gotten at Mary

Wells and me by giving us such quick little spots. As the show progressed, I could see that it was very well produced and fast-moving.

Linda Ronstadt and Smokey Robinson were great in their duet of "Ooh Baby Baby" and "Tracks of My Tears." The whole backstage then came to a halt when Michael Jackson arrived and stole the show with his rendition of "Billie Jean." My dear friend Claudette Robinson made a rare stage appearance with Smokey and the Miracles, and the Temptations and the Four Tops had fun with each other in a singing match of each other's hits.

I was very unhappy to see my song "Dancing in the Street" used as a backdrop for a number choreographed by Lester Williams and his dancers. I had to watch him featured as me singing lead to my "Dancing in the Street." That was my song, and he ended up with more stage time than I did. There were several other unhappy people there that evening.

I was backstage when Marvin Gaye came in with his entourage. He was heavier than I had ever remembered seeing him. This was before his decision to move to London. He looked puffy under his eyes, as if he had been crying or needed to have a good one.

I had rehearsed with Smokey Robinson the opening number that I was supposed to sing with Marvin. I recorded the rehearsal on a Walkman and handed it to Marvin, never to see it again. He was cordial, but preoccupied. He was probably composing the speech he was going to deliver before he sang his hit, "What's Going On." That evening was the last time I saw my friend, Marvin Gaye. It was only a year later that his father shot and killed him after a dispute.

We had heard that Diane's helicopter had arrived. She was scheduled to close the show and sing three songs with Mary and Cindy on a much-promoted reunion number. But Diane was full of surprises that evening. When Adam Ant was in the middle of singing the Supremes' "Where Did Our Love Go," Diane unexpectedly appeared onstage bumping and grinding and doing the old-fashioned "bootie-green." She never spoke to the rest of us that evening.

"Who is that?" we all asked one another in the wings. Adam was not amused when Diane stole his number with her antics, and he wanted to tape it over. Producer Suzanne de Passe declined because the show was so tightly scheduled and running late.

Richard Pryor and Bill Cosby were exchanging puns backstage, and when the Four Tops stole Bill Cosby's break–dancing routine, it was even funnier than at rehearsal.

Finally it was time for Diane's solo number on "Ain't No Mountain High Enough." Two of the Supremes' numbers had been cut by Diane, and now they were only going to do "Someday We'll Be Together." When she went out onstage, she was dragging this long white foxtail wrap. As Mary got ready to make her grand entrance in a red beaded gown, I warned her, "Don't you dare let her trip you with that fur!"

Mary strutted out onstage–and virtually stole the spotlight. Diane became so flustered that Mary had taken over the lead vocal, and we all watched in awe as Diane shoved Mary and pushed her microphone away from her mouth. Suddenly we were all hurried out onstage to defuse this fabulous diva fight. Most of this was edited from the final broadcast, of course. I saw egos fly all out of proportion.

The finale was one of pushing and shoving, but it was amazing to see how the Temptations, Four Tops, Jackson Five, Mary Wells, DeBarge, Stevie Wonder, and all of the rest of us jammed on that stage. The finale song was Ashford and Simpson's "Reach Out and Touch," and I shared a microphone with Stevie Wonder. Diane was so unhappy with her spot on stage that she was forced up in the back on the bandstand tower. When *Life* magazine captured us onstage for one grand photo, I was in the front row, in my own gold–lamé pants and sequined jacket, surrounded by producers Mickey Stevenson, Nick Ashford, Valerie Simpson, and Eddie and Brian Holland. Just like my early days at Motown, I always hung out with the producers, musicians, and songwriters.

The television special aired on May 16, 1983, and became a huge critical and ratings hit. It went on to win an Emmy Award as the Outstanding Variety, Music, or Comedy Program. When it was released on videocassette, it also became a big hit. Suddenly, I was back in the winner's circle again!

CHAPTER 12

I'm Ready for Love

I'M GETTING MY HEART REPAIRED BY A SPECIALIST

It took very little skill
     To teach me all about heartaches
It was just infatuation, then lonely regret
     But I had to step into deep water
Learn about life and get my footsies wet
     Years of petty misconceptions
That seemed long as a century
     I'm finally getting over
Mr. Fix-it has rescued me

I'm getting my heart repaired
     By a specialist
The best in his territory
     And what he is doing with me
Should win him Nobel prizes
     A certified degree
I'm so glad he finally got his hands on me

He comes highly recommended
     Meet him and know just what I mean
Both my mother and father dig him
     He's the finest I've ever seen
His middle name must be Patience
     He slowly took my pain away
He says it's a lifetime deal
     And I believe everything Mr. Goodness says.

From a very early age, I have enjoyed giving and receiving love from my songs.
(*Photo by Marc Raboy, 1993*)

One of my first publicity photos without the Vandellas, taken in 1972. My compliments to the art director, make-up artist, and photographer for this shot. I'm wearing a blouse by Jerome, designed by Jai Jackson, which features raw silk and sheer silk in green, blue, and pink. (*Martha Reeves Collection*)

I was surprised when a very strange photographer was sent to my doorstep at nine o'clock in the morning to shoot this photo. It was for the cover of my first Fantasy album. (*Mark Bego Archives*)

In 1974 I found this costume in a store called Strip Thrills. The Indian in me came out when I wore it. This was a fun two-piece outfit with authentic feathers and beads in natural chamois. (*Mark Bego Archives*)

I met with Wayne Newton at Woolie Bullie's in Detroit in 1993. There was a reception for Wayne, and a look-alike contest. (*Photo by Barbara Orto*)

Keith Stallworth of the Black Music Scholarship Fund, Eddie Kendricks, Martha, and David Ruffin. This was a happy 1990 reunion in Detroit at an awards ceremony. David, Eddie, and I were honored with awards as "local legends." (*Martha Reeves Collection*)

My son, Eric Jermel Graham, in 1990 when he received an honorable discharge from the United States Navy. (*Martha Reeves Collection*)

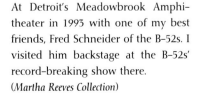

At Detroit's Meadowbrook Amphitheater in 1993 with one of my best friends, Fred Schneider of the B-52s. I visited him backstage at the B-52s' record-breaking show there. (*Martha Reeves Collection*)

(*Above*) "The Legendary Ladies of Rock and Roll":
(*back row*) Lesley Gore, Freda Payne, Shirley
Alston Reeves, Mary Wells, and Ronnie Spector;
(*middle row*) Grace Slick and Belinda Carlisle;
(*front row*) Brenda Lee and Martha. The evening's
emcee, Chubby Checker, stole the show.
(*Martha Reeves Collection*)

(*Right*) With Eddie Kendricks filming an interview by Dave Tucker for the show "Street Gold"
on Father's Day, June 21, 1992, at the Apollo
Theatre, New York City. Eddie kept tugging
affectionately at my dressing gown tie during
the interview. (*Martha Reeves Collection*)

(*Above*) Martha with Ike Turner and Casey Kasem in a Los Angeles recording studio in 1993. We had gathered to sing happy birthday to the Godfather of Soul, James Brown, on a session produced by Vonnie Sweeney.
(*Photo by Mark Bego*)
(*Right*) In 1993 the *Detroit News* and the *Detroit Free Press* wrote feature articles about the legendary Mrs. Powell, Motown's charm and modeling instructor. (*Martha Reeves Collection*)

Divas need their furs! Lois Reeves, Patti LaBelle, and Martha in 1993. Sandy Bomar is on the far right. This was after Patti's performance at the Masonic Auditorium in Detroit. The Reeves sisters' furs are by Bricker Tunis of Bloomfield Hills, Michigan.
(*Martha Reeves Collection*)

My 1990s Vandellas. First grouping: Delphine, Martha, and Lois Reeves, the sister act; second grouping: Rosalind, Martha, and Annette. *(Photo by Bendell Colding)*

With exciting hits like "(Love Is Like a) Heat Wave" and "Nowhere to Run" to call my own, I look forward to every show!
(Photo by Marc Raboy, 1993)

The 1993 Rhythm–and–Blues Foundation Awards in Los Angeles. At the press conference before the ceremony: Don Henley, Bonnie Raitt, Ruth Brown, Wilson Pickett, Martha Reeves, Lowell Fulsom, and Susan Jenkins. (*Photo by Jackie Sallow/The Rhythm-and-Blues Foundation*)

Martha Reeves and Mary Wilson on January 1, 1994. New Year's Eve brought us together in Scottsdale, Arizona, at four o'clock in the morning, and Mark Bego captured our moment of bliss.
(*Photo by Mark Bego*)

After thirty years of singing my biggest hits, I'm still "dancing in the street"!
(*Photo by Marc Raboy, 1993*)

Suddenly there was a huge resurgence in the interest of Motown music. The "Motown 25" special in 1983 really got the ball rolling. Later that year, when the movie *The Big Chill* was released, it heavily featured the music of Motown. The soundtrack album from *The Big Chill* went on to sell over a million copies, and "Dancing in the Street" was included on the CD version of it (and on Volume II of the vinyl edition). The music of Martha & the Vandellas has continued to be popular on the soundtracks of films. "Quicksand" was heard in *Carrie* (1976), and "Nowhere to Run" kicked off the soundtrack to *Good Morning, Vietnam* (1987), complete with Robin Williams introducing the song on camera in the film.

With the renewed interest in the group, I started auditioning background girls again. Just when I had thought that my career had ground to a halt, bookings began to pour in. In the audition process I met and hired Regina Carghill and Jacque Shelby, and I took them to England with me. However, while over there I found myself deluged with questions about where the original Vandellas were.

While in England I started to think about how I could get the Vandellas back together again. After all, I had always been the Vandellas' employer, and the only reason that I disbanded the group in 1972 was because there was a lack of work for us, and I couldn't afford full-time salaried Vandellas.

When I returned to Detroit I talked to my sister Lois, and she promised that she could work and perform with me on occasion. Her group Quiet Elegance had broken up, and the lead singer, Mildred, was off singing with Ortheia Barnes. After I had officially enlisted Lois, together we started to work at convincing my younger sister, Delphine, that it was her turn to work with me as a Vandella. Besides, I always enjoyed working with my family.

"I don't want to be a Vandella!" Delphine protested when I mentioned it to her. "I have a job with Blue Cross/Blue Shield and I don't have to put up with all that show business mess!"

"Oh come on, Delphine, I'm counting on you," I argued. "Since baby sister Eudora turned the road down for marital bliss, it is your turn, Delphine. Besides, Jessie's about ready to give birth, and her work schedule is unpredictable."

Delphine, like all of my immediate family, knew the music of Martha & the Vandellas inside out, because I had rehearsed and drilled countless other singers in front of them over the years. Since my music has been played around them all of their lives, of course they know it almost as well as I do! Well, Delphine came aboard. When she said yes, the Vandellas were reborn. (Although Delphine rebels and threatens to quit every time something goes awry, she loves it!)

Besides depending on good background vocals to accompany me, I was proud at how beautiful and talented my sisters turned out to be that I wanted to share the stage with them by my side. To complete the family affair element to my act, I began to employ my brother William as my road manager, and occasionally I had my other brother, Vic, on drums.

I also felt that I wanted my family around me because in 1983 I lost my dear father, Elijah Joshua Reeves, to his battle with cancer of the pancreas. It made me feel better having Lois, Delphine, William, and Vic right there with me whenever possible.

William Cornell Reeves, my baby brother, was aware of show business. He had traveled extensively with me in the past, so I knew he would be a seasoned and resourceful addition to the group. When I offered him the position as my road manager, he was more than willing to help me "go and get the bacon."

In my travels, I had met an independent promoter named Bruce backstage at a gig in New York, and he convinced me that he could put together a good tour with just his connections. Even though he was a stranger, I trusted him to be true to his promises, and took on the challenge.

I searched out and solicited the best musicians available. Duke Billingslea was to play bass, Ron English was on guitar, Alonzo McKenzie was my newly appointed music director on keyboard, and my brother Victor would be my drummer. We rehearsed briefly at Dave Hamilton's house. Dave is a very fine guitarist known around the jazz scene in Detroit. After that we were ready to rock.

Alonzo was a delight to watch, for he was quite young and had just graduated from Kim Weston's "Festival" program. Kim's project was created to allow underprivileged teenagers a chance to learn music firsthand from some of the best teachers available, like Teddy Harris, Earl Van Dyke, Ernie Rogers, and Arnold Clarrington. It was ingenious and kept a lot of music students out of trouble during their summer vacations from school.

William, affectionately known as Billy, was to be my road manager. He didn't know just what that entailed when we started out–but he soon found out. His first tour with me had us leaving Detroit in a blizzard headed for Washington, D.C. He quickly discovered that being road manager wasn't always as glamorous as one would imagine, and entails everything from repairing broken-down fuel pumps on a tour van as well as playing emcee onstage at showtime.

As my tour dates continued to pour in, I found myself as passionate about performing live onstage as ever before. Often it is the devotion of friends and fans that really fuels my love of the show business life. This brings to mind a very special friend of mine and how she risked her own safety just to come to one of my shows.

I am referring to my dear friend, Alice Dee Evans. It was in the mid–eighties when we first met on the phone. A mutual friend had given her my number, as she wanted to book me for a television show in Flint. They were planning a tribute to Motown Records, and we were selected from the few Motown stars still residing in Detroit. I was flattered, but I was suddenly working steadily and wasn't free.

After that she started up a friendship with me by calling regularly. I was beginning to think I knew her well when she casually asked me, "Did you know I'm visually impaired? Well, I thought you knew. I even attended college with Stevie Wonder's roommate. Maybe one day you can deliver a letter to Stevie from me." I assured her that if it was at all possible, I would. It took all of six months before we got to actually meet. When we finally got together, she vowed to attend my next concert performance anywhere in Michigan.

The opportunity arose on a snowy night at the Blind Pig in Ann Arbor. With the University of Michigan located there, the first show was sold out, and we had standing–room–only crowds and lines around the block in the snow. A facility that held only 300 comfortably now held 500, and the horn players–all four of them–stood in the exit door with microphones against a rail with barely enough room to blow their instruments. I had four Vandellas that night–Rosalind, Annette, Delphine, and Lois–because I like the full harmonies.

I had worried that Alice wouldn't make it because of the weather, but finally Al, my musical director, pointed them out in the crowd. I squeezed through the crowd of first show patrons leaving, only to see the bouncer attempting to put Alice and her friend Pat out. He was saying, "The place is totally sold out, and you don't have reservations or a ticket."

I felt he lacked compassion, for there they were–Alice without sight, and her friend Pat paralyzed from the waist down, though it was Pat who had driven them there in her specially equipped car. As I arrived at the door, Pat exclaimed, "Let Martha know we're here!" Alice, who was pushing the wheelchair, was terribly upset and was about to leave when I walked over to rescue them.

I ushered them to a front-row seat. The show, and the crowd, were just excellent that night. We held up the second show to get all of our snowed-on patrons unwrapped and seated. The club was so jammed with people that the dance floor was covered with music lovers seated on their scarves and sweaters awaiting the Motown Sound. We opened to cheers and shouts of approval. We sang "(Love Is Like a) Heat Wave," "I'm Ready for Love," "Jimmy Mack," and "My Baby Loves Me," while everyone sang along and clapped in their seat–there wasn't an inch of room to dance. We sang hit after hit, most of them fast songs, until I had to slow down a bit and do a ballad, "This Time I'll Be Sweeter."

I ventured out into the audience as we grooved on the vamp, and found Alice. Amid all of the confusion I could hear her singing. As I reached her, she kept singing some beautiful riffs, and after grasping the mike with her free hand, I hugged her. She slipped me something in a silk scarf, pulled the mike away, and whispered, "This is for you. Keep it always." I kept listening to her sing, as she had her own style, and the treatment that she gave the song added a spiritual touch. As she stood up and sang the song, she took it to a feverish peak and got a standing ovation. In other words: She burned me. That's the term we use when someone outdoes you in your own show! Well, after about three or four ovations, I knew if I wanted to continue and regain control of my show, I'd better get that mike back and return to the stage, and that I did, still clutching her gift.

After the show, I opened the scarf and her present. It was a beautiful miniature teddy bear. Because of our song "Come and Get These Memories," I have received a collection of teddy bears, and now I got a beautiful porcelain one, so small and precious.

It was then Alice informed me that when they were traveling to the show, Pat lost control on the icy highway and their car slid off the freeway into a ditch. It was down an embankment and out of sight of the other cars, and they had to figure out a way to get help. After attempting to help Pat out of the vehicle, Alice found herself totally blocked in and couldn't move. She had to hold one spot for forty-five minutes until help came. Now, those are what I consider to be devoted friends—to have gone through what they did just to catch my show.

As the excitement of 1980s "Motown mania" gained momentum, I found my schedule getting busier by the moment. In 1985 I was invited to be one of the singing stars on the television special "Motown Returns to the Apollo Theatre." Also on hand were the Four Tops, Stevie Wonder, Patti LaBelle, Sarah Vaughan, Mary Wells, the Commodores, Wilson Pickett, Joe Cocker, the Temptations, Boy George, Smokey Robinson, Al Green, Billy Eckstine, Bill Cosby, Debbie Allen, Thelma Houston, Diane Ross, the Drifters, George Michael, Marilyn McCoo, Luther Vandross, Jennifer Holliday, former Miss America Vanessa Williams, and Rod Stewart. It was an exciting star-studded evening of fun.

Quick to jump on the trend of compact discs, Motown Records put together a series of releases that they called *Compact Command Performances* on all of their biggest acts, including a Martha Reeves & the Vandellas package featuring twenty-four of our greatest hits. A pair of them were never-before-on-album gems of mine: "Third Finger, Left Hand" and "I Can't Dance to That Music You're Playin'." This release was further evidence that the company was making money off me and my recordings and I still wasn't paid a cent. Something would have to be done to rectify this situation.

In 1986 I recorded my first new album in several years. It was called *Martha Reeves: The Collection*, and it was my first direct-to-CD release. Recorded in Nashville, the album included new, stripped-down versions of my five biggest hits and several "cover" versions of some of my favorite songs from the 1960s that I never recorded before. I got a chance to sing some of my favorites: "Spooky" (the Classics IV), "In the Midnight Hour" (Wilson Pickett), "It's the Same Old Song" (the Four Tops), "Gotta See Jane" (R. Dean Taylor), and "Get Ready" (the Temptations). These were all among the songs that fans constantly requested me to sing, so I was happy to put them on record.

In 1987 I was one of the stars of a Cinemax TV special called "The Legendary Ladies of Rock and Roll." Taped in New York City at the former Latin Casino, it starred Lesley Gore, Mary Wells, Ronnie Spector, Grace Slick, Freda Payne, Brenda Lee, Belinda Carlisle, Shirley Alston Reeves of the Shirelles, and myself. We ladies all had a great time together, and even did some "Legendary Ladies" touring.

Motown's 1980s resurgence got so big that the original Hitsville U.S.A. building at 2648 West Grand Boulevard in Detroit was designated a historic site, and now houses the Motown Museum. Mrs. Esther Edwards, Berry Gordy's oldest sister, developed and heads the museum and its collected artifacts. Suddenly Motown took on a whole new aura of prestige in Detroit.

As my career continued to soar, there were some unhappy occurrences also. In 1987 my brother William was arrested. According to him, it was a "sting" operation, and he was wrongly detained in the middle of a cocaine deal. It was heartbreaking to see him get into this situation, but I remain in regular contact with him and await his release in 1996. I lost a good road manager in the process.

In 1987 I was part of a summer tour called the Dancing in the Street Tour, in which I starred along with Eddie Kendricks, David Ruffin, and Mary Wells. It was such fun to reunite with these old friends. All of us had kept busy ever since the "Motown 25" TV special had aired, and I was thrilled that it inspired tours like this one for us suddenly-in-demand Motown stars.

I had often worked on the same bill as Mary Wells. She had recorded a great album for Epic Records in 1982 called *In and Out of Love*, and had a hit with the song "Gigolo." David and Eddie had teamed up and recorded an album with Daryl Hall and John Oates called *Live at the Apollo, with David Ruffin and Eddie Kendricks*—a collaboration with Margo Lewis of Talent Consultants International. They sang on the 1986 anti-apartheid single "Sun City," and the following year released their own album, *Ruffin & Kendricks*, on RCA.

Another memorable tour from this era was one entitled "The King and Queens of Soul." It starred James Brown, Mary Wells, Etta James, and me. The tour was deluxe, with lots of extra comforts thrown in. That was one tour I wished could have gone on much longer. We were a real good combination—longtime friends who were appreciated by crowds of adoring fans. James gave all three of us ladies flowers and gifts every night, and he was a sheer pleasure to work with.

In 1988 I ran across my original Vandella, Annette Beard Sterling Helton, in a bowling alley in Detroit. She and her baby sister, Debra, stopped and we all talked. I had been in another part of the building at a club called the Probe. The dance floor was jumping, and I was there to judge a talent contest.

Right then and there I asked her to consider going out on the road with me again, and she said very definitely, "No thank you!"

Although Annette had quit the Vandellas in 1963 right after the success of "Dancing in the Street," I still ran into dedicated fans around the world who asked me, "Where are the *original* Vandellas?"

"Which ones are you talking about?" I'd ask. "Annette, Rosalind, Betty . . . ?"

They'd say, "I can't recall their names, but I know them when I see them. What are they all doing?"

That sparked an idea in my head. Now that I had located Annette, I began to wonder if I could get Rosalind out of Vandella retirement. Our last meeting had been to settle a lawsuit she filed against me after she left the group. Motown settled with her in my stead while I was on tour. I had learned a long time ago to forgive and forget. The money she won from me had no bearing on the fact that I loved her—always have, always will—whether or not I "like" her all the time. So, I called her up and proposed my idea. She was undecided.

Working on both of them, I finally convinced them to rejoin me on a part-time basis. They could still keep their regular office jobs in Detroit, but beginning in 1989, and every year since, Rosalind, Annette, and I have played several dates. Our debut of this reunited group took place on October 21, 1989, at the Talk of the Town Club in Manchester, England. Now we go on an annual tour of England as Martha Reeves & the Original Vandellas.

After thirty-five years, ever since 1958, I have come to think of both Rosalind and Annette as stepsisters. It's a fact that we love to sing with one another.

Since 1988 I have been blessed to be able to divide the concert dates equally among four Vandellas, at my discretion. Either I have Annette and Rosalind or Lois and Delphine with me. This way I let everyone retain their "day job," and they all use their vacation days, sick days, and holiday leave to come out on tour with me to "dance in the street" as my official Vandellas.

In 1989 Annette, Rosalind, and I decided to sue Motown Records for all of the back royalties that had amassed since 1972, the last year I saw a royalty check. With all of the albums that Motown had sold, released, repackaged, and sublicensed, I knew that there was a large chunk of change that was owed to them, and to me.

Ever since the "Motown 25" television broadcast, I had personally tried to get a telephone call through to Berry Gordy Jr., but never succeeded. I'm not ashamed to say that I have always dearly loved Berry Gordy and his family because he was a role model for all of us young performers. He made our lives successful. Most of us came from the ghetto and had nothing but our dreams. I loved him for the fact that he had a dream for Motown Records and included me in it. However, I was sometimes tight for cash while Motown raked in millions of dollars off our recordings. Finally it was time to do something about it. I hired a lawyer and sued Berry Gordy and Motown Records.

After fourteen years of being "royaltyless," I was blessed with the acquaintance of a lawyer I really trusted: Samuel Gary Spicer. Although he is primarily a corporate attorney, he has taken my scattered business and made a decent businesswoman out of me. A native of Nashville, Gary was the one who got me involved in my *Martha Reeves: The Collection* album. It was also through him I have become business wise.

The roller coaster that has been my career continued to speed up and slow down, and then speed up again. There are times in show business when you work so much you think that you will pop your cork, and then suddenly you can't find any work. During those dry spells I pray for miracles. That is just what happened one day in 1989 when I got a call from Broadway star Linda Hopkins (*Bessie* and *Black and Blue*). When Linda contacted me, she was helping a friend who owned a club in the Valley that she frequently played at. Her friend had played host to all of the divas of popular song, and she asked me if I would be a dear and take two weekends that the friend couldn't seem to book. It was little pay, but it beat a whole lot of nothing, so I rallied. I have always found prayer to bring quick results, and I knew that this engagement was heaven-sent.

I opened that Friday, and to my delight there was a full house, with little or no time to advertise. Energetic promoter that she is, Linda had filled the room with her friends and well-wishers. I was delightfully surprised to see both Esther Phillips and Linda herself there to cheer me on. The audience was polite as I started "Free Again" offstage. As the tempo picked up and we got into the groove, I could hear Linda's voice shouting words of encouragement. She openly responded to any lines I'd send out into the crowd, so I coaxed her to join me on the stage. I announced to the audience that it was Linda who was responsible for getting me this gig. She stepped into the spotlight with that babylike grin on her face and she sang an old blues song about her "ole man" being a "coal man." I just took an empty seat at one couple's table up front and enjoyed with the rest of the crowd as Linda took charge. When I returned to the stage, it took "Jimmy Mack" for me to get total control back, but the crowd was thoroughly entertained with the evening I spent with this fabulous star.

I began to notice some physical discomfort around this time, and after several medical tests, I underwent a total hysterectomy in 1989. After it was over I had to face the fact that things will never be quite the same. Although they have since developed less drastic laser surgery, I had an emergency hospital visit that included "the works." I had tumors growing on certain female organs, and the risk of complications was just too great.

My first evening in the hospital was one filled with unpleasant incidents. A short little unattractive nurse was sent into my room to take a blood sample, and she made me crazy with her unsuccessful attempts to find one of the veins in my arm.

After being poked with a needle several times, I had a badly bruised right arm, and I went off on her. "Take that needle out of my arm!" I yelled as I started to get to my feet. I suddenly didn't want to lie there anymore. I asked them to get out of my room, and if it took a fight to get rid of them, then I'd gladly oblige them. I wasn't half as sick as they were making me.

Following that, my doctor took it upon herself to start to lecture me about hospital procedures, and how every patient has to have certain tests. As my attention was diverted to the ringing phone at the side of my bed, I heard the nurse ask the doctor, "Have you ever heard of her before? I understand she's a singer."

"Yeah, girl," said the doctor, "years ago."

This made me even more unhappy about being there. When I was finished with my brief phone call, I announced to the doctor, "Get what you came in here for, hurry up, and get out!"

As she was leaving with her nurse and aide trailing behind her, another medical student pushed this big machine into the room, saying, "It's an EKG. I need your arms, chest, and legs exposed." She then pulled out this cold lotion and began saturating piles of cotton gauze to be rubbed on my body. Naked and cold, I start to rub the lotion around to warm it up in the overly air-conditioned room. "That ain't how this works," she snapped at me. "Do you want this or not?!"

I began to suspect that there was someone sitting on the desk down the hall telling everybody to expect a hard time from Miss Martha Reeves. Everyone who came to tend to me seemed to arrive with a big attitude. Or maybe my reputation preceded me.

Yes, I *was* being difficult! I was using the hospital personnel to air some of the anxiety about being here in the first place. It was making me have fits. Every time I thought of Dr. Charles Vincent "cutting up my stuff," going inside me and removing tumors, I would push the button for an attendant and voice a new demand.

I was glad when the whole ordeal was over and visiting time came around. All of my close friends and family members were there to make sure that I didn't want for anything. My woman-to-woman advice to anyone facing a similar operation would be to seek a second opinion about possible alternative procedures. Take it from Miss Martha: There was a lot taken out of me that I sorely miss!

In the summer of 1989 I again found myself on a tour bus for a show called "Dancing in the Street," starring Mary Wells, David Ruffin, Eddie Kendricks, and myself. I made the mistake of letting a strange man—a stranger to me, anyway—travel as a road manager. I don't know how I was ever duped into allowing this menace to come into my work environment and wreak havoc on my nerves. For revenge I nicknamed him "Satan's Baby." This was especially true when he decided to call my fellow entertainers in their rooms at all hours with crazy schemes and unorthodox deals. I felt I was being used to get to them. I even caught him signing my name to bills of credit, talking nonstop and pushing everyone we encountered to the point of retaliation by being overly flirtatious or aggressive.

To make matters worse, none of us was properly compensated for this six-week tour of twenty-eight one-nighters.

There were two buses for our convenience. Because you don't need two women trying to run the same house, Mary decided what bus she wanted to take and I agreed to take the other—so that she, Curtis Womack, and her children, Sugar and Harry, would be more comfortable. Eddie and his entourage shared the bus with Mary, too.

I traveled in the second bus with David, when he chose to ride. Most of the time he insisted on flying. He would always give us a fright, and show up just before it was time for him to walk onstage. Once he arrived, the original lead voices of the world-famous Temptations became the undisputed "stars" they rightfully deserved to be. Mary opened the show, I came on second, and the guys were the last act before we all came onstage for the finale song, "The Way You Do the Things You Do."

At showtime David Ruffin was ever-ready and always in good shape—*if* he showed up, that is. It was the offstage time when you wondered just what to expect. Several times he would arrive at the venue seconds before he was due onstage. Changing into his stage clothes in a flash, he would run directly to the stage. It was during these times that Eddie refused to look in his direction, let alone acknowledge his existence.

Afterward David would try to make Eddie look at him, smiling and trying to apologize for holding up the show—or sometimes for missing the show altogether the night before. His attempts to communicate with Eddie fell on deaf ears and blank stares. It was as if

Eddie had shut down. I once asked him the reason he ignored David that way, and Eddie, always a man of few words, said quickly, "He knows why."

On one occasion David suddenly decided to "streak" and run naked on our bus as a joke. He wore only a towel about his waist, and there before me I saw but a skeleton of a man. He was gifted and talented, yet was now wasting away. But our love and devotion to each other as fellow artists, and the family atmosphere that we grew up in at Hitsville, still existed throughout the tour.

I knew he was destroying himself, but I was unable to do anything to stop him. I knew firsthand that you cannot tell a person to stop doing drugs. They have to *want* to stop! The ironic thing was that it was David, who could barely take care of himself, who was often being protective of me. Not only did he keep this bogus road manager I had hired in check, but threatened to beat him up if he mistreated me in any way. David's concern touched me, though in the condition he was in, I don't think it would have taken very much to knock him over.

The atmosphere on this tour wasn't serious all the time. You couldn't take David seriously for long, because he was always making a joke, especially when he humorously changed your name. I became "Lou-Jean Authuris," and whenever we'd meet, we would go right into character. I mimicked a woman greeting her man at the door, and he would take me in his arms, dip me low, give me this big fake kiss on the neck, and we'd both have a good laugh.

When he was in a good mood, which was most of the time, he would sometimes be silly, but when he got onstage all of the foolishness would stop. He gave his singing performances everything he had. It came from within, and it was just magic. The range and vocal riffs he displayed every night were unforgettable. It was never the same routine two nights in a row.

Mary Wells held up as well as any mother on the road could. Her two-year-old daughter Sugar was still too young to walk on her own, so Mary carried her on her hip most of the time. She had bags and shoulder straps that her husband and Harry would help with–at her command. I became Sugar's godmother, and I would look after her when Mary was onstage. Sugar was a beautiful baby with glorious eyes. We would watch from the wings as her mother and father did their thing onstage. I gave Mary a lot of credit for having her baby with her on the road.

We often shared dressing rooms, and Mary was always on time for the show. That historic 1989 tour ended abruptly after a good number of promoters complained of no-shows by one of the actors. I thank God I had other booking agents who were working for me while I finished this bus tour from hell. After the tour was over, we went our separate ways and I returned my focus to my own career.

It disheartened me so to see the declining health of all three of my companions. This was the tour that could never again be, and what should have been a joyous reunion of four dear friends ended up a total fiasco.

CHAPTER 13

This Time I'll Be Sweeter

DETROIT

Everywhere I go I find you
Everywhere, there you are
Whatever I do
I look to find you
You are always near
My shining star

At intermission in the lobby of the Fisher Theater
At the Fox, and the Twenty Grand
Woodward Avenue when I go shopping
Eight Mile Road, even Northland
On a tour of the Ford Motor Company
An outing on Belle Isle
We should really get together
Because we go the same places
We could make our lives worthwhile

Tiger Stadium, the new County Building
Even at the crowded State Fair
Emancipation Celebration, the fireworks, Edgewater Park
I search and find you everywhere
Greektown, the Renaissance, and New Center
The zoo, and Cobo Hall and D.I.A.
General Motors, J. L. Hudson's and Bomac's
Music lovers one and all
Gather at the Motown Museum
Give a show at Music Hall

Grand Prix, Thanksgiving Day Parade
Hold on to the Roostertail
Call on history at Greenfield Village
Fairlane Mall, Ritz Carlton
Omni, Westin, Pontchartrain
Take a ride on the People Mover
Joe Louis Arena and back again

I can always find you
Detroit, you are a special friend
Wherever love is missing
    We can bring it back again.

Singing my way into the 1990s, it certainly has been a decade of changes. Some of them are for the better and some have been for the worse, but I face them all with my unwavering faith in God.

Mary Wells and I worked together on shows regularly for the last ten years of her life. We costarred on nearly every gig together those last three years she performed, from 1987 to 1989, and I saw her gradually get thinner and more and more ill, until there was nothing I could say or do to help her or stop her from smoking cigarettes. I listened to her voice grow more and more faint until she had no voice at all. Finally she just whispered the lyrics onstage.

In 1990 she was diagnosed with throat cancer, and it wasn't long before she could no longer sing. She had no savings account and growing medical bills, so several people who had grown up on her music donated large sums of money to help her–including Rod Stewart, Bruce Springsteen, and Phil Collins. It was wonderfully touching to see the outpouring of love for her. I contributed what I could.

She had a lot of personal problems that I always overlooked. When I talked to our mutual friend Ron from the Apollo, I asked him to speak about her. "I loved her for certain things," he told me, "and certain things I didn't love her for, because I felt she should have known better–yet she did self-destructive things anyway. Anybody who loves you is not going to go and do something for you that's gonna hurt you. That's why me and Mary fell out, because I didn't appreciate her asking me to get drugs for her and her man. Especially when they had Sugar on the road, I did not appreciate that. How many times did I have to go and get Sugar because she and her old man were fighting? Martha, how many times did you send me to go down there and see about Sugar because they were fighting? Then in ten minutes they were making mad passionate love, and everything was OK."

He was right, but I chose not to personally dwell on the choices she had made in her life. I did the only thing I knew how to do: I continued to pray for her recovery.

In March of 1991 I received wonderful news: Berry Gordy and Motown decided to settle my lawsuit. I finally got the chance to personally talk to Berry on the phone to deal with this matter.

"Martha, what's happening?" he said.

"I'd like to have some accounting of the money my records have earned," I asked him, "because I have grandchildren now. I have a little grandson named Eric Jr. and a two-year-old granddaughter named Loren Ashley whom my son, Eric, has blessed me with. I want to secure their futures."

He told me that he was sorry it had gone this far. I told him that I had no hard feelings, but I was certainly glad to have the problem finally solved. And it wasn't long before I had a sizable check for all of the records I had sold since the early 1970s.

I will always be grateful to my lawyer, S. Gary Spicer, for getting through to Berry Gordy himself. Because of this man's expertise, I can now look forward to receiving record royalties as long as my recordings continue to sell. Gary has carved a special place in my heart and changed my opinion of lawyers, and I can attest to the fact that he is definitely an honest one, and a wonderful friend.

Ace Lichtenstein, my manager, was there to help me through these stressful times, and he has changed my opinion of personal managers. He is my friend, and we exchange ideas and make joint decisions. My prayers to be surrounded by good people are being answered.

The decade of the nineties has brought me several new compliments. In 1991 the film *Thelma and Louise* was released. It starred Geena Davis and Susan Sarandon in the title roles, and is about two women who stand up for themselves and take control of their lives. My song "Wild Night" was part of the soundtrack album and was played as

Geena Davis decides to leave her husband and break wide. I am also pleased to see that Candice Bergen of TV's "Murphy Brown" has a photo of Martha & the Vandellas and the Supremes on the bookcase behind her desk. I'm glad to be associated with such strong, self-determined women–because that's what I have always tried to be.

I have continued to work steadily, and I still delight in getting to spend time with so many of my singing idols. The gorgeous "Mr. B"–Billy Eckstine--was in rare form as we watched him perform in 1991. He was finishing up his two–week appearance at the Four Queens Hotel in Atlantic City, and we were scheduled to appear there next. Fortunately, we arrived in time to catch his last set. After the show we went backstage. When we got there he was about to leave, but he immediately stopped what he was doing and greeted us warmly. He invited Lois and Delphine and I to join him in the dining room where everyone had gathered after this afternoon performance. We sat down at a table together, but little did I know that this would be the last chance in my life to sup with him. He was so debonair, and although in conversation he could swear a blue streak, those words somehow seemed necessary to express how he felt about things.

He talked about his days at Motown fondly, when both he and Barbara McNair were signed to the label in the late 1960s. He told us of many great times he had spent with Berry, Diane Ross, and the Gordy family in Detroit.

I thought this the perfect opportunity to ask him to tell me what the language was that I heard he and Sarah Vaughan speak that day in the dressing room during the taping of the TV special commemo-rating the Apollo's fiftieth anniversary. He threw his head back and laughed at me, saying that it was "bebop" and they were just greeting one another in jazz singer's language, making sure that each other was all right. It was double–talk of sorts, interlaced with profanity, yet it seemed full of warm and loving exchanges of devotion. He gave me a little example of it, though I was still left totally confused by this happy gibberish he recited. But how exciting it was to hear him rem-inisce that afternoon, and how blessed I was to have known both Billy Eckstine and Sarah Vaughan.

On June 1, 1991, David Ruffin was in Philadelphia. He and Eddie had gone there following a concert tour of England with Dennis Edwards. David reportedly had $35,000 in cash on him, the earnings from the British concerts. At 2:55 A.M. he was delivered to the emergency room of University of Pennsylvania Hospital. He had been dropped off by a chauffeur who helped him into the hospital and promptly disappeared. David died an hour later, but the money he supposedly had was never recovered. The coroner claimed that it was a drug overdose. David was one of the finest singers I've ever known. They say the good die young, and this good singer had done just that. Nobody could ever sing like David Ruffin.

I met Diane Showers, David's woman, at Detroit Metropolitan Airport, as she was accompanying his remains. I spent the day keeping her spirits up. We went to an "Attendance Plus" charity game at Joe Louis Arena, and that evening we were the guests of Brenda Wilson and Marv Johnson at a tribute to Brenda's dad, Jackie Wilson.

I attended David's funeral services at Detroit's New Bethel Baptist Church. The seven surviving Temptations all gathered in the pulpit to sing a tearful version of "My Girl." As Eddie walked off the stage and neared the front door, he was arrested on the spot for nonpayment of child support. The suit was filed by the mother of a child he had fathered out of wedlock. He was taken into custody right in front of the entrance to the church. I knew nothing about it until it was shown on the news that night: how he had been ushered into court and threatened with a jail sentence.

Well, that was all I could stand. The first thing in the morning I ran to the County Building in downtown Detroit, and after a minute of meditation with his family and friends gathered there, I called Berry Gordy Jr. and got him right away on the other end of the phone. Berry immediately sent the balance of the money needed to help free the star. It arrived fifteen minutes after I spoke to Mr. Gordy direct.

I had no sooner gotten off the phone when the local news reporters were all over me with cameras, asking questions: "What's happening with Eddie?" "Do you have the money to get him out?" "Why are you here?"

I was led back to see Eddie, who had spent the night in jail. He looked worried and deserted. I gave him a big hug and assured him, "It's going to be all right."

Fortunately, we had a friend at the bail desk, because that officer had grown up in my neighborhood, one of the Collins family. He devised an "escape" plan for us so that Eddie could avoid further embarrassment. I would walk out the front door while Eddie would be picked up in a private car at the back and could slip away undetected. As I pushed open the big front doors, we were confronted by the huge cameras of the four local TV stations. Poking microphones in our faces, they asked us question after question. That night on the news, I was shown proudly saying, "Yes, we got the money. *Berry Gordy* himself helped." The cameramen and reporters followed us all the way across the street to Clarence's car while Eddie was getting away.

About fifteen minutes later, we all rendezvoused at Rosalind's apartment to pray with Rev. Hunter. Then a call was placed to Berry and he and Eddie spoke on the phone for the first time in sixteen years. I felt good that I had been effective in getting these two big men to become childlike for a moment or two and put all of their years of differences behind them. I saw them make the world stop long enough to say to each other, "It's good to speak to you. Let's get together soon, man."

On September 10, 1991, I found myself in Puyallup, Washington, thinking about how successful last night's show had been. It surely was a treat anytime I got to see old friends like Freddy Cannon ("Palisades Park"), Lesley Gore ("It's My Party"), and the Diamonds ("Silhouettes"), after all of these years of performing.

There was one major aspect about this show that irritated me, though. Headlining the bill was a bogus group of "Coasting Drifters." By that I mean that these same singers would pretend to be either the Coasters or the Drifters according to whomever the bill called for. Someone had legally gotten hold of the trademarked groups' names and made money from this arrangement.

Martha Reeves & the Vandellas were billed comfortably in the middle. Although we were annoyed by these masquerading headliners, Rosalind, Annette, and I prayed and agreed to do our best, get paid, and get home to pay our bills. Who were we to complain or make a fuss? I lament the fact that the loyal days are over when the real Martha and her original Vandellas would be headliners above any fake group on the bill. Unfortunately, nobody in the audience seemed to care as long as they heard the classic songs and could be taken down memory lane.

Although I can rationalize it, I am still maddened by such things.

I had a fit when I saw that a trio of fake Supremes were touring Europe. Although Jean Terrell, Lynda Lawrence, and Scherrie Payne were each employed by Mary Wilson in the 1970s as her Supremes, I don't think that they should be allowed to use the Supremes' name to bill themselves. They only make it difficult for Mary Wilson, the original and dedicated member. I think it took a real lack of loyalty for them to get together and try to replace her on the European circuit. These three girls are all very talented women, but Mary Wilson deserves a lot of respect—much more than this *faux* group gives her.

There is also a group of young women who go around calling themselves the Marvelettes. In this way, original Marvelette Gladys Horton rarely gets to perform for her fans and do her own million-sellers. I get mad every time the fake "Marvelettes" are on the bill with me and I hear them go into their stage patter—having the audacity to say, "We recorded this song in 1963 . . ." when not one of these three girls was old enough to reach a microphone in 1963!

Thank goodness there is only one Martha Reeves—because without me there is no Martha & the Vandellas. I am really irritated by people pretending that they were real Motown artists or real members of classic groups they never had any part of creating. Oh well, that's show business, I guess—like it or not.

After seeing everyone off that morning in Washington State, I boarded an Alaska Airlines jet and headed for my once-hometown, Los Angeles. I had mixed feelings at the time. I knew it would be an opportunity to see many of my loved ones, yet I realized that two days would never be enough time to fit everyone in. Still, I vowed to give it my best efforts.

I was met at the airport by a pair of producers of a commercial project I was involved in. I had been hired to sing "(Love Is Like a) Heat Wave" on a radio advertisement for a jewelry store. Jim and Allan were gracious and delivered me to the Universal Hilton to rest and get prepared for the taping three hours later.

When I checked into my room, I telephoned as many people as time would allow. Among the business I had to take care of, I confirmed an appointment to see my mentor, Berry Gordy Jr., the next day. He was doing research for his book of memoirs about his career, and he asked me if I would share some of my memories and insights with him. I desperately wanted to get over to see Mary Wells, who was by then very ill, but it didn't look like I'd find the time. I was also a little reluctant, as I felt myself coming down with a cold and I didn't want to give it to her.

"Maybe on my next trip to L.A. I will have the privilege of seeing her," I thought to myself. Ever since she was stricken with cancer, I always kept her in my prayers.

The commercial taping went like a breeze. I sang with such grace that some of my delivery reflected my past vocals. I sounded as youthful as I did when I first sang the song in 1965. "(Love Is Like a) Heat Wave" has *always* been a winner, thanks to Holland–Dozier–Holland.

Later I was picked up by my friends Paul and Leslie, and they took me to the St. James Club, where there was a "sing" that night hosted by a sweet woman named Jan. We had a pleasant time, and I was announced in the audience. In spite of the fact that I was fighting off a cold, I was prompted to sing, and delivered a smooth rendition of "What a Difference a Day Makes." The crowd was filled with entertainers and professional people, and there was a lot of love for Motown music in the room that night. A finale of Mary Wells hits brought a lot of joy and fond memories to the crowd.

I awakened the next morning, and to my surprise, my 12:30 P.M. lunch with Berry Gordy was suddenly moved up to 11:00 A.M. I scurried around and got myself together. Roger, the longtime chauffeur of Mr. Gordy's, came by to pick me up in a limousine. I was more than just a little curious to see the Gordy mansion.

When I arrived, I found many familiar faces. Several of Mr. Gordy's original secretaries were still in his employ. I was greeted by Edna, who had aged very beautifully. I had a tour of the grounds, and there were quite a few oohs and aahs on my part. I had never seen such luxury before, but I expected it. Berry had come a long way from 2648 West Grand Boulevard.

As I was taken to one of the many houses on this grand property, I noticed that there was a computer screen in each and every room. All of the activity that happened around me was under the direction of Rebecca Giles, the secretary who let me into Hitsville U.S.A. when I first went there in 1962. She was always by Berry's side as his devoted secretary.

I met two more assistants, Mary and Brenda, and we all returned to the main house with a tape recorder to capture my thoughts. I was served tea on a grand tray that was laced with beautiful linens and roses. Every command to servants was smoothly performed with cordless telephones.

Sipping my tea, I reminded Rebecca that I had always loved her, and I reflected on how little my secretarial skills had been in those first days at Motown and how I had depended upon her guidance. I told her of how I tried to keep out of everyone's way but somehow managed to get the requests of the musicians for their pay, plus scheduling all of the sessions for the artists and repertory department.

As she began to ask me questions from a checklist of queries for Mr. Gordy's book, I asked her if we could hear some Motown music to trigger my memories of the old days, and she complied.

While we spoke, Berry suddenly appeared at the door. Unable to see him at first, I could feel an instant change on the faces of everyone in the room. I turned around and there he was, joking around and saying, "Who's telling lies about me?"

I immediately ran to hug and kiss my hero. We then sat and talked at length. Our rapport was so strong that it could have been 1961 instead of 1991. It was almost like the conversations we had during the old days, when he and I would sit in the front seat of his car parked outside of my parents' house in Detroit. Engrossed in our conversation, he reminded me of several things that I had long forgotten. When I spoke, I had my turn to share my memories with him. "Why did those good times ever have to end?" I asked myself. He still had that sparkling gleam in his eyes.

The following summer I was again appearing at the Apollo Theatre. Sadly, it was to be my last gig with Eddie. It was Father's Day, June 22, 1992, and he was recovering from a major setback. Stricken with cancer, he'd recently had one lung removed. During this booking he was resting between songs, sometimes singing from a stool just beyond the edge of the stage. As I stood behind him in the wings, I could hear that his voice was in perfect pitch and as clear as it had always been, only it wasn't as strong as his spirit was. He gave his audience all he had every time he performed, and he always had a charm and grace that set him apart from most. Tall and slimmer than I had ever seen him, he could barely stand. But once onstage he danced the entire routine, and made all of the Temptations' famous moves and gestures.

My friend Ron had worked as Eddie's personal valet, and we recently reminisced about him. "Eddie left the Temptations in 1971, and he recorded his Motown solo albums," Ron recalled. "When his contract with Motown was up, he had an offer from Arista Records. After saving up his money, he planned to open up a restaurant called the Three Little Pigs on the South Side of Detroit. He got a call on the road in the middle of the night, two days before the grand opening of the restaurant, and the news was that the restaurant had burned down to the ground. They said it was caused by faulty wiring. Eddie never seemed to be the same since that incident." Ron's observations were on target, and I had prayed for Eddie during that unfortunate time.

Mary Wells wasn't doing much better. By the summer of 1992, she had undergone radiation therapy in addition to a tracheotomy. She'd developed malignant polyps on her throat and spent her last year unable to speak, let alone sing. On July 26, Mary died in Los Angeles at the age of forty-nine. With Mary's passing, I lost a loving friend whom I dearly miss. I was unable to attend the funeral at Forest Lawn Memorial Park in Los Angeles, but sent flowers to her daughter, Sugar, from her godmother, Martha.

It was on Monday, October 5, at 10:35 P.M., when Eddie Kendricks departed this earth. He had lost his long battle with lung cancer, and I had lost another dear friend.

With all of this tragedy around me, I still found many things in my life to rejoice about. I have always thrived on the sound of my mother's voice. Sometimes I will get as close to her as I can and ask her things, just to hear her speak. One day my sisters Lois and Delphine and I got a real thrill. There was a Bobby "Blue" Bland song playing on Jay Butler's program. Jay only plays the blues, Mom's favorite kind of music next to gospel. Lois and Delphine were baking a cake, and I was just enjoying fellowshipping with my family. The three of us sisters started harmonizing like we always have, since we were all taught to sing, and heard Momma singing along. We all kept on going even after the song on the radio had ended. It was then that we heard Momma ad-libbing as she sat there in her favorite spot, the couch. Lois, Delphine, and I carried our notes as we all gathered around her. She kept the song going for about three minutes until we couldn't contain ourselves any longer. We were all over her kissing and hugging her, rejoicing.

I have discovered that if you stick around long enough, people start referring to you as a "survivor." And suddenly I find myself on the receiving end of several prestigious awards. I've been presented with the Dinah Washington Award from Detroit's Ballentine Belles, Dionne Warwick's annual Soul Award, and the Heroes and Legends Award. On February 25, 1993, I was onstage with the Vandellas at the Palace Theater in Hollywood receiving a Pioneer Award from The Rhythm-and-Blues Foundation. The celebrity hostesses that night were Ruth Brown and Bonnie Raitt. Together with four Vandellas–Rosalind Holmes, Annette Helton, Lois Reeves, and Betty Kelly–I was presented with this wonderful award by the group En Vogue.

I was proud to be honored alongside Little Anthony & the Imperials ("Goin' out of My Head"), Wilson Pickett ("Mustang Sally"), Carla Thomas ("Gee Whiz [Look at His Eyes]"), Hadda Brooks ("That's My Desire"), Solomon Burke ("Got to Get You Off My Mind"), Dave Clark (the R&B record promoter), Floyd Dixon ("Hey Bartender"), Lowell Fulson ("Tramp"), Erskin Hawkins ("Tuxedo Junction"), Jimmy Witherspoon ("Ain't Nobody's Business If I Do"), Panama Francis (the longtime drummer with Duke Ellington), and the Godfather of Soul himself, James Brown.

It was an exciting evening of reminiscing, and it was wonderful to see Martha & the Vandellas get their due respect on the pages of musical history. I felt proud for that which I have had the opportunity to achieve.

In September of 1993 Motown Records released a two-CD boxed set of forty-three of my greatest hits called *Martha Reeves & the Vandellas/Live Wire!: The Singles, 1962–1972*. It included not only our hit recordings, but several rare "B" sides as well. It also included me singing on a Vels' single as well as two of my previously unreleased Motown solo recordings. Motown did a beautiful job of packaging it, and it too received fabulous reviews. Motown threw me a huge release party at the Hard Rock Cafe in New York City, and Chubby Checker ("The Twist"), Fred Schneider of the B-52s ("Love Shack"), Lou Christie ("Lightnin' Strikes"), and a host of friends came to help me celebrate. I was in an especially good mood about this new release, since I could now look forward to receiving royalties from it! Motown still has over 150 unreleased songs of mine in their vaults.

My music is precious to me, because it represents "the Sound of Young America," as the back covers of our 1960s albums often proclaimed. I can't count the times I have been told by listeners that they have "made a lot of love" while listening to my records, or had a child pointed out to me as a "Motown baby." It's a real good feeling when you know that you are loved, and I'm glad to be of service, doing what I love to do!

COME ON AND GUESS THE FUTURE

Here's a crystal ball you'all
   Here's some grains of sand
Here's a lucky-numbers oil
   I'm holding in my hand
Here's polluted bubble gum
Here's some crazy dust
Here's a big strong wind
Coming after us
Looka here—all whose head is level
You who stand the strain
You who gather pigeons
While you're standing in the rain
Come on and guess the future,
I dare you
Come on guess the future
Let me hear ya

A highway protector
Held a light and saw nothing
Just a bottle here, a ribbon there
And a five-and-ten-cent ring
A lawyer after working
Left a notebook full of doodles
Gave a girlfriend a box of candy
And cursed his wife for cooking noodles
Can we control the insects
While they eat our collard greens?
Do we walk into a passing crowd
When we really need to scream?
Who are we to ask these questions
While we try to get along?
Think and cry and wonder why
We know what's been going on

Come on guess the future
I dare you
Come on, guess the future
Let me hear ya

Epilogue

As a young girl, God must have heard my prayers over the running of water, the tinkling of silverware, and the clanging of the pots and pans I was washing. Standing there at the sink in Detroit, I would blend my voice with the sounds of the kitchen, and I prayed real hard to one day become a successful person so that I could travel and sing before big audiences—and most of all, be loved.

Since that time, what I have received is a life that I could never have fully imagined or dreamed up. Along the way I have learned that you've got to have a dream before you can have one come true. If you learn patience, don't get discouraged when things don't exactly work out the way you'd like. Keep still and continue praying; you'll get exactly what you need.

I dreamed of having a distinguished singing career with wonderful songs I could call my own. Thanks to Motown, MCA, Arista, and Fantasy, I have an entire songbook of hits like "Jimmy Mack," "Come and Get These Memories" and "Nowhere to Run." There are some songs like "(Love Is Like a) Heat Wave" that still give me so much pleasure to sing, that doing so actually makes me light-headed. When I get to certain lyrics, I find myself lost in the fun and the frenzy of the song, so I always have to remember to brace myself and pray that I don't lose my balance! I welcome and expect healing through song.

Onstage I still get excited when it is time to share my music with my audiences. Before every performance I can look forward to giving and receiving some real to-the-heart love and gratitude for my efforts.

After years of making several wrong decisions in my life, in 1977 I found out that it was all right to be square, simple, and sober. I have found a wonderful peace of mind that I can dwell comfortably in. I don't worry about being in a hurry anymore, because my faith in God will always deliver me on time. That is not to say that I don't know how to have a good time as well. I'm learning to use my sense of humor, and I thoroughly enjoy God's grace.

I've learned many lessons in life, and one of the main ones that I stress is the value I put on having an education. As an adult, from time to time I am asked to address groups of students. Not only do I plead with them to get a proper education and to seek instruction from learned professions, I tell them about what struggles the students in the past have had. I tell them of how black students in the South were pursued with firemen's hoses, had dogs sicced on them, and were denied entry to schools and colleges. Nowadays, you almost have to defend the teachers who dare to educate. We need every American to be educated and at least have a high school diploma. Education is a right and a privilege guaranteed to all of us in the United States (and in Great Britain, too). People have come here from all over the world for a better life. All young people who don't take their education seriously are committing a crime against themselves. Some of my best friends have been teachers.

Today, I am pleased with myself and I'm satisfied to know that in all of the situations I have been in, I have proceeded to the best of my ability, regardless of the circumstances. I also know that it is always better to give, because in the end you are rewarded twofold.

Ever since I was a child in Detroit and Momma would encourage me with the words, "Sing it, baby!," I have derived untold pleasure in sharing and showing off my talents through my songs. As far as I'm concerned, I've only just begun.

In the 1990s my career keeps me as busy as ever, and that's the way I like it. I am still recording, writing, producing, and looking forward to greater things in the future. In my mind, I have yet to reach a career "utopia," so in this way I am always optimistic and faithfully looking forward to the next peak. I'm fortunate to have had so much success and love in my life so far, but I'm still living, loving, and perfecting my craft. I still have a long list of songs I want to sing, recordings I want to make, and love I want to share through them. I still have a vocal lesson every year. A few years ago Mr. Silver himself gave me an update!

I never miss any opportunity I am given to share my songs with you, because in my mind I'm not just singing an emotionally expressive tune to you, I'm letting God's light shine through me! Whenever we get together and the time is right to play some heavenly music, I'll be there. After four decades of singing my hits, I still look forward to many more years of "dancing in the street."

LET LOVE WIN

Try looking with your heart and not your eyes
When you're thinking of giving Love a try
It might be you who sees what you've longed to own
And the very thing that will do you wrong

If someone is different, try trading places
Could you stand it if you swapped faces?
God made us all perfect in his sight
Each as different as day and night

He made people in all sizes and colors
To attend to, not destroy one another
We can only grow ourselves
When we have nurtured someone else

This vast world has room for all
Whether we are big or small
The blessed assurance that it will continue to spin
Is that we open up our minds and let love win.

MARTHA REEVES
1994

Martha Reeves Discography

As the Del-Phis

- "I'll Let You Know" / "It Takes Two"
    (Checkmate Records, 1962)

As the Vels

- "You'll Never Cherish a Love So True ('Til You Lose It)" / "There He Is (at My Door)"
    (Mel-O-Dy Records, October 1962)

As Martha & the Vandellas

- "I'll Have to Let Him Go" / "My Baby Won't Come Back"
    (Gordy Records, September 1962)

- "Come and Get These Memories" / "Jealous Lover"
    (Gordy Records, February 1963)

- "(Love Is Like a) Heat Wave" / "A Love Like Yours (Don't Come Knocking Every Day"
    (Gordy Records, July 1963)

- "Quicksand" / "Darling, I Hum Our Song"
    (Gordy Records, November 1963)

- "Live Wire" / "Old Love (Let's Try It Again)"
  (Gordy Records, January 1964)

- "In My Lonely Room" / "A Tear for the Girl"
  (Gordy Records, March 1964)

- "Dancing in the Street" / "There He Is (at My Door)"
  (Gordy Records, July 1964)

- "Wild One" / "Dancing Slow"
  (Gordy Records, November 1964)

- "Nowhere to Run" / "Motoring"
  (Gordy Records, February 1965)

- "You've Been in Love Too Long" / "Love (Makes Me Do Foolish Things"
  (Gordy Records, July 1965)

- "My Baby Loves Me" / "Never Leave Your Baby's Side"
  (Gordy Records, January 1966)

- "What Am I Going to Do Without Your Love" / "Go Ahead and Laugh"
  (Gordy Records, April 1966)

- "I'm Ready for Love" / "He Doesn't Love Her Anymore"
  (Gordy Records, October 1966)

- "Jimmy Mack" / "Third Finger, Left Hand"
  (Gordy Records, February 1967)

- "Love Bug Leave My Heart Alone" / "One Way Out"
  (Gordy Records, August 1967)

As Martha Reeves & the Vandellas

- "Honey Chile" / "Show Me the Way"
  (Gordy Records, October 1967)

- "I Promise to Wait, My Love" / "Forget Me Not"
  (Gordy Records, April 1968)

- "I Can't Dance to That Music You're Playing" / "I Tried"
  (Gordy Records, July 1968)

- "Sweet Darlin' " / "Without You"
     (Gordy Records, October 1968)

- "(We've Got) Honey Love" / "I'm in Love"
     (Gordy Records, March 1969)

- "I Should Be Proud" / "Love, Guess Who"
     (Gordy Records, February 1970)

- "I Gotta Let You Go" / "You're the Loser Now"
     (Gordy Records, October 1970)

- "Bless You" / "Hope I Don't Get My Heart Broke"
     (Gordy Records, September 1971)

- "In and Out of My Life" / "Your Love Makes It All Worthwhile"
     (Gordy Records, December 1971)

- "Tear It On Down" / "I Want You Back"
     (Gordy Records, March 1972)

As Martha Reeves

- "Power of Love" / "Stand By Me"
     (MCA Records, March 1974)

- "Wild Night" / "Stand By Me"
     (MCA Records, 1974)

- "My Man (You've Changed My Tune)" / "Facsimile"
     (MCA Records, 1974)

- "Love Blind" / "This Time I'll Be Sweeter"
     (Arista Records, 1975)

- "Higher and Higher" / "Now That We Found Love"
     (Arista Records, 1976)

- "The Rest of My Life"
     (Arista Records, 1976)

- "You've Lost That Lovin' Feelin' "
     (Arista Records, 1976)

- "Love Don't Come No Stronger" / "You're Like Sunshine"
     (Fantasy Records, 1978)

- "Skating in the Streets (Dancing in the Streets)" / "You're Like Sunshine"
    (Fantasy Records, 1980)

- "Really Like Your Rap" / "That's What I Want"
    (Fantasy Records, 1980)

ALBUMS

An asterisk (*) indicates albums available on CD.

As Martha & The Vandellas

- *Come and Get These Memories*
    (Gordy Records, June 1963)

        "Come and Get These Memories"
        "Can't Get Used to Losing You"
        "Moments to Remember"
        "This Is When I Need You the Most"
        "Love Like Yours"
        "Tears on My Pillow"
        "To Think You Would Hurt Me"
        "Old Love (Let's Try It Again)"
        "There He Is (at My Door)"
        "I'll Have to Let Him Go"
        "Give Him Up"
        "Jealous Lover"

- *Heat Wave**
    (Gordy Records, September 1963)

        "(Love Is Like A) Heat Wave"
        "Then He Kissed Me"
        "Hey There Lonely Boy"
        "More (Theme From 'Mondo Cane')"
        "Danke Schoen"

"If I Had A Hammer"
"Hello Stranger"
"Just One Look"
"Wait Till My Bobby Gets Home"
"My Boyfriend's Back"
"Mockingbird"

- *Dance Party**
  (Gordy Records, April 1965)

"Dancing in the Street"
"Dancing Slow"
"Wild One"
"Nowhere to Run"
"Nobody'll Care"
"There He Is (at My Door)"
"Mobile Lil the Dancing Witch"
"Dance Party"
"Motoring"
"The Jerk"
"Mickey's Monkey"
"Hitch Hike"

- *Martha & the Vandellas Greatest Hits**
  (Gordy Records, May 1966)

"My Baby Loves Me"
"Come and Get These Memories"
"(Love Is Like a) Heat Wave"
"Dancing in the Street"
"Quicksand"
"Live Wire"
"You've Been in Love Too Long"
"In My Lonely Room"
"Love (Makes Me Do Foolish Things)"
"A Love Like Yours (Don't Come Knocking Every Day)"
"Nowhere to Run"
"Wild One"

- *Watchout!**
> (Gordy Records, December 1966)

>> "I'm Ready for Love"
>> "One Way Out"
>> "Jimmy Mack"
>> "Let This Day Be"
>> "Keep It Up"
>> "Happiness Is Guaranteed"
>> "I'll Follow You"
>> "No More Tearstained Make Up"
>> "Go Ahead and Laugh"
>> "What Am I Going to Do Without Your Love"
>> "Tell Me I'll Never Be Alone"
>> "He Doesn't Love Her Anymore"

- *Martha & the Vandellas Live!*
> (Gordy Records, August 1967)

>> "Introduction"
>> "I'm Ready for Love"
>> "Love But Leave My Heart Alone"
>> "For Once in My Life"
>> "(Love Is Like a) Heat Wave"
>> "Nowhere to Run"
>> "My Baby Loves Me"
>> "I Found a Love"
>> "Jimmy Mack"
>> "You've Been in Love Too Long"
>> "Love (Makes Me Do Foolish Things)"
>> "Do Right Woman/Respect"
>> Medley: "Dancing in the Street," "I Can't Help Myself
>>> (Sugar Pie, Honey Bunch)," "Sweet Soul Music,"
>>> "Uptight (Everything's Alright)"

As Martha Reeves & the Vandellas

- *Ridin' High*
> (Gordy Records, April 1968)

"I Promise to Wait My Love"
"Honey Chile"
"(There's) Always Something There to Remind Me"
"Leave It in the Hands of Love"
"Love Bug Leave My Heart Alone"
"I'm in Love (and I Know It)"
"To Sir, with Love"
"Forget Me Not"
"(We've Got) Honey Love"
"I Say a Little Prayer"
"Without You"
"Show Me the Way"

• *Sugar n' Spice*
    (Gordy Records, September 1969)

"Taking My Love (and Leaving Me)"
"Shoe Leather Expressway"
"You're the Loser Now"
"I'm a Winner"
"What Now My Love"
"Soul Appeal"
"Loneliness Is a Lonely Feelin' "
"I Love the Man"
"It Ain't Like That"
"I Can't Get Along Without You"
"Heartless"
"I Hope You Have Better Luck Than I Did"

• *Natural Resources*
    (Gordy Records, September 1970)

"Something"
"Easily Persuaded"
"Didn't We"
"I'm in Love"
"Love, Guess Who"
"Everybody's Talking"
"Put a Little Love in Your Heart"

"The Hurt Is Over (Since I Found You)"
"Take a Look"
"Won't It Be So Wonderful"
"I Should Be Proud"
"People Got to Be Free"

• *Black Magic**
    (Gordy Records, March 1972)

"No One There"
"Your Love Makes It All Worthwhile"
"Something"
"Benjamin"
"Tear It on Down"
"(I've Given You) the Best Years of My Life"
"Bless You"
"I Want You Back"
"In and Out of My Life"
"Anyone Who Had a Heart"
"Hope I Don't Get My Heart Broke"

• *Martha Reeves & The Vandellas Anthology*
    (Motown Records, August 1974)

"I'll Have to Let Him Go"
"Come and Get These Memories"
"(Love Is Like a) Heat Wave"
"A Love Like Yours (Don't Come Knocking Every
    Day)"
"Quicksand"
"There He Is (at My Door)"
"Live Wire"
"Dancing in the Street"
"Wild One"
"Nowhere to Run"
"Motoring"
"You've Been in Love Too Long"
"Love (Makes Me Do Foolish Things)"
"My Baby Loves Me"
"I'm Ready for Love"

"Jimmy Mack"
"Love Bug Leave My Heart Alone"
"Honey Chile"
"I Promise to Wait My Love"
"(We've Got) Honey Love"
"I Gotta Let You Go"
"Bless You"
"In and Out of My Life"
"Benjamin"
"Tear It on Down"

• *Martha Reeves & the Vandellas: Motown Superstar Series, Volume 11**
    (Motown Records, 1980)

Medley: "Nowhere to Run," "Dancing in the Street,"
    "(Love Is Like a) Heat Wave," "I'm Ready for
    Love," "Jimmy Mack"
(*Note:* This medley is a remix of five hits to a newly
    added dance beat.)
"Honey Chile"
"My Baby Loves Me"
"Love (Makes Me Do Foolish Things)"
"A Love Like Yours (Don't Come Knocking Every
    Day)"
"Bless You"
"I Promise to Wait My Love"

• *Martha Reeves & The Vandellas: Compact Command Performance (CD only)**
    (Motown Records, March 1986)

"Come and Get These Memories"
"(Love Is Like a) Heat Wave"
"A Love Like Yours (Don't Come Knocking Every
    Day)"
"Quicksand"
"Live Wire"
"In My Lonely Room"
"Dancing in the Street"
"Wild One"
"Motoring"

"Nowhere to Run"
"You've Been in Love Too Long"
"Love (Makes Me Do Foolish Things)"
"My Baby Loves Me"
"I'm Ready for Love"
"Jimmy Mack"
"Third Finger, Left Hand"
"Love Bug Leave My Heart Alone"
"Honey Chile"
"I Promise to Wait My Love"
"I Can't Dance to That Music You're Playin' "
"Sweet Darlin' "
"(We've Got) Honey Love"
"I Gotta Let You Go"
"Bless You"

• *Martha Reeves & the Vandellas/Live Wire!: The Singles, 1962–1972**
  (Motown Records, September 1993)

"You'll Never Cherish a Love So True ('Til You Lose
    It)"
"There He Is (at My Door)"
"I'll Have to Let Him Go"
"My Baby Won't Come Back"
"Come and Get These Memories"
"(Love Is Like a) Heat Wave"
"Quicksand"
"Darling, I Hum Our Song"
"Live Wire"
"In My Lonely Room"
"A Tear for the Girl"
"Dancing in the Street"
"Wild One"
"Nowhere to Run"
"Motoring"
"You've Been in Love Too Long"
"Love (Makes Me Do Foolish Things)"
"My Baby Loves Me"
"Never Leave Your Baby's Side"

"What Am I Going to Do Without Your Love"
"I'm Ready for Love"
"Third Finger, Left Hand"
"Jimmy Mack"
"Love Bug Leave My Heart Alone"
"One Way Out"
"Honey Chile"
"Show Me the Way"
"I Promise to Wait My Love"
"Forget Me Not"
"I Can't Dance to That Music You're Playin' "
"I Tried"
"Sweet Darlin' "
"(We've Got) Honey Love"
"Taking My Love (and Leaving Me)"
"I Should Be Proud"
"Love, Guess Who"
"I Gotta Let You Go"
"Bless You"
"In and Out of My Life"
"Your Love Makes It All Worthwhile"
"Tear It on Down"
"I Won't Be the Fool I've Been Again"
"Baby (Don't You Leave Me)"

• *Martha Reeves & The Vandellas: Motown Legends**
   (Motown, 1993)

"Jimmy Mack"
"In and Out of My Life"
"(Love Is Like a) Heat Wave"
"Tears on My Pillow"
"I Love the Man"
"In My Lonely Room"
"To Think You Would Hurt Me"
"I Should Be Proud"
"Mickey's Monkey"
"I Promise to Wait My Love"
"Easily Persuaded"

As Martha Reeves

• *Martha Reeves: Produced by Richard Perry*
         (MCA Records, April 1974)

                    "Wild Night"
                    "You've Got Me for Company"
                    "Facsimile"
                    "Ain't That Peculiar"
                    "Dixie Highway"
                    "Power of Love"
                    "My Man (You've Changed My Tune)"
                    "Sweet Misery"
                    "I've Got to Use My Imagination"
                    "Storm in My Soul"
                    "Many Rivers to Cross"

• *The Rest of My Life*
         (Arista Records, 1976)

                    "Higher and Higher"
                    "The Rest of My Life"
                    "Second Chance"
                    "This Time I'll Be Sweeter"
                    "Love Blind"
                    "Thank You"
                    "Now That We Found Love"
                    "Love Strong Enough to Move Mountains"
                    "You've Lost That Lovin' Feelin' "

• *We Meet Again**
         (Fantasy Records, 1978)

                    "Free Again"
                    "You're Like Sunshine"
                    "I Feel a Magic"
                    "One Line from Every Love Song"
                    "Love Don't Come No Stronger"
                    "What Are You Doing the Rest of Your Life?"
                    "Dedicated to Be Your Woman"
                    "Special to Me"

- *Gotta Keep Moving**
  (Fantasy Records, 1980)

  "Skating in the Streets (Dancing in the Streets)"
  "That's What I Want"
  "Really Like Your Rap"
  "Gotta Keep Moving"
  "Then You Came"
  "If It Wasn't for My Baby"

- *Martha Reeves: The Collection** European release of new 1980s recordings.
  (Object Enterprises, 1986)

  "Jimmy Mack"
  "Quicksand"
  "(Love Is Like a) Heat Wave"
  "Dancing in the Street"
  "Nowhere to Run"
  "Spooky"
  "In the Midnight Hour"
  "It's the Same Old Song"
  "I Want You Back"
  "I Say a Little Prayer"
  "Come See About Me"
  "Get Ready"
  "I Heard It Through the Grapevine"
  "Gotta See Jane"

APPEARANCES ON SOUNDTRACK ALBUMS

As Martha Reeves & the Vandellas

- *Cooley High*
  (Motown Records, 1975)

  "Dancing in the Street"

- *The Big Chill** (CD version or *Big Chill II* vinyl)
  (Motown Records, October 1983)

  "Dancing in the Street"

- *Good Morning Vietnam**
  (MCA Records, 1987)

  "Nowhere To Run"

As Martha Reeves & the Sweet Things

- *Willie Dynamite*
  (MCA Records, 1974)

  "Willie D"
  "King Midas"
  "Keep on Movin' On"
  "Willie D" (short version)

As Martha Reeves

- *Thelma and Louise**
  (MCA Records, 1991)

  "Wild Night"

APPEARANCES ON OTHER ALBUMS

As Martha & the Vandellas

- *Recorded Live: The Motor Town Revue, Vol. 2*
  (Motown Records, 1964)

  "Quicksand"
  "It's Alright"
  "(Love Is Like a) Heat Wave"

• *Motor Town Revue in Paris*
   (Motown Records / 1965)

   "If I Had a Hammer"
   "Nowhere to Run"
   "Dancing in the Street"

As Martha Reeves & the Vandellas

• *In Loving Memory*
   (Motown Records, 1968)

   "Were You There"

• *From the Vaults: Never-Before-Released Recordings by Motown Stars of the '60's*
   (Natural Resources/Motown Records, 1979)

   "Undecided Lover"

• *Motown Superstars Sing Motown Superstars*
   (Motown Records, 1983)

   "Tracks of My Tears"

• *Never-Before-Released Masters From Motown's Brightest Stars—The 1960s*
   (Motown Records, 1986)

   "Can't Break the Habit"

Index

Abner, Ewart, 177
Acklin, Barbara, 158
Aikens, Charlie, 80
"Ain't It the Truth," 112
"Ain't No Mountain High Enough," 156, 223
"Ain't Nothing Like the Real Thing," 156
Alabama, 16–18, 68
Aldred, Michael, 125
Ales, Barney, 58
Ali, Muhammad, 77
Allen, Debbie, 231
Allen, Johnny, 109, 166
Allen, Richard "Pistol," 160
"All the Way for Love" (Reeves), 102
"American Bandstand," 67
Andantes, 59, 136, 172
Ant, Adam, 221, 222
Apollo Theatre, 78–79, 87–91, 92, 112, 148, 149, 156, 157, 243, 250
    television specials on, 231, 245
Arista Records, 195, 251, 256
Ashford, Jack, 105
Ashford, Nickolas, 153, 156, 157, 172, 185, 223
Ashford, Rosalind, see Holmes, Rosalind Ashford
Atkins, Cholly, 88, 109
Axton, Hoyt, 192

"Baby (Don't You Leave Me)," 172
"Baby I Need Your Loving," 103
"Baby Love," 103
Bailey, Pearl, 88
Ballard, Florence, 5, 39, 45, 56, 69, 117, 126, 145, 148, 176, 220

Ballentine Belles, 252
Barnes, J. J., 47, 147
Barnes, Ortheia, 228
Bass, Fontella, 158
Bateman, Robert, 55
Beach Boys, 66
Beagle, Irv, 58
Beard, Annette, see Helton, Annette Beard Sterling
Beatles, 7, 103, 124, 172
"Beauty Is Only Skin Deep," 155
Bell, Madelyn, 119, 120
Benjamin, Benny, 5, 53–54, 105–6, 160
Bergen, Candice, 245
Bermas, Joe, 22
B-52s, 252
Big Chill, The, 227
Billboard, 83, 104
Billings, Vic, 115
Billingslea, Duke, 229
Billingslea, Joe, 72–73
Birdsong, Cindy, 220, 222
Black Magic, 184–85
Bland, Bobby "Blue," 251
"Bless You," 185
Blind Pig, 230
Bonds, Gary U.S., 113, 215
Boston, Mass., 40–44
Bottom Line, 194
Bowles, Thomas "Beans," 68–69, 74, 75, 112
Boy George, 231
Bradley, Bernadine, 35
Bradley, JoAnne, 35
Branch, Margaret, 149
Britain, see England

Brooklyn Fox, 112, 113–19
Brown, Billie Jean, 96, 154
Brown, Fred, 44, 46, 50
Brown, James, 70, 80–81, 82–83, 157, 167,
    233, 252
Brown, Katie, 46, 50
Brown, Wenny, 145, 146
Buckner, Milt, 41, 42
Burke, Solomon, 215, 252
Butler, Jay, 251
Butler, Jerry, 157
"Buttered Popcorn," 56
"Bye Bye Baby," 48

Cairo, 198–203
Choker Campbell and His Show of Stars
    Band, 68
Cannon, Freddy, 247
"Can't Get Used to Losing You," 80
Carghill, Regina, 227
Carlisle, Belinda, 232
Carlo, Tyran (Billy Davis), 91, 92, 97
Carrie, 227
Charles (boyfriend), 137–38
Charles, Ray, 51, 135
"Cheap Ed," 166, 167–68
Checker, Chubby, 252
Checkmate Records, 47, 50
Cher, 211, 214
Christie, Lou, 252
City Wide Cleaners, 47, 48, 50, 55, 67
Clark, Dick, 67, 221
Clarrington, Arnold, 229
Classics IV, 232
Clayton, Merry, 192, 211
Coasting Drifters, 247
Cobo Hall, 185
Cocker, Joe, 231
Coconut Grove, 204–5
Coffey, Dennis, 192
Cole, Natalie, 211
Cole, Nat "King," 59
Coles, Honi, 87–88
Collins, Phil, 243
Come and Get These Memories, 80
"Come and Get These Memories," 59,
    65–66, 67, 79, 83, 84, 91, 119, 132, 217,
    231, 256
"Come Home, My Sweet" (Reeves), 210
"Come On and Guess the Future"
    (Reeves), 255
"Come See About Me," 103
Commodores, 184, 231

Compact Command Performances, 231
Conley, Connie, 88–90, 91
Contours, 68, 69, 70, 72–73, 74, 79, 80
Cooke, Sam, 128
Cooper, Buzz, 143, 159
Copacabana, 159–60, 163–64, 176
Cosby, Bill, 221, 222–23, 231
Coudy, Douglas, 163
Crosby, Hank, 154, 211
Crystals, 80, 82
Culver, Veola, 29
Curtis Mayfield & the Impressions, 35,
    157–58

Dance Party, 135
"Dance Party," 135
"Dancing in the Street," 4, 7, 104, 114, 119,
    124, 129, 135, 147, 164–65, 192, 193,
    214, 222, 227, 233
Dancing in the Street tour (1987), 232
Dancing in the Street tour (1989), 6–7,
    236–39
"Dancing Slow," 135
"Danke Schoen," 84
Dave Clark Five, 135
Davis, Billy (Tyran Carlo), 91, 92, 97
Davis, Clive, 195
Davis, Geena, 244–45
Davis, Sammy Jr., 145
Dean, Debbie, 154
Deans, Mickey, 164
DeBarge, 223
"Dedicated to Be Your Woman," 212
Dee, Willie, 190–91
Del-Phis, 44–47, 50–51, 58, 130, 137
    become Martha & the Vandellas, 45,
    60–62
    as Gaye's backup singers, 59, 60
de Passe, Suzanne, 219, 222
DeShannon, Jackie, 172
"Detroit" (Reeves), 242
Detroit, Mich., 14, 25, 28, 40
    Martha's return to, 215–19
    Motown's move from, 176–77, 185
    riots in, 147, 153
    see also Motown
Diamonds, 247
"Didn't We," 172
Dinah Washington Award, 252
"Disco-itis" (Reeves), 213
"Dixie Highway," 192
Dixon/Propas, 195
"Don Kirshner's Rock Concert," 196

"Do Right Woman," 149
"Do You Love Me," 70
Dozier, Lamont, 60, 65, 103, 123, 155, 214
    see also Holland–Dozier–Holland
Drifters, 80–81, 135, 220, 231, 247
Durio, Mickey, 211–12
"Dusty Springfield Presents: The Sound of
    Motown," 124, 127–29

Easy, 157
Eaves, Paul, 196–97, 216
Eckstine, Billy, 88, 97, 231, 245
Edwards, Dennis, 156, 245
Edwards, Eddie, 75
Edwards, Esther Gordy, 66, 75, 95, 110,
    112, 232
Edwards, George, 95
Egypt, 197–203
Ellis, Shirley, 158
England, 123–24, 257
    Martha's solo tour of, 195
    Martha & the Vandellas' popularity in,
        123, 124, 141, 153, 164–65
    Martha & the Vandellas' tours of, 139,
        175, 234
    Motown Revue tour of, 124–29
English, Ron, 229
Evans, Alice Dee, 229–31
Everett, Betty, 158
"Everybody's Talking," 172

"Facsimile," 192
Fairy Tales, 197
Fakir, Duke, 215
Fame, Georgie, 128
Fantasy Records, 211, 212–13, 256
Fascinations, 34–35
"Festival" program, 229
"Fever," 31
"Fingertips, Part 2," 130
Fitzgerald, Ella, 65, 192
Flame Show Bar, 97
Flint, Mich., 45–46
Ford Auditorium, 32
Ford Motor Company, 96, 135–36
"Forget Me Not," 153, 154
Foster, Al, 163
Four Tops, 7, 40, 103, 135, 136, 176, 215,
    220, 222, 223, 231, 232
Fox Theater, 146, 147
Foxx, Charlie, 80, 81
Foxx, Inez, 80, 81
Foxx, Redd, 156

Franklin, Aretha, 149–50, 172
Franklin, Brenda, 149
Franklin, Carolyn, 149, 150
Franklin, Melvin, 89, 130, 185
"Free Again," 212, 235
Fuller, Perry, 81, 216
Funk Brothers, 104–7
Fuqua, Harvey, 96

Garland, Judy, 164
Gary Lewis & the Playboys, 135
Gaye, Marvin, 5, 7, 58–60, 66–67, 70–71,
    80, 82, 89, 103, 104, 110, 111, 116, 123,
    135, 176, 179
    death of, 222
    Martha & the Vandellas as backup
        singers for, 59, 60, 66, 67, 70, 79, 80,
        82, 84, 117, 118, 135
    on Motown Revue tour, 68, 69, 70–71,
        79–80
    on "Motown 25" television special, 220,
        222
    Terrell and, 156, 157
Gentry, Bobbie, 163
Gerald (boyfriend), 173–75
"Get Ready," 190, 232
"Gigolo," 232
Giles, Rebecca, 51, 249, 250
Gilmore, Ben (great–great uncle), 14
Gilmore, "Big Daddy" Grover
    (grandfather), 13, 16, 18
Gilmore, "Big Mama" Jessie
    (grandmother), 13, 16, 18
Gilmore, Jewel (aunt), 13
Gilmore, Juanita (aunt), 13
Gilmore, Junior (uncle), 13
Gladys Knight & the Pips, 109–10, 153,
    176, 193–94
Goden, Dave, 124
Golden World Records, 147–48
Good Morning, Vietnam, 227
Gordon, Billy, 73, 74
Gordy, Anna, 58, 95–96, 97, 111
Gordy, Berry, Jr., 51, 55, 57–58, 60–62, 66,
    68, 89, 96–97, 103, 105, 107, 111, 112,
    129, 131, 132, 219–20, 245
    artist development program created by,
        109
    in Chinese restaurant, 93–94
    dancing of, 94
    dreams of, 57, 94–95, 97, 127, 234
    England tour and, 124, 125, 127, 128
    Kendricks's arrest and, 246–47

Gordy, Berry, Jr. (*cont.*)
    Martha & the Vandellas' earnings and,
        165, 166, 234, 244
    Martha's disintegrating relationship
        with, 155, 157, 166, 176, 184
    and Martha's fight with Supremes,
        118–19
    Martha's hospitalization and, 184
    Martha's lawsuit against, 234, 244
    Martha's love and respect for, 57–58,
        94–95, 118, 131, 184, 234
    memoirs of, 248, 249–50
    Motown Revue and, 69, 76
    Motown started by, 97
    "Motown 25" television special and,
        219, 221
    musical direction of, 94, 96
    on New York trip, 91–94
    Ross and, 130, 157, 176
    songwriting of, 97
    Supremes promoted by, 125, 128, 129,
        130, 131
Gordy, Berry, Sr., 57
Gordy, Berry, III, 58
Gordy, Esther, *see* Edwards, Esther Gordy
Gordy, Fuller, 96
Gordy, Gwen, 92, 95, 96, 97, 111
Gordy, Iris, 96
Gordy, Joy, 58
Gordy, "Momma Bertha," 96
Gordy, "Pops," 96
Gordy, Raynoma, 58, 92
Gordy, Terry, 58
Gordy, Thelma, 58
Gore, Lesley, 116, 232, 247
Gorman, Freddie, 55
Gotta Keep Moving, 214
"Gotta Keep Moving," 214
"Gotta See Jane," 232
Grant, Pat, 195
Greco, Chris, 160
Green, Al, 189–90, 231
Greene, Shecky, 163
Griffin, Herman, 112
Gunther, Junior, 73
Guthrie, Gwen, 195

Hale, Faye, 95
"Half Loved" (Reeves), 86
Hall, Daryl, 232
Hamilton, Dave, 229
Hard Rock Cafe, 252
Harlem, 78, 88, 90, 91, 92

Harris, Little Joe, 39
Harris, Teddy, 229
Harrison, George, 192
Heard, Fran, 95
Heat Wave, 84
"Heat Wave," *see* "(Love Is Like a) Heat
    Wave"
Heavy D & the Boyz, 195
"Hello Stranger," 84
Helton, Annette Beard Sterling, 4, 66, 69,
    79, 87, 88, 90, 92–93, 99, 230, 233–34,
    247, 252
    in Del-Phis, 45, 46, 59, 60, 61
    marriage and pregnancies of, 97–98,
        130
    Martha & the Vandellas left by, 98, 130,
        233
    Motown sued by, 234
Herman's Hermits, 135
Heroes and Legends Award, 252
"Higher and Higher," 195
"Hitch Hike," 66, 69, 118, 135
Hitsville U.S.A., *see* Motown
Holiday, Billie, 15, 65
Holland, Brian, 60, 65, 103, 123, 131, 155,
    223
    see also Holland–Dozier–Holland
Holland, Eddie, 48, 65, 155, 223
    see also Holland–Dozier–Holland
Holland, Jack, 219
Holland, Jim, 219
Holland–Dozier–Holland, 84, 87, 104, 108,
    123, 136, 141, 155, 171–72, 249
Holliday, Jennifer, 231
Holmes, Rosalind Ashford, 4, 45, 66, 69,
    79, 87, 88, 90, 92–93, 98, 108, 117, 126,
    130, 135, 142, 144, 146, 164, 230,
    233–34, 247, 252
    Cheap Ed and, 166, 167
    in Del-Phis, 44, 45, 46, 59, 60, 61, 66,
        130, 137
    lawsuits filed by, 233, 234
    Martha's firing of, 171
"Honey Chile," 148, 153, 154
Hopkins, Linda, 211, 235
Horne, Lena, 19, 50
Horton, Gladys, 56, 248
Houston, Thelma, 231
Hull, Ted, 75
Humperdinck, Engelbert, 190
Hunter, Ivy Jo, 104, 119, 135, 136
Hunter, Joe, 105
"Hurt So Bad," 84

"I Call It Pretty Music (but Old People Call It the Blues)," 70
"I Can't Dance to That Music You're Playin'," 154–55, 231
"I Can't Get Along Without You," 172
"I Feel a Magic," 212–13
"If I Had a Hammer," 84, 129
"I Heard It Through the Grapevine," 214
"I Hope You Have Better Luck Than I Do," 172
"I'll Have to Let Him Go," 60, 61, 62, 83
"I'll Let You Know," 47
"I'm a Winner," 172
"I'm Getting My Heart Repaired By a Specialist" (Reeves), 226
"I'm Gonna Take Advantage of You" (Reeves), 38
Impressions, 35, 157–58
"I'm Ready for Love," 141, 214, 230
"I'm Ready For You Now" (Reeves), 134
In and Out of Love, 232
"In and Out of My Life," 175, 185
"In My Lonely Room," 103, 104
"In the Midnight Hour," 232
"I Promise to Wait My Love," 153, 154, 211
"I Say a Little Prayer," 154
"I Should Be Proud," 172, 211
Island Records, 195
Isley Brothers, 119
"It Ain't Like That," 172
"It's the Same Old Song," 232
"It's What's Happening, Baby," 135–36
"(I've Got to Use My) Imagination," 193
"I Want to Hold On To Your Love" (Reeves), 2
"I Wish It Would Rain," 155
"I Won't Be the Fool I've Been Again," 172

Jackson, Chuck, 135
Jackson, Deon, 147
Jackson, Michael, 220, 222
Jackson Five, 172, 220, 223
Jaison (backup singer), 197, 200, 201, 203
Jamerson, Anne, 107
Jamerson, James, 5, 53, 54, 105, 106–7, 192, 196
James, Etta, 143, 233
James, Rick, 217
"Jamie," 48
Jan & Dean, 135

Jasmin, Elaine, 182–83
Jay & the Americans, 116
Jenkins, Susan, 3–4, 7
"Jerk, The," 135
Jet, 141
"Jimmy Mack," 7, 141, 214, 230, 235, 256
John, Elton, 125, 214
John, Little Willie, 31, 78
Johnson, Hubert, 5
Johnson, J. J., 191
Johnson, Marv, 48, 246
Jones, Tom, 135
Jones, Uriel, 105, 107, 160
Joyce, Gwen, 111
"Just One Look," 84

Kaufman, Murray (Murray the K), 113–14, 116, 135–36
"Keep on Movin' On," 192
Kelly, Betty, 4, 98–99, 108, 117, 126, 130, 135, 140, 142, 144, 172, 233, 252
  Martha's firing of, 145–46, 159
Kendricks, Eddie, 5–8, 130, 155, 156, 186, 221, 245, 250–51
  arrest of, 246–47
  cancer of, 4, 7, 250, 251
  on Dancing in the Street Tour, 6–7, 232, 237–38
  death of, 5, 7, 251
  Temptations quit by, 8, 251
Khan, Chaka, 211
Kinfolks, 143, 158–59
King, Ben E., 81
King, Carole, 192
King, Clydie, 192, 211
King, Martin Luther, Jr., 8
King, Maurice, 109–10, 149, 163, 166
"King and Queens of Soul" tour, 233
"King Midas," 192
Kinnebrew, Dee Dee, 82
Kitt, Eartha, 126–27

LaBelle, 124
LaBelle, Patti, 204, 211, 231
Lance, Major, 107–8, 125
Larkins, Pops, 50
Lawrence, Lynda, 248
"Leader of the Pack," 119
Lee, Brenda, 232
"Legendary Ladies of Rock and Roll, The," 232
Legrand, Michel, 212
"Let Love Win" (Reeves), 258

"Let Me Be Your One-Stop Lover"
    (Reeves), 188
"Let Me Go the Right Way," 70, 119
Let's Get It On, 179
"Let's Get It On," 179
Lewis, Joe, 28
Lewis, Margo, 233
Lewis, Rudy, 81
Lichtenstein, Ace, 244
Life, 223
Little, Hattie, 54, 55
Little Anthony & the Imperials, 80, 113,
    135, 252
Little Joe and the Peps, 39
*Live at the Apollo, with David Ruffin and Eddie
    Kendricks*, 233
"Live Wire," 87, 103–4
Lockett, Beatrice, 18–19
"Lonely Teardrops," 97
Los Angeles, Calif., 141, 248–49
    Martha's move to, 191, 215
    Motown's move to, 176–77, 185
"Love (Makes Me Do Foolish Things),"
    136, 144
"Love Blind," 195
"Love Bug Leave My Heart Alone," 147,
    154
"Love Don't Come No Stronger," 212
"(Love Is Like a) Heat Wave," 7, 69, 84, 87,
    91, 108, 131, 192, 214, 220, 230,
    248–49, 256
Lulu, 154
Lymon, Frankie, 148–49

McClain, Michael, 97
McCoo, Marilyn, 231
McKenzie, Alonzo, 229, 230
McNair, Barbara, 245
McPhatter, Clyde, 81
Malveaux, John, 217
Mance, Melvelyn, 48
Martha & the Vandellas:
    awards given to, 252
    birth of, 61–62
    Carghill in, 227
    change in sound of, 130
    compact disc releases of, 231, 252–53
    debut album of, 80
    Delphine Reeves in, 228, 230, 234
    disbanding of, 185, 227
    earnings of, 165–66, 167, 234, 244
    England and, 123, 124, 139, 141, 153,
        164–65, 175, 234

on film soundtracks, 227, 244–45
    final concert of, 185
    as Gaye's backup singers, 59, 60, 66, 67,
        70, 79, 80, 82, 84, 117, 118, 135
    Grammy nomination of, 131
    Kinfolks as touring band for, 143,
        158–59
    Lois Reeves in, 146–47, 153, 159, 160,
        163, 164, 166, 167, 171, 172, 185, 230,
        234, 252
    Motown contracts of, 61, 65, 112, 165
    Motown's abandoning of, 172, 184, 185
    "music video" of, 135–36
    name changes of, 45, 60–62, 148
    New York Street Band and, 177–79
    origin of name, 62
    rebirth of, 227–34
    Shelby in, 227
    Tilley in, 4, 171, 172, 174–75, 185, 215
    Trimble in, 204
    two-sided hits of, 136, 153
    see also Helton, Annette Beard Sterling;
        Holmes, Rosalind Ashford; Kelly,
        Betty; Reeves, Martha
Martha & the Vandellas' Greatest Hits, 139
Martha & the Vandellas "Live," 144, 147, 149
Martha Reeves, 190, 191–95
Martha Reeves: The Collection, 231–32, 234
*Martha Reeves & the Vandellas: Superstar Series
    Vol. 11*, 214
Martha Reeves & the Vandellas Anthology, 219
*Martha Reeves & the Vandellas/Live Wire!: The
    Singles, 1962-1972*, 252–53
Marvelettes, 5, 7, 48, 50, 56, 69, 103, 123,
    176, 221
    fake, 248
    on Motown Revue tour, 68, 69, 73, 74,
        76, 79–80
Mary Jane Girls, 217
Mathis, Johnny, 135
Mayfield, Curtis, 35, 191
MCA Records, 194–95, 256
    Martha Reeves, 190, 191–95
Mellowtones, 55
Michael, George, 231
Michigan State Fair, 66
"Mickey's Monkey," 108, 130, 135
Middle East, 197–204
"Mike Douglas Show, The," 145
Miracles, *see* Smokey Robinson & the
    Miracles
"'Misty' Martha Reeves" (Reeves), 170
Mitchell, Willie, 189

Mitchum, Robert, 142–43, 215
"Mobile Lil, the Dancing Witch," 135
"Mockingbird," 81, 84
"Money," 50, 97
"Monkey Time," 107
Moonglows, 96
Moore, Archie, 77
Moore, Johnny, 81
"More," 84
Morris, Richard, 148, 154, 155
Morrison, Van, 192
Moses, Gilbert, III, 191
Motown (Hitsville U.S.A.), 4, 5, 7–8, 40, 50,
    67, 88, 94–95, 123, 124, 176, 182–83,
    192, 193–94, 211, 219–20, 229, 233,
    256
  artist development department of,
    109–11, 150
  birth of, 97
  CD releases of, 231, 252–53
  competitiveness at, 116, 119
  contracts of, 8, 105, 112, 165
  disco and, 214
  expansion of, 95, 96, 97, 109, 153, 176
  fake groups and, 247–48
  family atmosphere at, 95, 96, 116, 117,
    119
  film studios compared to, 110
  Golden World Records bought by,
    147–48
  government investigation of, 165
  group name changes and, 148
  labels of, 95
  Los Angeles move of, 176–77, 185
  Martha & the Vandellas abandoned
    by, 129, 172, 184, 185
  Martha & the Vandellas' contracts
    with, 61, 65, 112, 165
  Martha & the Vandellas' lawsuit
    against, 234, 244
  Martha as secretary at, 51–57, 58, 60, 65,
    67, 69, 76, 105, 250
  Martha's "audition" at, 48–52
  Martha's disintegrating relationship
    with, 153, 154–55, 165–66, 176, 190
  Martha's hospitalization and, 183, 184
  Martha's solo recordings at, 172, 252,
    253
  monopoly created by, 165
  profits of, 8, 165–66, 167, 219, 231, 234,
    244
  resurgence of interest in, 227, 231, 232
  session work at, 56–57

  talent contests and, 45
  war protest songs and, 172
Motown Appreciation Society, 124
Motown Museum, 232
"Motown Returns to the Apollo Theatre,"
    231
Motown Revue (Motor Town Revue;
    Motor City Tour), 6, 67–80, 82, 125
  at the Apollo Theatre, 78–79, 87, 88, 92
  in England, 124–29
  in Paris, 129
Motown Sound, 8, 66, 95, 103, 104, 105,
    131, 214
"Motown 25–Yesterday, Today,
    Tomorrow," 219–23, 227, 232, 234
Moy, Melvin, 153
Moy, Sylvia, 148, 153, 155
"Mr. Sandman," 58
Mullins, Benny, 49
"Murphy Brown," 245
Murray, Bill, 68
Murray the K, 113–14, 116, 135–36
"My Baby Loves Me," 136, 139, 175, 230
"My Baby Won't Come Back," 62
"My Boyfriend's Back," 84
"My Girl," 130, 246
"My Guy," 7, 103, 112
"My Man (You've Changed My Tune),"
    194

Natural Resources, 172
"Needle in a Haystack," 98
New York, 91–94
  Brooklyn Fox, 112, 113–19
  Harlem, 78, 88, 90, 91, 92
  Martha's parents in, 160–63
  see also Apollo Theatre
New York Street Band, 177–79
  drug incident and, 179–84
New York Times, 194
"Night Time Is the Right Time, The," 51
Nilsson, Harry, 172, 192
Novak, Sidney, 58
"Nowhere to Run," 123, 129, 136, 139, 165,
    193, 214, 227, 256
"Now That We Found Love," 195
Number One with a Bullet (Jasmin), 182–83

Oates, John, 232
"Ode to Billie Joe," 163
"Oh My My," 192
O'Jays, 195
"Ooh Baby Baby," 222

Originals, 45
Orlons, 171
Otis, Clyde, 172

Paradise Theater, 18–19
Paris, 129, 130, 131
Parliaments, 147
Patti LaBelle & the Blue-Belles, 112, 124,
    125, 135, 220
Paul, Clarence, 53, 54, 55, 130
Payne, Freda, 204, 211, 232
Payne, Scherrie, 211, 248
"People Got to Be Free," 172
Peppermints, 39
Perry, Richard, 192, 193, 194, 195, 219
Phillips, Esther, 235
Pickett, Wilson, 231, 232, 252
"Pick of the Pops," 165
Pioneer Award, 252
"Please Mr. Postman," 50, 55, 56
Podell, Jules, 159, 160, 163
Powell, Maxine, 109, 110–11
"Power of Love, The," 192, 194
Preston, Billy, 192
Price, Louis, 215, 220
"Pride and Joy," 66
Primes, 45
Primettes, 39, 45
Pryor, Richard, 156, 215, 221, 222
"Put a Little Love in Your Heart," 172

"Quicksand," 7, 87, 192, 227
Quiet Elegance, 185, 189, 190, 227

Rare Earth, 190
Rascals, 172
Rawls, Lou, 156, 215
"Reach Out and Touch," 223
"Ready Steady Go!," 124
"Really Like Your Rap," 214
"Really Saying Something," 98
Recorded Live: The Motor Town Revue, Vol. 2,
    80
Recorded Live at the Apollo: The Motor Town
    Revue, Vol. 1, 80
Record World, 83, 195
Reed, Jimmy, 80
Reed, Vivian, 88
Reese, Della, 62, 97
"Reet Petite (the Finest Girl You Ever
    Want to Meet)," 97
Reeves, Adron (uncle), 14, 34
Reeves, Arvester (cousin), 15

Reeves, Benny (brother), 14, 18, 20, 21–22,
    23, 31
Reeves, Ben Thomas (uncle), 14
Reeves, Bernice (aunt), 19, 49
Reeves, Bertha (cousin), 15
Reeves, Delphine (sister), 4, 23, 31, 245,
    251, 252
  as Vandella, 228, 230, 234
Reeves, Elijah Joshua "E. J.," Jr. (father),
    13–16, 20, 22, 23, 24, 25, 33, 50, 181,
    218
  accident of, 30
  death of, 228
  illnesses of, 162, 216–17
  Martha's Boston "gig" and, 42, 44
  Motown and, 51, 55, 56
  in New York, 160–63
  singing and guitar playing of, 13, 16,
    17, 30
Reeves, Ella Mae (aunt), 14, 15
Reeves, Eloise (cousin), 15
Reeves, Eric, Jr. (grandson), 244
Reeves, Eric Jermel Graham (son), 177,
    178, 179, 180, 181, 183, 185, 186, 189,
    218, 219, 244
  birth of, 175–76
Reeves, Eudora (sister), 23, 31, 228
Reeves, Eunice (aunt), 32
Reeves, Eunice (cousin), 15, 218
Reeves, Florence (sister-in-law), 184
Reeves, Irene (cousin), 15, 218
Reeves, Jessie Pecola (sister), 22, 25, 31,
    228
Reeves, Juanita (cousin), 15
Reeves, Loren Ashley (granddaughter),
    244
Reeves, Marie (cousin), 31–32
Reeves, Martha:
  acting classes taken by, 191
  aspirations of, 31, 50, 65, 256
  attack on, 218–19
  awards received by, 252
  birth of, 14
  cars of, 175, 184
  as cheerleader, 31, 33
  childhood of, 13–35, 256
  childhood singing of, 18, 21, 30, 31, 32,
    34, 256
  cover songs avoided by, 149
  creative input of, 155
  current career of, 257
  dancing of, 138–39
  "difficult" reputation of, 155, 236

drugs used by, 144, 158, 161–62, 168, 179–84, 196, 197, 201, 206, 207
early music gigs of, 34–35, 40, 44–49
earnings of, 165–66, 167, 219, 231, 234, 244, 253
film debut of, 197
on film soundtrack, 191–92
first direct-to-CD release of, 231–32
in first singing group, 34–35
fur coats of, 217–18
high school graduation of, 32–33, 40
husbands of, 140–41, 143, 144, 190–91, 195
hysterectomy of, 235–36
illnesses of, 88, 199, 200–201
jobs and job-hunting of, 33–34, 40, 42, 44, 47, 48, 50, 55, 67
love affairs of, 136–39, 139–41, 145, 173–75, 174, 190–91, 215
in mental hospital, 180–84
poems and songs of, 2, 12, 38, 64, 86, 102, 122, 134, 152, 170, 178, 183, 188, 192, 193, 195, 210, 213, 226, 242, 255, 258
pregnancy of, 174–75, 176
religious faith of, 201, 206–7, 243, 257
robbing of, 217–18
in school choirs, 31, 32, 39
schooling of, 20–22, 27–33, 39
as secretary, 51–57, 58, 60, 65, 67, 69, 76, 105, 250
as session musician, 56–57, 67
show business almost quit by, 131, 184, 185–86, 186, 189
solo career of, 189, 190, 191–95, 197–98, 201–2, 204–5, 211–14, 215
solo debut album of, 190, 191–95
son of, *see* Reeves, Eric Jermel Graham
spiritual rebirth of, 206–7, 211, 212, 215, 217, 219
stage name of, 47, 48, 49, 65
suicide attempt of, 174
in talent contests, 45, 47, 48, 65
unreleased solo recordings of, 172, 252, 253
Reeves, Melvin Douglas (brother), 15, 23, 31, 153
Reeves, Ola (aunt), 15
Reeves, Ruby Gilmore (mother), 13–16, 17, 23, 24, 25, 28, 29, 30, 65, 181, 183, 218, 219
illness of, 216–17
Martha's career and, 40, 42, 44, 51, 65, 257

Martha's graduation and, 32–33
Martha's schooling and, 20, 21, 22
Martha's visit to, 216–17
in New York, 160–63
singing and guitar playing of, 13, 15–16, 17, 30, 251–52
Reeves, Samuel Elijah (brother), 15, 23, 31
Reeves, Sandra Delores "Lois" (sister), 4, 15, 31, 175, 227–28, 245, 251, 252
Gerald and, 173–74
Green and, 189–90
as Vandella, 146–47, 153, 159, 160, 163, 164, 166, 167, 171, 172, 185, 230, 234, 252
Reeves, Shirley Alston, 232
Reeves, Shirley Ann (sister), 15
Reeves, Sylvester (uncle), 14, 15, 19, 49
Reeves, Thomas (brother), 14, 17, 19–20, 21–22, 31, 138, 183–84, 196
Reeves, Victor Tyrone (brother), 22, 23, 31, 162, 173
as drummer, 159–60, 195, 228, 229
Reeves, William Cornell "Billy" (brother), 23, 31, 218, 232
as road manager, 228, 229, 232
Regal Theatre, 157–58
Reid, John, 125
Reno Sweeney's, 195, 196
"Respect," 149
Rest of My Life, The, 195
"Rest of My Life, The," 195
Reunion, 221
Rhythm-and-Blues Foundation, 3–4, 7, 252
Richards, Deke, 154–55
Ridin' High, 153–54
Righteous Brothers, 113, 135
Ringo, 192
Rio de Janeiro, 119–20, 123
Robinson, Claudette, 39, 68, 69, 73, 130, 206, 222
Robinson, William "Smokey," 8, 39, 89, 95, 130, 131, 158, 176, 206, 214, 231
on Motown Revue tour, 68, 69, 73, 78
on "Motown 25" television special, 220, 221, 222
Smokey Robinson & the Miracles, 7, 39, 48, 50, 68, 70, 89, 108, 124, 128, 130, 148
on Motown Revue tour, 68, 70, 73, 74, 79–80
on "Motown 25" television special, 220, 222

Rogers, Bobby, 39, 69, 72–73, 74, 89
Rogers, Ernie, 229
Roland, Gilbert, 142, 215
Rolling Stone, 193, 194
Rolling Stones, 124
Ronettes, 116
Ronstadt, Linda, 221, 222
Roostertail, 143–44, 147
Ross, Diana (Diane), 39, 56, 66, 69, 126,
    128, 148, 155, 185, 231, 245
  Gordy and, 130, 157, 176
  Kitt and, 127
  Martha's fight with, 116–19
  on "Motown 25" television special, 221,
    222, 223
  singers' ad-libs stolen by, 119
Ruffin, David, 5, 6–8, 68, 89, 130, 185, 221,
    245–46
  on Dancing in the Street Tour, 6–7, 232,
    237–38
  death of, 246
  drug problem of, 6, 7, 238
  expelled from Temptations, 8, 155–56
  Terrell's affair with, 156–57
Ruffin & Kendricks, 233
Russell, Brenda, 211
Russell, Nipsey, 156

Sample, Joe, 192
Sands, Diana, 191
Sarandon, Susan, 244
"Saturday Night Live," 195, 196
Schneider, Fred, 252
Searchers, 116
Seltzer, Ralph, 58
Seymour, Robin, 147
Shangri-Las, 112, 116, 119
Shelby, Gene, 112
Shelby, Jacque, 227
"Shindig," 103, 139
Shirelles, 232
"Shop Around," 50, 79
Showers, Diane, 246
Sills, Beverly, 212
Silver, Abraham, 32, 39, 258
Simon, Carly, 192
Simpson, Valerie, 153, 156, 157, 172, 185,
    223
Sinclair, Maurice, 42, 43
"Skating in the Streets," 214
Slick, Grace, 232
"Smiling Faces Sometimes," 39
"Someday We'll Be Together," 223

"Something," 172
"Soul," 156
Soul Award, 252
Soulful Mood of Marvin Gaye, The, 59
"Special to Me," 212, 213
Spector, Ronnie, 232
Spicer, Samuel Gary, 234, 244
"Spooky," 232
Springfield, Dusty, 114–16, 119–20, 124,
    125–26, 127–29
Springfield, Tom, 119, 120, 124
Springsteen, Bruce, 243
"Stand By Me," 193
Starr, Edwin, 172
Starr, Ringo, 192, 194
Sterling, Annette, *see* Helton, Annette
    Beard Sterling
Stevenson, William "Mickey," 48–49,
    51–52, 59, 60, 62, 105, 107, 108, 119,
    126, 135, 136, 155, 223
  "Dancing in the Street" and, 104
  Martha as secretary to, 52–56, 59, 65
Stewart, Rod, 214, 231, 243
Strain, Sammy, 113
Strasberg, Lee, 191
Strasner, Ron, 190, 191, 192, 194–95
Streisand, Barbra, 192, 212, 214
Strong, Barrett, 48, 50, 97
"Stubborn Kind of Fellow," 59, 66, 67, 70
Sugar n' Spice, 171–72
Summer, Donna, 214
"Sun City," 233
Superfly, 191
Supremes, 7, 56, 70, 103, 110, 123, 135,
    176, 206, 214, 220, 245
  England toured by, 124, 125, 126,
    127–28
  fake, 248
  Gordy's plans for, 125, 128, 129, 130, 131
  Martha's fight with, 116–19
  on Motown Revue tour, 68, 69, 70, 73
  on "Motown 25" television special, 220,
    221, 222, 223
  name changes of, 45, 148
  see also Ballard, Florence; Ross, Diana;
    Wilson, Mary
"Sweet Darlin'," 154, 156
"Sweet Misery," 192
Sweet Things, 192
Swiss Cottage, 185

"Take a Look," 172
"Taking My Love (and Leaving Me)," 165

Talk of the Town Club, 234
Tamla Records, 95, 123
Taylor, James, 192
Taylor, R. Dean, 232
Taylor, Ron, 88–89, 90, 91, 157, 243
"Tear It on Down," 185
"Tears on My Pillow," 80
Temptations, 6, 7, 45, 68, 79, 89, 103, 110,
    123, 124, 130, 135, 155, 156, 176, 185,
    214, 220, 221, 231, 232, 237, 246, 251
    on "Motown 25" television special, 220,
    222, 223
    see also Kendricks, Eddie; Ruffin, David
Terrell, Jean, 248
Terrell, Tammi, 5, 153, 156–57
"Thank Your Lucky Stars," 124
That Stubborn Kinda' Fellow, 66
"That's Why (I Love You So)," 97
Thelma and Louise, 244–45
"Then He Kissed Me," 84
"There He Is (at My Door)," 60, 80
"Thinking You Were For Real" (Reeves),
    152
"Third Finger, Left Hand," 141, 231
Third World, 195
"This Time I'll Be Sweeter," 195, 230
Thomas, Charlie, 81–82
Thomas, Yvonne, 47
"Throw the Old Away" (Reeves), 12
Tilley, Sandra "Sandy," 4, 5, 171, 172, 173,
    174–75, 185, 215
Tillman, Georgeanna, 5, 74
"To Be Loved," 97
Tomlin, Lily, 212
"Too Many Fish in The Sea," 103
Tory, Doris, 81
"To Sir with Love," 154
Townsend, Ed, 179
"Tracks of My Tears," 222
Trimble, Jean, 197–98, 200, 201–2, 203,
    204, 205, 206
Troubadour, 194, 214
Troy, Doris, 80, 211
20th Century Records, 112
Twenty Grand, 47–49, 147
"Twist and Shout," 119
"Two Lovers," 70

Undisputed Truth, 39
"Use Your Head," 112

Vandross, Luther, 231
Van Dyke, Earl, 5, 104, 105, 172, 229

Vaughan, Sarah, 65, 97, 231, 245
Vels, 61, 252
Velvelettes, 98, 171
Vider, Larry, 105
Vietnam War, 153, 172
Vincent, Charles, 236
Voice Masters, 45

"Wait 'Til My Bobby Gets Home," 84
Wakefield, Loucye Gordy, 5, 83, 95
Walker, David T., 143, 145, 159
    Martha's affair with, 154, 159, 174
Walker, Shirley, 34–35
"War," 172
Ward, Singin' Sammy, 68, 69
Warfield Theater, 45
Warwick, Dee Dee, 211
Warwick, Dionne, 135, 154, 211, 252
Watchout!, 141
Waters, Richard, 143, 159
"Ways of Love, The" (Reeves), 64
"Way You Do the Things You Do, The," 7,
    103, 237
Webb, Jimmy, 172
Wells, Mary, 5, 48, 56, 60, 62, 69–70, 103,
    106, 123, 231, 232, 233, 243–44, 248–49
    on Dancing in the Street Tour, 6–7, 232,
    237, 238–39
    death of, 7, 8, 251
    Motown left by, 8, 111–12
    on Motown Revue tour, 68, 69–70,
    71–72, 73, 78, 79–80
    on "Motown 25" television special, 220,
    221–22, 223
    throat cancer of, 6, 7, 243, 249, 251
We Meet Again, 212
Weston, Kim, 31, 104, 123, 124, 229
"(We've Got) Honey Love," 154
"What a Difference a Day Makes," 249
"What Am I Going to Do Without Your
    Love?," 136, 141
"What Are You Doing the Rest of Your
    Life," 212, 213
"What Do You Do With a Love Affair?"
    (Reeves), 122
What's Going On, 179
"What's Going On," 222
"Where Did Our Love Go," 103, 117, 131,
    222
White, Robert, 105
White, Ron, 128
White, Slappy, 156
"Why?" (Reeves), 178

Wickham, Vicki, 124, 128
"Wild Night," 192, 194, 196, 244
"Wild One," 119
Wiley (first husband), 140–41, 143, 144
William (fiancé), 136–37
Williams, André, 53
Williams, Andy, 80
Williams, Elsie, 31
Williams, Evelyn, 25–27
Williams, Lester, 222
Williams, Otis, 8, 130, 185
Williams, Paul, 5, 130
Williams, Robin, 227
Williams, Vanessa, 231
Williamson, Gloria Jean, 44, 45, 46, 51, 59, 60, 61
Willie ("friend"), 177, 179, 181
"Willie D," 192
Willie Dynamite, 191–92
Willis, Eddie, 105
Wilson, Brenda, 246
Wilson, Bunny, 206
Wilson, Flip, 156
Wilson, Frank, 206, 211
Wilson, Hosea, 158
Wilson, Jackie, 97, 195, 246
Wilson, Mary, 8, 39, 45, 56, 59–60, 66, 69, 73–74, 117, 126, 176, 248
    on "Motown 25" television special, 220, 222, 223
Wilson, Nancy, 149

Wine Head Willie, 40–42, 43
"Wishin' and Hopin'," 114, 128
Womack, Curtis, 237
Wonder, Stevie, 7, 70, 124, 130, 153, 176, 206, 229, 231
    on Motown Revue tour, 68, 70, 74–75, 77
    on "Motown 25" television special, 220, 223
"Won't You Let Me Know," 47
Wright, Syreeta (Rita), 153, 155
Wright, Tracey, 143, 145, 146, 159

"You Beat Me to the Punch," 5, 7, 69–70
"You Don't Know How Glad I Am," 149
"You'll Feel the Magic in Me," 197
"You'll Never Cherish a Love So True ('Til You Lose It)," 60, 61
"You'll Never Walk Alone," 207
"You Messed Me Up" (Reeves), 183
Young, Wanda, 74
"You're All I Need to Get By," 156
"You're a Wonderful One," 103
"You're Like Sunshine," 212
"Your Love Is So Wonderful," 54
"You've Been in Love Too Long," 136
"You've Got Me for Company," 192
"You've Lost That Lovin' Feelin'," 195
"You've Really Got a Hold on Me," 70

Z-Man, 179, 182, 184

About the Authors

Martha Reeves, the lead singer of Martha & the Vandellas, lives in Detroit. She gives local seminars, delivers lectures, travels extensively, and actively records her own compositions. This is her first book.

Mark Bego is the author of over twenty-five books on popular music and show business, including the best-seller *Michael!*; *Madonna: Blonde Ambition*; and *I'm a Believer: My Life of Monkees, Music and Madness*, with Mickey Dolenz. He frequently writes for national magazines and appears on television, entertainment, and news shows. He lives in Tucson, Arizona.

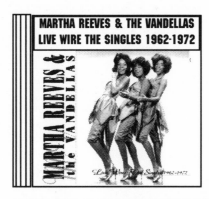

AVAILABLE ON MOTOWN COMPACT
DISCS AND **HQ** CASSETTES

Listen to the music that made Martha Reeves a legend with Motown's recently released album, *Martha Reeves & The Vandellas–Live Wire! The Singles: 1962–1972.* A 43–song anthology on Motown CDs and cassettes, the album traces Martha's hit-filled career from her first Motown recordings as one of the Vels, to her first Top Ten hit as Martha & The Vandellas–"Come and Get These Memories"–to her never–before–released solo recordings. Including smash hits like:

- "(Love Is Like a) Heat Wave"
- "Nowhere to Run"
- "Quicksand"
- "My Baby Loves Me"
- "Live Wire"
- "Dancing in the Street"
- "I'm Ready for Love"
- "Honey Chile"
- "Jimmy Mack"

With over a dozen rare singles, "B" sides, and album tracks on CD for the very first time, including "Taking My Love and Leaving Me," "My Baby Won't Come Back," "A Tear for the Girl," "I Tried," and "I Should Be Proud," Motown invites you to experience the energy and excitement of Martha Reeves with *Live Wire! The Singles: 1962–1972*–a specially boxed two–CD or two–cassette package from the original Motown diva!